ANCIENT HISTORY AND THE ANTIQUARIAN

WARBURG INSTITUTE COLLOQUIA
Edited by W. F. RYAN

2

ANCIENT HISTORY AND THE ANTIQUARIAN

ESSAYS IN MEMORY OF ARNALDO MOMIGLIANO

EDITED BY

M. H. CRAWFORD and C. R. LIGOTA

THE WARBURG INSTITUTE
UNIVERSITY OF LONDON
LONDON 1995

This book contains the papers given at the colloquium held in memory of
Arnaldo Momigliano at the Warburg Institute, 6–7 December 1991

ISBN 0 85481 095 1
ISSN 1352–9986

Designed and computer typeset at the Warburg Institute and the University of London Computer Centre
Printed by Henry Ling, The Dorset Press, Dorchester, Dorset

Table of Contents

Contributors

L. CAPOGROSSI COLOGNESI   Università di Roma

T. J. CORNELL   University College London

M. H. CRAWFORD   University College London

A. C. DIONISOTTI   King's College, London

JEAN-LOUIS FERRARY   École Pratique des Hautes Études, Paris

ANTHONY GRAFTON   Princeton University

CHRISTIANE KUNST   Freie Universität, Berlin

C. R. LIGOTA   Warburg Institute, London

Introduction

Where next? *The Classical Foundations of Modern Historiography*, as T. J. Cornell observes, undertakes the task 'of analysing the principal features of modern historical writing, an amalgam of very recent formation, and tracing the origin of its far from self-evident components back to their classical roots'. To this story, the attempt to integrate what can be described as the results of antiquarian research into a historical discourse is central. The story might well, of course, have been very different if it had not been for the unfortunate survival of Livy. One has only to compare him with what survives of his predecessors or with Dio Cassius to see that already in Rome a quite different kind of historical discourse existed, embracing, beside politics and war, religious institutions, the civil law, the peoples of Italy, coinage and money. It is salutary to be reminded, via the figure of Claude de Seyssel, that some of the Renaissance readership of the great classical historians, Thucydides included, thought that they were an alternative to romances. Otherwise, the papers in this volume explore aspects of the history of scholarly work on the institutions of antiquity: the early study of the history of Roman legislation, the beginning of the deployment in this country of archaeological and epigraphical evidence, the investigation of chronology, the exploration of the Roman field surveyors. But if we are still a long way from a complete fusion of antiquarian research and political history, the question 'Where next?' poses itself with greater insistence. Perhaps historians cannot easily 'read' many of the 'texts' that speak of institutions. In part the reason is no doubt a reluctance on the part of historians to make the effort to understand the 'texts' concerned as possessing a language and structure of their own that has to be respected, in part a desire by the guardians of specialisms to maintain their exclusiveness. Few coinages of the ancient world have been presented in such a way as to be a 'text' that can be read as historical evidence, few bodies of ancient legislation, few series of pottery styles: the examples could be multiplied. And even when a single text has been transmitted and does not need to be painfully reconstructed, whether Festus or Varro, the editions we use are insufficient precisely because a historical dimension is missing. Historians of antiquity currently enjoy access to a range of models and parallels of extraordinary sophistication. At the same time, they often make use of a body of evidence from the ancient world that is quite startlingly impoverished. The historical exploitation of the sources that survive from the ancient world has only begun.

M. H. CRAWFORD

Ancient History and the Antiquarian Revisited:
Some Thoughts on Reading
Momigliano's *Classical Foundations*[1]

T. J. CORNELL

Momigliano's Sather Lectures, delivered in 1962 but published posthumously only in 1990, form an original and thought-provoking study that deserves the careful consideration of all historians who care about the past, and, perhaps more importantly, about the future, of their profession. It is important to state that the book is not just an elegant synthesis of Momigliano's well-known and previously published views, although much of what it contains can naturally be found elsewhere in his writings. Equally, it is not a simple account of the work of the classical historians and their later influence, although this is how some critics have described it. The fact that it has little or nothing to say about historians such as Xenophon, Sallust and Livy, and (perhaps more surprisingly) not much about Polybius, should be sufficient to dispel that idea.

Most emphatically, it is not a history of classical scholarship, or 'Wissenschaftsgeschichte'. It is about historiography, a very different matter.[2] It is also a truly historical work (an examination of a subject that has a history), concerned above all with the practice, rather than the theory, of historical writing—although as we shall see it has important theoretical implications.[3] Finally, it is about the practice of historiography in general, not just the study of the ancient world. Momigliano set himself the task, never previously attempted, of analysing the principal features of modern historical writing, an amalgam of very recent formation, and tracing the origin of its far from self-evident components back to their classical roots. The general point can be exemplified by a consideration of the book's central chapter (ch. 3), dealing with the rise of antiquarian research. Momigliano's discussion of the antiquarians, and their role in the history of historiography, is one of his most important (but in my view least understood) contributions to the subject.

---

[1] A. Momigliano, *The Classical Foundations of Modern Historiography*, Berkeley, 1990. All references to Momigliano's other work, except where otherwise indicated, are taken from the fourteen volumes of his collected essays, the *Contributi alla storia degli studi classici (e del mondo antico)*, I–X, Rome, 1955–95 (the first *Contributo* is not numbered).

[2] This distinction is simply not understood by W. M. Calder III in his review of *The Presence of the Historian: Essays in Memory of Arnaldo Momigliano*, ed. Michael P. Steinberg (1991), *Bryn Mawr Classical Review*, 3, 3, 1992, p. 226.

[3] On the relationship between history and historiography in the work of Momigliano see further my comments in the introduction to A. Momigliano, *Studies on Modern Scholarship*, ed. G. W. Bowersock and T. J. Cornell, Berkeley, 1994, pp. xi–xviii.

I

Modern accounts of the history of ancient historiography, going back to Vossius
in the early seventeenth century, have tended to adopt the categories and concepts
of the ancients themselves, and therefore to accept the narrow definition of
history and the historian that was established in the centuries after Thucydides.
According to this definition, which was retained until the later years of the
nineteenth century, history dealt essentially with political and military events, and
was written in chronological order. Accounts of other social phenomena, such as
private life, customs, and religious ceremonies, were excluded from history, as
were systematic treatments of public life, laws and even political and military
institutions. These were the ingredients of antiquarian research, which, although
never subsumed under a single name in antiquity, was recognized as something
distinct from, and inferior to, true history.

This narrow view of history and the historian's task goes back to Thucydides,
as Momigliano showed. It was not implicit in Herodotus, and there is no reason
to suppose that later historians would have excluded geography, the description
of customs, research into the remote past, and extrapolitical events generally, if
Thucydides had not 'put himself between Herodotus and his readers' (p. 40). The
result was to drive a wedge between history in the narrow political sense, and
other forms of research into the past which became the preserve of antiquarians
and scholars, but were generally avoided by historians. This distinction was
reflected in the classical canon of historians, from Herodotus and Thucydides to
Ammianus Marcellinus and Procopius. No one in antiquity or in any subsequent
age would include a writer on religious rites, barbarian laws, obsolete names or
local history among the great historians of the classical world. 'Everyone sensed
that writers of this kind were something other than historians', even though '...
there would have been no clear answer to the question as to who they actually
were' (p. 60).

Momigliano argued that the distinction would not have arisen without
Thucydides' intervention, and that it is therefore unnecessary and, at least in part,
artificial or even arbitrary. But modern students of Greek and Roman historiography have nevertheless followed the lead of the ancients and concentrated
exclusively on the writing of political history. In one way this was inevitable,
since for many the object of study has been not ancient historiography as such,
but the ancient historians, a fact reflected in the titles of their books, from
Vossius's *De historicis graecis* (1624) and *De historicis latinis* (1627), to more
recent works on *The Greek Historians* (J. B. Bury), *The Greater Roman
Historians* (M. L. W. Laistner), and others of the same type.[4] Books on ancient

[4] J. B. Bury, *The Ancient Greek Historians*, Cambridge, Mass., 1908; M. L. W. Laistner, *The Greater
Roman Historians*, Berkeley, 1947. Among books in English notice M. I. Finley, *The Greek Historians*, London,

historiography, or the art of history, beginning with Creuzer's *Die historische Kunst der Griechen*, are not as a rule very different, and tend to concern themselves largely or exclusively with the canonical list of Greek and Roman historians. Antiquarian research is either ignored or relegated to a footnote. This is still true of recent works, such as Charles Fornara's sensitive and stimulating book, *The Nature of History in Ancient Greece and Rome*, which devotes no more than half a page to antiquarian studies.[5]

Like all modern students of the subject, Fornara took his cue from Jacoby, who organized his great project of editing and interpreting the fragments of the Greek historians in accordance with ancient categories, giving pride of place to political history, and relegating what he called 'historical-antiquarian writings' to a sub-category of local history, to be included in part VI of his planned compilation.[6] The fact that Jacoby did not live to complete his great work has served only to diminish still further the status of antiquarian writings, consigning them to a footnote in the history of Greek historiography.

The situation is, if anything, even worse where the Romans are concerned. The texts of the major antiquarian writers, particularly the great Varro, are still virtually unobtainable, and have not been seriously studied in recent times.[7] Verrius Flaccus is similarly neglected, and it is fair to say that the whole subject of Roman antiquarianism is still in urgent need of serious research.[8] This neglect has had far reaching effects on the study of Greek and Roman antiquity in general, and goes beyond the confines of historiography as such.

In his Sather Lectures Momigliano freed himself from the restrictions of an approach based on the ancient differentiation of history and antiquarian research,

1959; T. A. Dorey (ed.), *Latin Historians*, London, 1966); S. Usher, *The Historians of Greece and Rome*, London, 1969; M. Grant, *The Ancient Historians*, London, 1970.

[5] C. W. Fornara, *The Nature of History in Ancient Greece and Rome*, Berkeley, 1983. Among other good books see e.g. K. von Fritz, *Die Griechische Geschichtsschreibung*, Berlin, 1967. On Creuzer see Momigliano, *Contributo* (n. 1 above), pp. 233–48 (= 'Friedrich Creuzer and Greek Historiography', *Journal of the Warburg and Courtauld Institutes*, 9, 1946, pp. 153–63).

[6] See his important programmatic article 'Über die Entwicklung der griechischen Historiographie und den Plan einer neuen Sammlung der griechischen Historikerfragmente', *Klio*, 9, 1909, pp. 80–123, esp. p. 120 f.

[7] The only usable text of the fragments of the *Res humanae* is that of P. Mirsch, *Leipziger Studien*, 5, 1882, p. 1 ff. For the *Res divinae* see B. Cardauns (ed.), *M. Terentius Varro. Antiquitates rerum divinarum*, Mainz, 1976. Fragments of other important antiquarian works: B. Riposati, *M. Terenti Varronis de vita populi romani*, 2nd edn, Milan, 1972; P. Fraccaro, *Studi Varroniani. De gente populi Romani*, Padua, 1907. As for modern scholarly discussions, the situation is no better now than in 1950, when Momigliano noted the lack of a serious study of Varro in the history of antiquarian studies: *Contributo*, p. 72 n. 10 (n. 1 above). The standard account is still that of H. Dahlmann in *Paulys Realencyclopädie der classischen Altertumswissenschaft*, suppl. VI, 1935, cols 1172–277. More recently notice E. Rawson, *Roman Intellectual Life in the Late Roman Republic*, London, 1985, pp. 235–47 and *passim*.

[8] On Verrius Flaccus the standard scholarly works are R. Reitzenstein, *Verrianische Studien*, Breslau, 1887; W. Strzelecki, *Quaestiones Verrianae*, Warsaw, 1932, in Latin; A. Dihle in *Paulys Realencyclopädie der classischen Altertumswissenschaft*, VIII A, 2, 1958, cols 1636–45. Neglect is an understatement.

and demonstrated, more clearly than in any of his previous studies, that modern historiography amounts to a combination of both types. The work is not, as some superficial comments have suggested, an account of ancient historians and their modern successors; rather, it sets out to demonstrate that the foundations of modern historiography extend far beyond the confines of ancient historical writing as traditionally understood. Since the late nineteenth century we have managed to escape 'from the iron tower in which Thucydides want[ed] to shut us, having shut himself in it' (p. 53).

The complex story of how this happened is set out with characteristic lucidity in *Classical Foundations*, although the groundwork was laid in a series of pioneering articles which Momigliano published during the 1950s. The rediscovery of the ancient distinction between history and antiquities was a feature of the Renaissance. During the fifteenth and sixteenth centuries Thucydidean history was more esteemed than systematic learned research; but it was discredited when the historians took sides in political and religious disputes and directed their efforts to partisan causes. In the later seventeenth century this provoked a reaction in the form of a movement known as historical Pyrrhonism, which threatened to undermine the very foundations of history by questioning whether anything certain could be known about the past. As Momigliano was the first to observe, in a paper published in the *Journal of the Warburg and Courtauld Institutes* over forty years ago, it was the antiquarians who came to the rescue by showing that secure historical facts could be obtained by other means than relying on the statements of historians, by the careful investigation of primary evidence, and particularly through the study of coins, inscriptions and documents.[9]

The prestige of the antiquarians increased as a result, and in the eighteenth century historians such as the remarkable Scipione Maffei realized the importance of using non-literary evidence. But it was above all Gibbon who succeeded in incorporating the methods and erudition of the antiquarians into a major work of political and military history, and in doing so paved the way for the final synthesis that occurred in the course of the nineteenth century.[10] In the age of Niebuhr and Boeckh it was evident that historians had adopted the entire panoply of antiquarian learning, and were prepared to make use of evidence of all kinds; moreover it became obvious that there was no longer any point in a formal division between chronological order as the natural arrangement for history, and systematic or descriptive organization as the preserve of antiquarians. Such a

---

[9] 'Ancient History and the Antiquarian', *Journal of the Warburg and Courtauld Institutes*, 13, 1950, pp. 285–315 (= *Contributo* [n. 1 above], pp. 67–106).

[10] On Maffei see further Momigliano, *Secondo contributo* (n. 1 above), pp. 255–72 ('Gli studi classici di Scipione Maffei', *Giornale storico di letteratura italiana*, 133, 1956, pp. 363–83); and, on Gibbon, *Contributo* (n. 1 above), pp. 195–211 ('Gibbon's Contribution to Historical Method', *Historia*, 2, 1954, pp. 450–63).

distinction could hardly be rigidly maintained when traditional antiquarian subjects were being tackled chronologically, as in the *Geschichte des griechischen Kriegswesens von der ältesten Zeit bis auf Pyrrhos* by W. Rüstow and H. Köchly (Aarau, 1852), and when systematic description was being applied to the history of Greek civilization by Burckhardt.[11]

Nevertheless the final result was not a complete fusion of antiquarian research and political history; Momigliano clearly felt that the end of the story was uncertain and indeed that it had not yet been reached (pp. 76–9). He was undoubtedly right about this, but it is not easy to see why, and I doubt if I am alone in sensing that he himself was rather puzzled. The question is worth examining in some detail because, as Momigliano clearly saw, it raises fundamental issues about the nature and purpose of historical study, which we cannot afford to ignore.

II

The problem can be tackled on a number of levels. First there is the matter of academic conservatism, or rather, and this is perhaps another way of saying the same thing, the continuing failure of historians to think clearly about their own subject and to make up their minds about what they are doing. The antiquarian mentality is still very much alive, but in these days of conservationism and the 'heritage industry' that is perhaps not altogether surprising. In any case, we are all familiar with professional colleagues who value obscure facts for their own sake, and are incapable of distinguishing between relevant and irrelevant details. The most common manifestation of the type is the person who chooses a narrowly restricted topic, in ancient history usually a city, region, or province, and proceeds to collect 'all the evidence' relating to it. The result resembles nothing so much as a response to the famous injunction, in a children's examination, to 'write down everything you know' about a given subject.[12]

Equally there are still historians who confine themselves to political history based largely on literary evidence. These days a person who attempts to write on, say, the romanization of Italy, without visiting the country and without making extensive use of archaeological evidence, is unlikely to be taken seriously; but there are still areas of ancient political and military history where documents, archaeological evidence and the direct use of material artefacts are of minimal importance. Nevertheless there is no longer any chance that a serious historian could approach the ancient sources guided solely by the ideas and assumptions

[11] See further *Secondo contributo* (n. 1 above), pp. 283–98 (Introduction to the Italian edition of Burckhardt's *Griechische Kulturgeschichte*, 1955. English translation in Momigliano, *Studies on Modern Scholarship* (n. 3 above), pp. 44–53).

[12] Cf. M. I. Finley, *Ancient History: Evidence and Models*, London, 1985, p. 61. The whole chapter, 'How it really was', is relevant.

of the classical historians. Thucydides, Polybius and Tacitus can no longer supply us with the kinds of questions we want to ask. 'In this century historians have gone into the study of the ancient world with ideas and problems derived from other areas and other epochs', wrote Momigliano, dating the beginning of the change to around 1860.[13]

This crucial development finally severed the direct link between the historians of the classical world and their modern successors. What is more, historians of this century have been wholly conscious of the break with the classical past: no one any longer thinks of himself (or herself) as a new Thucydides. True enough, this idea took some time to die. Thucydides was still the model historian for Ranke, and even for Eduard Meyer, who died in 1930, but after that the break with the classical past was complete. It is possible that an exception should be made in the case of Sir Ronald Syme, but this cannot be certain, given the difficulty of understanding precisely what it was that Syme intended to achieve, as a historian, by his imitation of Tacitus. The answer is far from obvious if only because Syme was the last person to offer any explicit clarification of what he thought he was doing, or why.[14]

Although the antiquarian mentality is still with us, the distinction between the historian and the antiquarian is dead because there is no longer any justification for the exclusive definition of history as political history in the Thucydidean sense. What we are left with, and it was this that made Momigliano uneasy, is an incomplete aggregation of different types of history, each with its own distinctive methods and approaches. The dilemma is particularly evident in the contrast, which all historians have to face and must resolve in one way or another, between chronological narrative and systematic or descriptive analysis—what it is fashionable nowadays to call 'diachronic' and 'synchronic' history. The synchronic mode, once the exclusive preserve of the antiquarians, has now been adopted by historical sociologists and social anthropologists. Momigliano was even able to point to a direct link between modern sociology and ancient antiquarian studies through Emile Durkheim, who was taught by Fustel de Coulanges, and Max Weber, the favourite pupil of Mommsen. There is playful irony in this paradoxical suggestion, which must have been appreciated by the greatest modern exponent of Weberian history, Sir Moses Finley, who did not hesitate to use 'antiquarian' as a term of abuse, and whose contempt for the antiquarian mentality knew no bounds.

---

[13] *Settimo contributo* (n. 1 above), p. 30 (= 'The Place of Ancient Historiography in Modern Historiography', in *Les Études classiques aux XIXe et XXe siècles*, Entretiens Fondation Hardt, Geneva, 1980, pp. 127–57).

[14] See Momigliano's discussion in *Terzo contributo* (n. 1 above), pp. 729–37 (= Introduction to the Italian edition of Syme's *Roman Revolution*, 1962; English translation in *Studies on Modern Scholarship*, pp. 72–9).

Historians are well aware that they are no longer treading in the footsteps of their classical predecessors. Recent work, especially that dealing with rhetorical aspects of ancient historiography, has tended to stress the ways in which the Greek and Roman historians differed in their aims and methods from their modern counterparts. Particular attention has been drawn to their rhetorical aims (and their habit of composing fictitious speeches), their failure to acknowledge, criticize and evaluate their sources (i.e. their reluctance to offer anything equivalent to footnotes), and their unwillingness to make use of documents or archaeological evidence.[15] What has not been fully appreciated, however, is Momigliano's contention that the features that separate us from the classical historians are precisely those that bring us close to the antiquarians. One has only to mention their love of research, their delight in revealing new facts (preferably from newly discovered sources), their use of archives and relics, and the systematic arrangement of their works, to make the point clear.

A history of historiography that attempts to define the origin of what modern historians do, and why they do it, must take account of these elementary facts. Momigliano's *Classical Foundations* is the first to do this by giving serious attention to the role of the antiquarians. There is no guarantee, however, or even likelihood, that practising ancient historians will grasp the point (initial reactions to the book do not make one optimistic), any more than they did during the preceding forty years during which Momigliano published various articles on the subject. We have already seen that recent work on ancient historiography has neglected the antiquarians no less than in the past, a fact which must itself tend to justify Momigliano's disquiet about whether the fusion of history and antiquarian studies is really complete or secure.

A further reason for doubting whether the fusion has been properly effected is that there are forces at work in modern intellectual life that threaten to continue the separation or even to provoke a new separation along similar lines to the old. These forces have for the most part only become evident in the years since Momigliano delivered his Sather Lectures, which indicates how right he was to be dubious. One such tendency is represented by the so-called New Archaeology, the movement which first emerged in the 1960s and had the effect of formalizing an incipient division between history and archaeology. The more extreme versions of this tendency aimed to make archaeology an independent discipline concerned solely with 'material culture', and to deny altogether its function of providing historical information.[16]

---

[15] See e.g. T. P. Wiseman, *Clio's Cosmetics*, Leicester, 1979; A. J. Woodman, *Rhetoric in Classical Historiography: Four Studies*, London, 1988.

[16] The classic texts are L. R. and S. R. Binford, *New Perspectives in Archaeology*, Chicago, 1968, and D. L. Clarke, *Analytical Archaeology*, London, 1968. For a more recent (and rather pretentious) statement, M. Shanks, C. Tilley, *Re-Constructing Archaeology: Theory and Practice*, 2nd edn, London, 1992. For a useful

What is striking in this sort of formulation is its underlying assumption that material culture and historical evidence are distinct, indeed incompatible, entities. This was indeed the origin of the archaeologists' complaint, namely that historians tended to subordinate archaeology to the study of literary texts, calling upon it only when it had some bearing on political or military events, or relegating it to footnotes and appendices on supposedly marginal topics such as the arts and daily life. Given the reactionary character of much of what has passed for historiography during this century the complaint was understandable and entirely justified; and it was equally legitimate to argue that archaeologists (especially classical archaeologists) had collaborated with this backward-looking historical regime.

But the new archaeologists failed to see that the problem was not simply a matter of freeing archaeology from the tyranny of the historians, but of persuading the historians to approach their own subject differently. The best practitioners had clearly indicated the way forward. The efforts of the great historians of the nineteenth and early twentieth centuries, from Burckhardt and Mommsen to Beloch and Rostovtzeff, had shown historians how to escape from Thucydides' 'iron tower'. The point is that history, if it is not to be restricted to battles and political conflicts, must cover all the aspects of society and culture that were formerly the province of antiquarians, including those areas of material life that are illuminated by archaeological evidence.

By the same token, it must be recognized that the issues that concern the best modern archaeologists—the organization of settlements, demographic patterns, production, exchange and cultural processes—are historical issues, and ought to concern historians too. Archaeological research, if it is not to become a mindless application of mere technique, must be directed to answering historical questions. Rather than turn their backs on each other, historians and archaeologists should recognize that they are engaged in the same activity, but using different methods. It follows that written sources, if available, cannot and should not be ignored by archaeologists, any more than historians can avoid archaeological evidence. Attempting to write purely 'archaeological history' is misguided.[17] That route will lead inevitably to a revival of the most blinkered form of antiquarianism and will tend to drive the historians back into the tower.

It should be obvious enough that this brief discussion amounts in general to an argument against excessive specialization and to a plea for historians and archaeologists to work more closely together. The danger of over-specialization is that the proliferation of different techniques and approaches will lead once

---

guide through the maze, B. Trigger, *A History of Archaeological Thought*, Cambridge, 1989.

[17] See for example N. Spivey, S. Stoddart, *Etruscan Italy: An Archaeological History*, London, 1989, a deliberate attempt to give an account of the Etruscans without reference to written sources. The book is a *tour de force*, but the method is doomed to failure.

again to the creation of artificial barriers like the one that for so long separated history from antiquarian research, to the great detriment of both.

The second threat is more insidious, coming as it does at least partly from within the historical profession itself. This is the notion, deriving ultimately from literary theory and what is sometimes called post-modernism, that the work of the historian, being undeniably a text, is like all texts a rhetorical construct, and can make no claim to represent objective reality, the 'truth', or 'what really happened', concepts which are themselves held to be deeply problematic.[18] The idea that history is constructed by historians is of course true in the obvious sense that historians create their accounts of past events and situations by selection, interpretation and presentation of historical data. But this banal observation, sometimes hailed as a discovery, has given rise to the suggestion that all historians' constructs are fictional, and that, the truth being either not recoverable or even non-existent, no historical account can be regarded as more (or less) true than any other. The result is that all historical writing is relativized (a matter of 'competing fictions'), and comes to be regarded as no more than an expression of the ideological context in which it was produced. This kind of relativism is not in itself new; it is after all a feature of the more extreme forms of historicism.[19] But the current relativism of the deconstructionists is accompanied by a deep scepticism about the value of evidence and the possibility of establishing, or even pursuing, the truth about the past.

The threat is a serious one, as all historians know (or should know), and represents a challenge that is every bit as damaging as that of the seventeenth-century Pyrrhonists—if not more so, given the wide diffusion of this new Pyrrhonism in intellectual circles, and the sophistication of its proponents. The principal flaw in the argument, however, lies in the idea that 'history' is somehow locked up in the works of historians, and that the past cannot be approached except through their rhetorically constructed (and ideologically conditioned) narratives. This is evidently another way of getting historians back into the tower; it implies a concept of historical writing as something that must either be based on the work of earlier historians whose veracity cannot be controlled, or as something created *ex nihilo* by a contemporary historian who then becomes an

[18] See in particular the work of Hayden White, *Metahistory*, Baltimore, 1973; *Tropics of Discourse*, Baltimore, 1978; *The Content of the Form: Narrative Discourse and Historical Representation*, Baltimore, 1987; also R. Rorty, *Contingency, Irony and Solidarity*, Cambridge 1989. For a convenient summary of what these ideas amount to see K. Jenkins, *Re-Thinking History*, London, 1991.

[19] As pointed out by Momigliano in *Rivista storica italiana*, 73, 1961, pp. 104–32 (= *Terzo contributo* [n. 1 above], pp. 267–84; English translation, 'Historicism in Contemporary Thought', in *Studies in Historiography*, 1966, pp. 221–38).

uncontrollable source for future historians.[20] In short, it implies that historians are still engaged in classical historiography of the Thucydidean type.

Stated thus, the problem becomes soluble. As Momigliano himself argued in a lecture in 1982, the new Pyrrhonism, like its seventeenth-century counterpart, can be countered by the trusted old remedy, namely erudite research.[21] It need only be pointed out that there are recognized methods of checking historical evidence, and that traces of the past survive in a wide variety of forms which can be investigated and assessed by tried and tested procedures. True enough, the evidence has to be interpreted: it does not speak for itself. But it nevertheless exists independently of the historians, who can and must be judged on how well their interpretations account for the evidence (which need not be the same as that selected by the historians themselves).

To conclude this brief discussion of a complex issue we may note that the principal weakness of the prevailing scepticism is its failure to appreciate what modern historiography is really like. The feature that distinguishes the modern practice of history most clearly from its classical counterpart (and also from the kind of history presupposed in modern literary theory) is its use of methods pioneered by the antiquarians. In a discussion of the work of Hayden White, one of the leading theorists in question, Momigliano mentioned a piece of historical research he was then (in 1981) involved in, as a way of exemplifying 'what I believe to be the difference between the History we historians practise and the Metahistory the theoreticians attribute to us'. His conclusion was that 'the contrast between what I was doing and what White supposed I was doing was really too much'.[22] The research in question concerned an archaic Latin inscription which had been unearthed in an excavation a couple of years earlier. No seventeenth-century *érudit* could have bettered that.

III

As far as theory is concerned, then, there can be no doubt about the importance of antiquarian studies in Momigliano's general picture, and about their central place among the classical foundations of modern historiography. But the antiquarians and their methods are also vitally important in the actual practice of

---

[20] The following statement is typical: 'No account can recover the past as it was because the past was not an account, but events, situations, etc. As the past has gone, no account can ever be checked against it but only against other accounts. We judge the 'accuracy' of historians' accounts *vis-à-vis* other historians' interpretations and there is no real account, no proper history that, deep down, allows us to check all other accounts against it: there is no fundamentally correct 'text' of which other interpretations are just variations; variations are all there are.': Jenkins, *Re-thinking History* (n. 18 above), p. 11.

[21] *Settimo contributo* (n. 1 above), p. 255 (= 'Considerations on History in an Age of Ideologies', *The American Scholar*, 51, 1982, pp. 495–507.)

[22] *Settimo contributo* (n. 1 above), p. 52 (= 'The Rhetoric of History and the History of Rhetoric: on Hayden White's Tropes', *Comparative Criticism*, 3, 1981, pp. 259–68).

reconstructing the history of antiquity. This point can be illustrated by a brief examination of a topic to which Momigliano devoted much of his scholarly activity, the history of archaic Rome.

The history of early Rome is a classic example of a topic on which the modern investigator is held to be at the mercy of the ancient historians who provide the most detailed and coherent accounts of it. Everything, so it is said, depends on the reliability and honesty of Livy, Dionysius of Halicarnassus and Plutarch, and beyond them, of the earlier historians (the so-called 'annalists') who are believed to have been their main sources. If this annalistic tradition is unreliable, or even if it cannot be shown to be reliable, then the whole subject lies beyond the reach of serious historical inquiry. This, I believe, represents a widely held scholarly view, and is used to justify a sceptical or at best agnostic position on the early centuries of Rome.

The approach is unjustified, however, because its initial premise is mistaken. The annalists do not represent the only source of evidence for archaic Rome. This observation is valid in two distinct ways. First, the surviving literary sources can now be set against a growing body of archaeological evidence, including contemporary inscriptions, which can put the modern historian directly in touch with the material conditions, and sometimes with other aspects, of archaic Roman society. As we have seen, it was precisely this use of non-literary evidence that enabled the antiquaries of the seventeenth and eighteenth centuries to confront, and eventually to overcome, the assaults of the Pyrrhonists. 'They turned to coins, inscriptions and charters when chronicles and histories were distrusted. Ultimately, when the panic was over, the critics found that they had learned that not all chronicles and histories were to be distrusted.'[23] The same thing can be said, today, of the literary tradition concerning archaic Rome. The study of non-literary evidence has shown that Livy, Dionysius of Halicarnassus and Plutarch (and therefore the annalistic sources on which they are presumed to have drawn) are not after all as unreliable as was once thought.[24]

The second and rather different way of establishing the same point starts from the observation that the evidence for early Roman history cannot be simply defined as a combination of historical accounts and non-literary sources. The literary sources themselves give us much more than annalistic historical accounts. In fact they contain a great deal of information about archaic Rome that is independent of the historians and free from their real or supposed shortcomings. I am referring, of course, to the work of the antiquarians, who tend to be ignored

[23] *Settimo contributo* (n. 1 above), p. 255.

[24] A balanced statement of the case can be found in J. Heurgon, *The Rise of Rome to 264 BC*, London, 1973, p. 244 ff. On the impact of archaeological discoveries see most recently M. Pallottino, *Origini e storia primitiva di Roma*, Milan, 1993. I have discussed the issues at length in my book *The Beginnings of Rome*, London, 1995 (forthcoming).

in discussions of the sources for early Roman history, even in works that rely heavily on them. For many modern scholars, including experts on early Rome who ought therefore to know better, the literary tradition means the annalists. It is true that the annalists provide the essential narrative framework, but only the antiquarians give us any idea of what that framework might be based on. If it were not for the antiquarians, we should know nothing about, for example, the banquet songs or the *Annales Maximi*.[25] Our knowledge of Roman institutions, customs, monuments and so on is immeasurably enriched by antiquarian sources; without them, we should have a very different, and much dimmer, picture of archaic Rome.

It should be remembered that what the antiquarians tell us is not necessarily to be taken as more historical than what the annalists tell us. However learned they may have been, the Roman antiquarians were often credulous and facile (as their feeble etymologies so amply attest), and did not possess the kind of skill and expertise that a modern scholar would be able to bring to an ancient inscription or monument. Nevertheless the materials they were working with were genuine enough. Some modern books give the impression that in the late Republic very little survived from the city's ancient past. This absurd view is the exact opposite of the truth. The amount of evidence available to anyone in the late Republic who wished to investigate the archaic period was simply overwhelming.[26] However poorly they understood what they found, the antiquarians are important because they can put us in touch with countless genuine vestiges of a remote past that is, almost by definition, missing from the elaborated narratives of the annalists.

The evidence studied by the antiquarians was far more abundant than the admittedly rather meagre documentation that would have been available, even on the most optimistic interpretation, to the historians. This was because, unlike the historians, they did not confine themselves to material relating to political and military events. Religious texts (like the *carmen saliare*, the calendars, and the procedural books of the priestly colleges), building inscriptions, dedications, private documents and legal texts—all were grist to the antiquarian mill. For instance it was the antiquarians, rather than the historians, who studied the Twelve Tables, and observed, quite rightly, that they provided evidence not only about early Roman law, but about all kinds of social and cultural realities. Cicero, for example, realized that the funerary regulations in the Tables provided evidence for early Roman burial practices.[27]

---

[25] Discussed briefly in *Classical Foundations*, p. 92 ff. Momigliano's article on the banquet songs, 'Perizonius, Niebuhr and the Character of Early Roman Tradition', *Journal of Roman Studies*, 47, 1957, pp. 104–114 (= *Secondo contributo* [n. 1 above], pp. 69–88), is now a classic.

[26] See my *Beginnings of Rome* (n. 24 above), *passim*.

[27] Cicero, *De legibus*, 2.55 ff. On Cicero as an antiquarian see E. Rawson, 'Cicero the Historian and Cicero the Antiquarian', *Journal of Roman Studies*, 62, 1972, pp. 33–45 (= *Roman Culture and Society*, Oxford, 1991,

Apart from documents, there were many physical reminders of the city's ancient past in the buildings, monuments and other relics that surrounded the Romans on every side. Other survivals persisted in a more abstract form. They included institutions, customs and practices which the Romans had inherited from their ancestors, and on which they placed great value precisely because of their antiquity. Above all, the Romans preserved a vast amount of invaluable information about the past in the performance of their religious customs.

At this point it is worth noticing a curious feature of Momigliano's published work. Is it not strange that a scholar who devoted so much of his time and energy to the history of historiography on the one hand, and to the study of archaic Rome on the other, never chose to combine these two strands by examining the historiographical tradition of archaic Rome? The fact remains, however, that Momigliano never wrote an article on the Roman annalists, or chose to do for Livy or Dionysius of Halicarnassus what he so memorably did for Herodotus, Thucydides, Polybius, Ammianus Marcellinus, Cassiodorus, and so many others. The only exception is Fabius Pictor, the first Roman historian, to whom Momigliano was naturally drawn as a pioneer who wrote in a language that was not his own and reacted in a positive way to a political and moral crisis in his society. For Momigliano, the significance of Fabius Pictor lay in the fact that he introduced Greek-style history to Rome, and thereby transmitted it to us, rather than in what he had to say about early Rome as such. The fact is, of course, that almost nothing is known about Fabius' account of the archaic period.[28]

It remains true, however, that apart from his studies of Fabius Pictor, Momigliano never wrote about the other republican annalists or even Livy, an omission so striking that it must have been deliberate. The reasons are undoubtedly complex. The failure to study the republican historians in a direct way extends to Caesar and Sallust, and cannot be explained solely in relation to the problem of the sources for the archaic period.[29] Nevertheless I suspect that one of the reasons was the fact that the bulk of the literary evidence we actually use in discussions of early Rome derives not (or not in the first instance) from the annalists, but from the antiquarians. This is a crucial point. Momigliano's own research on this subject has its roots in the antiquarian tradition because he was not concerned to write a political and military narrative of the early centuries of

---

pp. 58–79).

[28] As Momigliano firmly pointed out (*Quarto contributo* [n. 1 above], pp. 488–9). The article 'Linee per una valutazione di Fabio Pittore', *Rendiconti della Accademia dei Lincei*, ser. 8, 15, 1960, pp. 310–20 (= *Terzo contributo* [n. 1 above], pp. 55–68) is the starting point for any study of Rome's first historian.

[29] For a brief glimpse of what we have missed see 'The Crisis of the Roman State and the Roman Historians (from Sallust to Tacitus)', an unpublished lecture of 1942, now printed in *Nono contributo* (n. 1 above), pp. 503–19. Further remarks on the republican historians will appear in 'Aspects of Roman Political Thought. From Seneca to Tacitus', a series of unpublished lectures given in 1947, to be published in the forthcoming (1995?) *Decimo contributo*.

Rome, but by using erudite methods to reconstruct and analyse its social organization and its political and religious institutions.

A small but significant pointer to the nature of Momigliano's method can be found in his account of the sources in the justly famous 'Interim Report on the Origins of Rome', published in 1963.[30] Here he singled out, as the principal types of evidence, the literary sources, archaeological evidence, linguistic evidence, and 'evidence from religious customs'. Strictly speaking this is illogical since the evidence from religious customs is itself derived from literary sources (note also that there is an inconsistency in the numbering of the sub-headings at this juncture). But Momigliano's point was clearly that the (essentially antiquarian) information about customs and institutions is so distinctive, by contrast with the annalistic narratives, that it forms a separate (and of course more reliable) body of evidence.

Momigliano's work on early Rome, which consistently focuses on the interpretation of minute and obscure texts as evidence for a broader social reality, is a perfect demonstration of the way in which modern historiography has incorporated the methods of the antiquarians, and in which profound and far-reaching historical conclusions can be extracted from the findings of systematic learned research.

---

[30] *Journal of Roman Studies*, 53, 1963, pp. 95–121 (= *Terzo contributo* [n. 1 above], pp. 545–98). For a later synthesis, incorporating the results of nearly twenty years of subsequent research and reflection, see 'The Origins of Rome', chapter 3 of the revised *Cambridge Ancient History*, VII.2, Cambridge, 1989, pp. 52–112 (= *Settimo contributo* [n. 1 above], pp. 379–436).

Tradition and Technique in Historical Chronology

ANTHONY GRAFTON

When I want to feel sure that technical chronology matters, I go to the Campo de' Fiori, where Giordano Bruno died in February 1600. Between the grim shadow of his monument and the bright window of one of Rome's liveliest bookshops, Fahrenheit 451, I recall the list of heresies for which he went to the stake. According to Caspar Schoppe, Bruno identified the Holy Spirit with the *anima mundi*. He unmasked Moses, Jesus and the Apostles as magicians who had performed tricks rather than miracles. And he took a heretical position on biblical chronology. Bruno insisted that only the Jews were descended from Adam and Eve; the rest of the human race went back to the first man and woman, who were created the day before Adam and Eve.[1] In 1600, in other words, chronology mattered a great deal; so much that it seemed worth dying for. Though eccentric in many ways, Bruno was not the only heretic who believed this. At the other end of Christian Europe, in England, Christopher Marlowe also ventured brave pre-Adamite remarks about the incompleteness of the Old Testament account of human history.[2] So did the less learned French heretic Noël Journet, who died for his views a few years before Bruno.[3] If some heretics were chronologers, however, most chronologers were not heretics. Across the river from the square in which Bruno died, a team of scholars and mathematicians had worked hard and well in the Vatican to devise the reformed Gregorian calendar of 1582.[4] And historical as well as practical chronology fascinated the most original Roman humanists from Pomponio Leto to Onofrio Panvinio.[5] Rome, moreover, was only a particularly prominent node on the networks of correspondence and polemic that bound students of historical chronology everywhere in Europe into a large and quarrelsome community. From the court of St James in London to the

---

[1] See *Documenti della vita di Giordano Bruno*, ed. V. Spampanato, Florence, 1933, pp. 199–202, esp. p. 201, letter of Caspar Schoppe to Conrad Rottershausen: 'solos Hebraeos ab Adamo et Eva originem ducere, reliquos ab iis duobus quos Deus pridie fecerat'.

[2] See P. Kocher, *Christopher Marlowe*, Chapel Hill, 1946, pp. 34–5 (quoting the report on Marlowe to the Privy Council known as the Baines note): 'That the Indians and many Authors of antiquity haue assuredly writen of aboue 16 thousand yeares agone wheras <Moyses> Adam is <said> proued to haue liued within 6 thowsand yeares...'

[3] See R. Peter, 'Noël Journet detracteur de l'Écriture Sainte (1582)' in *Croyants et sceptiques au XVIe siècle*, ed. M. Lienhard, Strasbourg, 1981, pp. 147–56.

[4] See *Gregorian Reform of the Calendar*, ed. G. V. Coyne et al., Vatican City, 1983, with full references to earlier literature; N. Courtwright, 'The Vatican Tower of the Winds and the Architectural Legacy of the Counter Reformation' in *IL 60. Essays Honoring Irving Lavin on His Sixtieth Birthday*, New York, 1990, pp. 117–31.

[5] See W. McCuaig, 'The Fasti Capitolini and the Study of Roman Chronology in the Sixteenth Century', *Athenaeum*, 79, 1991, pp. 141–59; P. Jacks, *Urbs and civitas*, forthcoming.

Hradčany in Prague, from the Calvinists' University of Leiden to the Jesuits' Collegio Romano, scholars and scientists sweated and mumbled over the intricate tables and difficult texts that Joseph Scaliger and a host of his forgotten predecessors and rivals had brought into play. They tried to squeeze coherent information from the mysterious numbers of the Hebrew kings and the even more mysterious calendars of the ancient Athenians. And they produced an immense and rebarbative literature, perhaps the least amusing, but certainly the most formidable, component of that antiquarian tradition of which Arnaldo Momigliano was the unrivalled master.[6]

The intellectual world in which these Renaissance chronologers dwelt has received few large-scale maps and no detailed studies in modern times. This neglect does not stem from the obscurity or unimportance of the subject. Technical chronology reconstructs the calendars and dates the main events of ancient and medieval history. In the Renaissance it won the interest of many of the most innovative thinkers and gave rise to several sophisticated debates. It probably enjoyed more esteem than textual criticism, which threatened to degenerate into sterile quarrels over petty details, or epigraphy, which suffered from the proliferation of attractive fakes. Europeans plastered their walls and filled their rucksacks with calendars and charts of world history. They produced and consumed majestic books and tiny monographs on both the structure and the details of historic time. They argued heatedly over the nature of lost calendars, the dates of eras and battles, and the historicity of Greek and Roman myths. By the early seventeenth century they had identified what remain the central sources and data for the study of technical chronology. They had constructed the armature of precise Julian dates to which we still affix the events and movements of ancient and medieval history—though their version began, unlike ours, with the Creation, and included the life of Heracles and the fall of Troy as well as the first Olympic games and the Peloponnesian War. And they had studied, sometimes fragmentarily but sometimes presciently, the rich body of religious beliefs and practices which underlay ancient calendars. No Renaissance science, perhaps, reached more dramatic or more lasting results.

Even in the Enlightenment, when many intellectuals across Europe lost faith in the extravagant erudition of late humanism, chronology provoked and stimulated. Bolingbroke and Vico devoted sharp treatises, admittedly of very different kinds, to attacking the Latinate citadels of seventeenth-century erudition. They insisted that no one could actually carry out the task that Scaliger and Petavius, Selden and Marsham had taken on: building a sturdy framework of dates for the whole history of the human race. 'In short', Bolingbroke wrote, '... all these systems are so many enchanted castles, they appear to be something, they are nothing but appearances: like them too, dissolve the charm, and they

---

[6] See in general A. Grafton, *Defenders of the Text*, Cambridge, Mass. etc, 1991, ch. 4.

vanish from the sight'.[7] Vico, more specifically, traced the failure of Scaliger and Petavius directly to the principles from which they began. Despite their 'stupenda erudizione', they had insisted on basing their chronologies on 'the astronomical year'. This the primitive men with whom Vico populated early history had not understood, and in any case astronomy could impose order only on celestial, not terrestrial, events. Vico thought the erudite chronology of the great seventeenth-century scholars as futile, in the end, as the astrological chronology of that fifteenth-century polymath, Pierre d'Ailly.[8]

Other *philosophes* found chronology more to their liking. As a child Edward Gibbon made the dynasties of Egypt 'his top and cricket-ball'.[9] As a grown man he lay awake in bed, worrying about the mysteries of the Metonic cycle and the date of the Battle of Gaugamela, and rose to reassure himself by reading Edmond Halley's excellent digest of a treatise by the learned but turgid Dodwell.[10] Heroic polymaths like Dodwell made easy targets for ridicule, even for their sympathisers (Gibbon said of him that his enormous mass of learning extinguished the flickering candle flame of his intellect). But their work lived, even in the libraries of men of the coffee-house and the salon.[11]

In the Latin-speaking world of university scholarship, moreover, technical chronology of the traditional style retained a central role in the eighteenth century. It was taught and practised at a high level in Gatterer's Historical Institute at Göttingen. More important, it survived the transition from *Polyhistorie* to *Neuhumanismus*. F. A. Wolf included chronology in his philological encyclopedia, and his followers in Berlin and elsewhere—above all Ideler and Böckh—did a great deal of sophisticated work on chronological texts and problems. In particular, they took advantage of the rapid expansion of epigraphic evidence to study local chronologies throughout the ancient world, rather than confining themselves, as earlier scholars largely had, to the history and calendar of Athens. But they also continued to do original and insightful work on problems that had become acute in the sixteenth century, and they still read Scaliger.[12] One of the most distinguished pieces of chronological work produced in nineteenth-century Berlin was Ewald Scheibel's edition of Scaliger's

---

[7] Henry St John, Viscount Bolingbroke, *Letters on the Study and Use of History*, London, 1752, I, pp. 8–9.

[8] G. B. Vico, *La Scienza Nuova giusta l'edizione del 1744*, ed. F. Nicolini, Bari, 1911–16, II, p. 679.

[9] E. Gibbon, *Memoirs of my Life*, ed. G. Bonnard, London, 1966, p. 43.

[10] *The Miscellaneous Works of Edward Gibbon, Esq.*, ed. John, Lord Sheffield, London, 1837, pp. 453–55; for Halley's treatise see F. Brokesby, *The Life of Mr. Henry Dodwell*, London, 1715, II, pp. 615ff.

[11] For Gibbon on Dodwell see *Miscellaneous Works* (n. 10 above), p. 431.

[12] For Wolf's views on chronology see his *Vorlesungen über die Alterthumswissenschaft*, ed. J. D. Gürtler and S. F. W. Hoffmann, Leipzig, 1839, I, 372–6; for two examples of Böckh's remarkable insight into traditional problems see A. Grafton and N. Swerdlow, 'Greek Chronography in Roman Epic: The Calendrical Date of the Fall of Troy in the *Aeneid*', *Classical Quarterly*, 36, 1986, pp. 212–18 and Ptolemy, *Almagest*, ed. G. J. Toomer, London, 1984, pp. 13–14.

'Ολυμπιάδων ἀναγραφή—a remarkable commentary on a remarkable text, written in Greek, in which Scaliger reconstructed what a Hellenistic chronicle would have looked like so effectively that later scholars as learned as Lessing and Heyne mistook it for the real thing.[13] Scheibel's vast commentary explicated Scaliger's annalistic text year by year and point by point, in the light of all his other work; it remains the only profound, first-hand study of Scaliger's practices as a chronologer.

Work on Greek and Roman chronology burgeoned in the academies and universities of the nineteenth century. The subject attracted the interest of the most creative scholars in Germany: Niebuhr, Bernays, Theodor Mommsen. It spawned a vast literature of treatises and Gymnasium programs, periodical articles and pamphlets. *Quaestiones desperatae* like the date of the founding of Rome, the nature of the original *Bauernkalender*, and the development of calendrical cycles attracted scholar after scholar. Many of them, unfortunately, were as cranky as they were erudite, and many of their debates as acid as they were intricate. It was only typical that Mommsen devoted the second edition of his *Römische Chronologie* to refuting the systems of that particularly injudicious innovator, his brother August. The experts swaddled each central problem, half-digested, in sticky layers of new scholarship, like flies in a spider's web. And at some point in the later nineteenth century the strips of new *Literatur* finally concealed the older Latin treatises. Chronologers genuflected to Scaliger in their introductory chapters, where they laid out the genealogy of their field in order to prove its age and respectability. But they did not read his books. They usually forgot that he had had many predecessors and colleagues. And they almost never realised that some of their shiniest new theories were reinvented Renaissance wheels.

Between 1880 and 1920, syntheses emerged. Tempers continued to run hot, and debates still raged. But iron men like Fotheringham, Gelzer, Ginzel, Jacoby, Mahler, P. V. Neugebauer, Oppolzer and Rühl framed and synthesized the results of a hundred years of hard scholarly labor in two sorts of works that remain the central tools of the chronologer's trade: editions of the basic primary sources and manuals of the basic techniques. As late as the early part of this century, in other words, technical chronology remained a central component of classical scholarship.

After the first World War, however, chronology almost atrophied. The newer manuals of Kubitschek and Bickerman showed a dramatic falling-off in technical competence. The one field that still received intense cultivation—the Athenian calendar—was not fertilized by the scholarly *son et lumière* that crackled and flickered over the agora for half a century, only to leave us still unable to convert

---

[13] See Joseph Scaliger, 'Ολυμπιάδων ἀναγραφή, ed. E. Scheibel, Berlin, 1852.

an Attic to a Julian date. A few individuals—notably Helm, O. Neugebauer, Pritchett and Rose—continued to make substantial, lasting contributions to the technical literature. But most twentieth-century classical scholars have been more inclined to denigrate chronology than to study it. The very name has often served, like 'antiquarianism', as a code word for useless, irrelevant scholarship. To paraphrase Sir Kenneth Dover, many scholars who would be appalled to make a false quantity will say three impossible things about the Athenian calendar before breakfast, with perfect equanimity.[14] Early modern chronology has naturally become even more obscure, a literal no-man's-land.

This attitude of uncomprehending disdain can be explained. Chronology requires of anyone who would understand it a willingness to master techniques and terms that do not form part of a normal classical education. One must study a small amount of classical astronomy, learn one's way around eclipse tables, and become familiar with the vagaries of the solar and lunar years. In early modern times, the necessary information formed part of the fabric of common life. It belonged to the art of the computus, which the vast majority of intellectuals knew intimately. After the spring equinox many Europeans turned naturally to reckoning by the moon until Easter had come and gone, and then turned as naturally back to their normal, solar calendar for the rest of the year.[15] Men whose rituals were still governed by the moon readily took an interest in her ancient complaint, recorded by Aristophanes, that the Athenians had failed to observe her phases and starved the gods by celebrating their festivals on the wrong days.[16]

In the eighteenth and nineteenth centuries, the art of the computus became the preserve of clerical antiquaries, the sort of dry-biscuit subject that the protagonist of an M. R. James story might study before being attacked at midnight by the ghost of a long-dead cathedral canon. But serious scholars, at least in the German-speaking world, enjoyed a secondary education that combined Greek, Latin and mathematics, all at a high level. Classicists like Böckh and Eduard Schwartz did not suffer from math anxiety; indeed, many of them were expert computers. Astronomers like Ideler, Ginzel, Oppolzer and Fotheringham, for their part, could read the classical texts in the original languages. Collaboration and discussion seemed easy. Chronology, in fact, was probably the last academic study in which the two cultures of the modern university shared a territory. But

---

[14] See *Les Études classiques aux XIXe et XXe siècles*, ed. W. Den Boer, Vandoeuvres, 1980, pp. 123–4: 'But it is absurd to dismiss with contempt—as I was brought up to do—a man who is mistaken over the quantity of the vowel in the first syllable of *omittere*, while treating with far greater tolerance another who "knows his quantities" but overlooks or cannot understand the relation between the Attic calendar and the solar year'.

[15] See E. Le Roy Ladurie, *Carnival in Romans*, tr. M. Feeney, New York, 1979, p. 189.

[16] Aristophanes, *The Clouds*, 615–26.

by the end of the nineteenth century, the pedagogical as well as the computistical foundations of chronology had been undermined. Technical and classical education became separate tracks. Nowadays few scholars or scientists have even encountered the ecclesiastical calendar in a prayer book. Many have never computed or looked up a date for Easter.[17] Tables alienate philologists, and texts astronomers, to an extent that would have astonished and pained the giants of German *Neuhumanismus*. The very language of chronology has become foreign.

Since the 1960s, happily, the study of ancient chronology has floated again, borne on two of the larger currents that have recently stirred the once calm waters of classical studies. A revived interest in ancient religion has alerted many scholars to the importance of calendars and the officials who controlled them. And a revived interest in the Hellenistic and late antique worlds has led many scholars to concentrate on the periods, milieus and textual traditions in which chronological scholarship flourished. The Alexandrian Museum, late antique historiography, and Byzantine historiography and science have all received renewed attention. If we do not yet have a new chronology, we certainly have many new instruments with which to shape one. Sharp new manuals have been written.[18] The tradition of chronography has undergone a thorough and constructively scrutiny. The texts of Censorinus, Geminus and Syncellus have been newly established, and the first two newly translated into modern languages.[19] And many scholars have devised ingenious and plausible solutions to long-standing technical problems.

As scholars have turned back to the ancient texts and problems, moreover, they have realised that the syntheses and debates of the nineteenth century had a history of their own—and that they had often been shaped to a surprising extent by the assumptions and theories of early modern scholars. Most nineteenth-century historians accepted Scaliger's belief that Eusebius drew his chronological methods and materials from the lost work of Julius Africanus. But Alden Mosshammer's revisionist analysis has restored a substantial measure of creativity and learning to the author of the *Chronicle* that we still have, and raised disturbing questions about the achievement of his putative source.[20] Scaliger also dismissed the Byzantine chronologer George Syncellus, whose work he was the first to exploit, as a learned idiot who had tripped over good sources, a scholar

---

[17] Cf. the moving words of Professor Trevor-Roper, in his *Catholics, Anglicans and Puritans*, London, 1987, p. 159.

[18] E.g. A. E. Samuel, *Greek and Roman Chronology*, Munich, 1972.

[19] For Censorinus see the edition by N. Sallmann, Leipzig, 1983, and the translation with notes by G. Rocca-Serra, Paris, 1980; for Geminus the edition and translation by G. Aujac, Paris, 1975; for Syncellus the edition by A. A. Mosshammer, Leipzig, 1984.

[20] A. A. Mosshammer, *The Chronicle of Eusebius and Greek Chronographic Tradition*, Lewisburg, 1979; see also T. D. Barnes, *Constantine and Eusebius*, Cambridge, Mass. etc, 1983, ch. 7.

even more foolish and a writer even more derivative than Eusebius. Yet William Adler's recent work has shown that Scaliger's lack of sympathy with his intermediate source sometimes prevented him and his successors from understanding the text before them. In fact, Syncellus and other late Christian chronographers had a considerable degree of method in their apparent madness.[21]

These enterprises clearly take chronology very much in Momigliano's spirit: as a coherent intellectual tradition, one that must be studied directly and from end to end if any segment of it is to be properly labelled, fixed and explicated. Mosshammer and Adler have brushed the dust from Scaliger's great folio of 1606, the *Thesaurus temporum*. And instead of enfolding his work in another cloud of meaningless adjectives, they have begun to strip it of its worn but clinging layers of old rhetoric and to examine it in detail. Scaliger's biases and errors, it turns out, have done as much as his vast learning and insight to shape generations of inquiry into both the Christian chronography of the age of the Fathers and the earlier, pagan chronography that the Christians appropriated and replaced. The history of modern chronological scholarship has already become a source of revitalization in the study of ancient scholarship.

My report, accordingly, is hopeful; but it is also tentative. Far more can be done both to explicate the early modern sources and to use them to refine and enrich our approach to the classical ones. Two case studies will suggest how stimulating it can be to force chronological texts from different periods to speak to one another in new ways. Sometimes, indeed, applying Momigliano's method may even require the modification of Momigliano's views—a result that underlines, rather than undermines, the power of his work.

From Scaliger to Pfeiffer and Momigliano, scholars have treated the classical origins of technical chronology in the same way. They have attributed it to the work of Hellenistic scholars—above all Eratosthenes, the great Alexandrian philologist who also did remarkable work in mathematics and astronomy. They have described it as a typical Alexandrian study: technical, esoteric, rigorous, dependent on the many skills and texts that could be brought to bear on a single subject in the Alexandrian Museum. Erasistratus's discovery of the valves in the heart, we are told, had to take place in Alexandria. Only there could scholars read older texts while medical virtuosi practised dissection and vivisection. There, moreover, the physicist Ctesibius invented both the valve and the pump—thus providing Erasistratus with a mechanical model all previous medical thinkers had lacked.[22] Only in Alexandria, similarly, could scholars bring to bear on records from many cities a knowledge of mathematics and astronomy. Alexandrian

[21] W. Adler, *Time Immemorial: Archaic History and its Sources in Christian Chronography from Julius Africanus to George Syncellus*, Washington, D.C., 1989; see also G. H. Huxley, 'On the Erudition of George the Synkellos', *Proceedings of the Royal Irish Academy*, 81.C.6, 1981, pp. 207–17.

[22] See G. Maino, *The Healing Hand*, Cambridge, Mass. etc., 1975, ch. 8.

philologists possessed not only a unique store of materials but also an acute sense of history. Aristarchus refused to explain away the unfortunate bits of Homer by allegoresis. Eratosthenes dismissed the scholars who tried to work out the real locations of Odysseus's landfalls in the *Odyssey*. His rigorous scientific chronology, which arranged a vast amount of data on the firm time-line provided by the Olympiads and refused to treat the age of myth before the foundation of the Olympics as part of history, was a native product of Egypt's foreign city.

This reconstruction has been restated memorably by many great scholars. Gottfried Bernhardy, the pupil of Wolf who produced the first systematic collection of *Eratosthenica*, praised his hero's precision, his willingness to undertake the most ant-like of labors in the pursuit of truth.[23] Eduard Schwartz, almost a century later, drew an inspiring profile of Eratosthenes's tireless efforts and 'wissenschaftlicher Scharfblick'. Schwartz criticized the great chronologer only for his effort to provide dates for the Trojan war. This error, Schwartz lamented, proved that epic exerted a spell over the Greek 'scientific spirit'.[24] Similar views inspired Rudolf Pfeiffer's eloquent account of Eratosthenes —though he defended Eratosthenes's effort to provide dates for Troy's fall and Homer's *floruit*.[25]

These accounts have only one flaw: they rest on almost no evidence. The lack of material certainly reflects no lack of interest. From the beginnings of modern chronology, scholars realized that they could recreate the dates and intervals of ancient history only by reconstructing the lost works of ancient chronographers. Even the forger Annius of Viterbo, whose products did so much to bring the whole study of history into disrepute, derived some of his wares from the tradition of chronography that he encountered in the *Chronicle* of Eusebius and Jerome and elsewhere.[26] The fragments of Eratosthenes's work on chronology attracted interest by the middle of the sixteenth century. Even before Scaliger wrote, Abraham Bucholzer had made Eratosthenes's list of eras, preserved by Clement of Alexandria,[27] the basis of his chronology, and the Genevan fanatic Matthieu Béroalde had attacked the text—as he attacked Herodotus—as a pagan fantasy.[28] Scaliger, who made one of the first collections of the fragments of early

---

[23] *Eratosthenica*, ed. G. Bernhardy, Berlin, 1832, p. 238: 'Eratosthenes tamen minus quam pro molestia et difficultatibus illius argumenti gloriae videtur reportasse; verum ne hic quidem diligentiam aut acumen viri desideres consuetum...'

[24] Ed. Schwartz, *Charakterköpfe aus der antiken Literatur*, 2nd ser., 2nd edn, Leipzig, 1911, pp. 101–3.

[25] R. Pfeiffer, *Geschichte der klassischen Philologie von den Anfängen bis zum Ende des Humanismus*, tr. M. Arnold, 2nd edn, Munich, 1978, pp. 203–5.

[26] Grafton, *Defenders of the Text* (n. 6 above), ch. 3.

[27] F. Jacoby, *Die Fragmente der griechischen Historiker* (hereafter *FrGrHist*), I–II, Berlin, 1925–30; III, Leiden, 1950–58; I, 2nd edn, Leiden, 1957 (repr. 1968), 241 F 1a.

[28] A. Bucholzer, *Isagoge chronologica*, n.p., 1580, ff. 39ᵛ–40ᵛ; M. Béroalde, *Chronicum, Scripturae sacrae auctoritate constitutum*, Geneva, 1575, pp. 211–12.

Greek historians, studied Eratosthenes with care, printed a text of his era list, and followed Dionysius of Halicarnassus (*FrGrHist* 241 F 1b) in insisting on the excellence of his technique as a chronologer.[29] Two great German scholars, Bernhardy in the nineteenth century and Felix Jacoby in the twentieth, have trawled the same waters. Yet their fine-meshed nets have caught only enough fragments to fill ten pages in Jacoby's *Die Fragmente der griechischen Histor-iker*. If we return, as Momigliano taught us to, from modern structures of interpretation to the unadorned blocks of evidence they rest on, it will become clear that the two are often insecurely joined, and that the tradition of scholarship may have grown both awry and away from the evidence.

One text raises at least mild qualms. The world chronicle of Syncellus contains a list of thirty-eight Egyptian kings attributed to Apollodorus. He received it, supposedly, from Eratosthenes, who translated it at the order of the king from the Egyptian records of the scribes at Diospolis.[30] In the seventeenth and eighteenth centuries this list proved Eratosthenes's erudition. Scaliger, who considered Eratosthenes as expert in non-Greek as in Greek history, noted it.[31] In the mid-seventeenth century John Marsham made the list the foundation of his influential chronology; a century later, in the age of the *Magic Flute*, P. E. Jablonski used the text to prove that Eratosthenes had known the Egyptian language very well indeed.[32] Bernhardy accepted the list as genuine Eratosthenes and founded on it his belief that the best Alexandrian chronologers had taken a cosmopolitan interest in Egyptian as well as Greek history.[33] All of these judgements reflect a desire to find an ancient antecedent for modern scholarship rather than an effort to put the text back into its context—the maze of Hellenistic and later Greek texts, purportedly of Near Eastern origin. The claims to have been translated from originals in recondite languages that appear in such texts are usually the signatures of the men who forged them, and who hoped by claiming merely to serve as translators to add veracity to what would otherwise have been

---

[29] For Scaliger's text of the Eratosthenes era list see *Thesaurus temporum*, 2nd edn, Amsterdam, 1658, pt. 3, p. 396. For his view of Eratosthenes see his *Opus de emendatione temporum*, 3rd edn, Geneva, 1629, p. 536: 'Canones Eratosthenei omnium optimi'; and his *Elenchus utriusque orationis chronologicae D. Davidis Parei*, Leiden, 1607, pp. 41–2, 80–1.

[30] F. Jacoby, *Die Fragmente der Griechischen Historiker,* I–II, Berlin,1925–30; III, Leiden, 1950–58; I, 2nd edn, Leiden, 1957 (hereafter *FrGrHist*), 244 F 85: 'βασιλέων τῶν...Θηβαίων, ὧν τὰ ὀνόματα Ἐρατοσθένης λαβὼν ἐκ τῶν ἐν Διοσπόλει ἱερογραμματέων παρέφρασεν ἐξ Αἰγυπτίας εἰς Ἑλλάδα φωνήν...'

[31] See *Thesaurus temporum* (n. 28 above), pt. 3, p. 18, and *Canones isagogici*, ibid., p. 136.

[32] J. Marsham, *Chronicus Canon Aegyptiacus Ebraicus Graecus et disquisitiones*, London, 1672; A. Des Vignolles, *Chronologie de l'Histoire Sainte*, Berlin, 1738, II, pp. 735–65.

[33] *Eratosthenica* (n. 23 above), pp. 238, 256: 'Post Graecorum chronologiam Aegyptiis quoque dynastis suum tribuisse locum Eratosthenes videtur'.

bald and unconvincing prefaces.[34] The most informative reactions, however, are those of the two most profound students of Eratosthenes's work: Jacoby and Schwartz. Jacoby condemned the list as a fake, unconnected with either Eratosthenes or Apollodorus.[35] Schwartz by contrast praised the list as a relic of cultural interaction; he singled Eratosthenes out as the first Greek scholar who had asked native Near Eastern scribes to translate historical records for him.[36] Yet though the two men disagreed on the provenance and worth of this text—the longest single text attributed to Eratosthenes, it amounts to more than ten per cent of his surviving chronological work—they agreed absolutely on the nature and value of Eratosthenes's larger scholarly project.

Consider the situation. A piece of evidence that seemed central to earlier students of Eratosthenes, a queen or at least a rook in the game of interpretation, serves one modern player as queen, while the other knocks it from the board. Yet neither its presence nor its absence has had much effect on the outcome of the game. Even Schwartz, who thought the piece genuine, insisted that a rigorous scholar like Eratosthenes would not have tried to synchronize the dates of Greek and Egyptian history. But he had no more evidence than we do to go on, and it is hard to imagine what Eratosthenes would have used an Egyptian dynasty list for, except his chronology. Evidently the tradition of modern scholarship—the Renaissance construction of Eratosthenes as a polyglot figure rather like Scaliger or Salmasius (who was actually called a modern Eratosthenes)—has done as much as the texts themselves to shape our estimate of this great but shadowy figure.

One worries even more keenly that textual damp may be rising when one examines the chief foundation for Eratosthenes's claim to scientific rigour. This is preserved not in Greek but in Latin, in Censorinus, *De die natali,* 21:

> I shall now deal with the period that Varro calls *historical*. He divides time into three periods. The first stretches from the beginning of mankind to the first cataclysm; because of our ignorance it is called 'obscure'. The second stretches from the first cataclysm to the first Olympiad; because many myths are recorded in it, it is called 'mythical'. The third stretches from the first Olympiad to us. Because the events in it are contained in true histories, he calls it 'historical'. As to the first period, whether it had a beginning or lasted from eternity, and certainly how long it was, cannot be known. The second is not known precisely, but it is believed to have been about 1600 years long. For from the first cataclysm, which they call that of Ogygus, to the reign of Inachus, there are around 400 years; [I omit a phrase that occurs in angled brackets in the modern editions: A.G.] and from then to the first Olympiad there are just over 400. And as these years, though

---

[34] See A. Grafton, *Forgers and Critics*, Princeton, 1990.

[35] The fragment appears as pseudo-Apollodorus in *FrGrHist* 244 F 85.

[36] Schwartz, *Charakterköpfe* (n. 24 above), p. 96.

they are the last ones in mythical time, are the closest to the memory of historians, some have tried to define them more precisely. Sosibius wrote that this period was 395 years long, Eratosthenes that it was 407, Timaeus that it was 417, Aretes that it was 514, and others have computed it in other ways. Their disagreement shows that it is uncertain.[37]

This text has long seemed memorable and incisive. It inspired Scaliger, who repeatedly quoted Varro's periodization and praised his insistence that history began with the Olympic games. Jacoby and others have argued that it must represent a version of Eratosthenes's argument, borrowed by Varro, for using the Olympic chronology.[38] But the passage is deeply problematic. As it stands, its sums do not add up; 400 years and a little more than 400 cannot make a total of 1600. Scaliger did not raise—much less resolve—this problem. Lindenbrog, who did point to it in his commentary on the text, had no remedy to offer: 'I seriously doubt the correctness of this passage', he remarked, 'but my scruples prevented me from changing it without manuscript authority'.[39]

Only after Böckh and others interpolated their versions of a whole clause, which set an interval of 800 years between Inachus and the fall of Troy, did the mathematics work. One basic piece of evidence for Eratosthenes's method, in short, is a piece of Latin prose composition done in nineteenth-century Germany, when the nature of that method had supposedly been established from other evidence. The argument for Eratosthenes's precision is circular. Moreover, the passage from Censorinus is itself tied to Eratosthenes only by another scholarly conjecture.

And even if we grant the connection between Eratosthenes and Censorinus, the passage remains ambivalent. It divides the age of myth into periods and both reflects and criticizes efforts to define the last of these very precisely. The original passage could thus have served as a warrant for, as well as a critique of, chronological argument about the mythical time that preceded the first Olympiad.

---

[37] Censorinus, *De die natali*, 21: 'Nunc vero id intervallum temporis tractabo, quod ἱστορικόν Varro appellat. hic enim tria discrimina temporum esse tradit: primum ab hominum principio ad cataclysmum priorem, quod propter ignorantiam vocatur ἄδηλον, secundum a cataclysmo priore ad olympiadem primam, quod, quia multa in eo fabulosa referuntur, μυθικόν nominatur, tertium a prima olympiade ad nos, quod dicitur ἱστορικόν, quia res in eo gestae veris historiis continentur. Primum tempus, sive habuit initium seu semper fuit, certe quot annorum sit, non potest conprehendi. secundum non plane quidem scitur, sed tamen ad mille circiter et sescentos annos esse creditur: a priore scilicet cataclysmo, quem dicunt et Ogygii, ad Inachi regnum annos circiter quadringentos <computarunt, hinc ad excidium Troiae annos octingentos>, hinc ad olympiadem primam paulo plus quadringentos: quos solos, quamvis mythici temporis postremos, tamen, quia a memoria scriptorum proximos, quidam certius definire voluerunt. et quidem Sosibius scripsit esse CCCXCV, Eratosthenes autem septem et quadringentos, Timaeus CCCCXVII, Aretes DXIIII, et praeterea multi diverse, quorum etiam ipsa dissensio incertum esse declarat'.

[38] See Jacoby's commentary on *FrGrHist*, 241 F 1c.

[39] Censorinus, ed. H. Lindenbrog, Leiden, 1642, p. 157: 'De integritate huius loci vehementer dubito: mutare tamen quicquam absque auctoritate veterum codicum religio fuit'.

Many of Eratosthenes's fragments deal with myth. And indeed, if we return to
Scaliger, we will find that he read the passage exactly in that latter sense. True,
he sometimes used it as Jacoby did, as confirmation of the value of Olympiad
dating. But in the *Thesaurus temporum* of 1606 he made it the model for his own
effort to provide astronomically precise dates for such 'mythical' events as the
fall of Troy and the Olympic Games of Pelops and Hercules. Records of the time
of myth, he explained more than once, combined fable and history; good critical
method could reduce them to a 'certum Chronicon'. Scaliger even suggested that
'heroic' might be a more appropriate term than 'mythical' for these earliest
accessible centuries of Greek history.[40] In fact, four of the ten eras ascribed to
Eratosthenes by Clement of Alexandria date such 'mythical' events as the descent
of the Heraclidae and the founding of Ionia (*FrGrHist* 241 F 1a). Even that sober
text, in other words, could support Scaliger's ambiguous reading of the Censorinus passage. The chief textual basis for Eratosthenes's reputation is corrupt in
substance, problematic in authorship and ambiguous in argument. And the
Alexandrian sense of history proves to be a rather less solid and visible intellectual tool than modern accounts suggest. The history of scholarship once again
reveals death-watch beetles in apparently sound beams.

Historiography, however, need not serve only critical ends; it can also enlarge
our inquiries, if we treat it as Momigliano did, in a broad-minded way, dropping
the assumption that the figures whose names we remember and the traditions we
consider central are the only ones relevant to our inquiries. Consider Giordano
Bruno, with whom we began. He had a theory about chronology, which he
expressed in characteristically mordant terms in his *Spaccio de la bestia trionfante*. Here he made Zeus show that the world was far older than the Bible
allowed. The Greeks, the Druids and the 'tables of Mercury' recorded 20,000
years' worth of events. The New World peoples had records going back 10,000
years and more. These, Zeus insisted, were full solar years. And they could not
be cleverly manipulated into conformity with the Bible, as 'certi magri glosatori'
thought, by being taken as equivalent to mere lunar months—a procedure which
would transform 10,000 years to fewer than a thousand, placing the origins of the
New World well within the span of history since the biblical Flood.[41]

---

[40] J. J. Scaliger, *Thesaurus temporum*, Lugduni Batavorum, 1606, Canones isagogici, p. 340: 'quanquam
secundum intervallum mixtum est ex fabuloso et historico. Quia enim eos, de quibus falso praedicatur, non
dubium est fuisse, propter eos quidem historicum fuerit, propter falso attributa fabulosum. Proinde nobis placuit
heroicum potius vocare, quam mythicon...'

[41] G. Bruno, *Spaccio de la bestia trionfante*, ed. M. Ciliberto (Milan, 1985), p. 281: 'perché (lascio altre
maladette raggioni da canto, quanto a gli Greci, Druidi e tavole di Mercurio, che contano più di vinti mila anni
non dico de lunari, come dicono certi magri glosatori, ma di que' rotondi simili a l'annello, che si computano
da un inverno a l'altro, da una primavera a l'altra, da uno autunno a l'altro, da una staggione a l'altra medesima)
é frescamente scuoperta una nuova parte de la Terra che chiamano Nuovo Mondo, dove hanno memoriali di
diece mila anni e piú, gli quali sono, come vi dico, integri e rotondi...'

Bruno had a clear set of opponents in his sights, as Giuliano Gliozzi has shown in his magnificent study *Adamo e il nuovo mondo*.[42] From the early sixteenth century, many scholars had found it irresistibly tempting to connect the New World with Plato's Atlantis (after all, as Gómara pointed out, many Indian words and place names ended with the revealing suffix *-atl*). Some identified the two. Others followed Plato more literally and assumed that Atlantis had once provided the bridge for human and animal traffic between the Old World and the New, only to sink in the cataclysm Plato described. But anyone who made either argument in more than a passing way had to confront a serious chronological difficulty. Plato's description of Atlantis supposedly recorded events that took place 9,000 years before his time—and more than 5,000 years before the biblical Creation (*Timaeus*, 23e; *Critias*, 108e; cf. *Laws*, 656d-657a). Surely his story was as much a myth as the myth of Er in the *Republic*; so, at least, one might expect Christian readers to respond to such claims.

Juan Luis Vives—a 'glosator', if hardly a lean one—responded in exactly that way in his massive commentary on the *City of God*. He rehearsed as many ancient long chronologies as he could find, Chaldean and Egyptian alike, and then denounced them as mendacious. He cited, among other countervailing evidence, the argument that the Egyptians had called lunar months years—exactly the excuse that Bruno denied to Christian scholars.[43] And he found many readers in the later sixteenth and seventeenth centuries, not all of whom shared his pious assumptions. Ironically, his commentary provided fertile soil in which the very speculations he hoped to extirpate grew like weeds. Montaigne borrowed the ancient claims Vives denounced—but not the arguments with which Vives had tried to remove their sting—when he revised his *Apology for Raymund Sebond*.[44]

But the reduction of Egyptian and Aztec years to months was not simply an exercise in theological chronology. In Christian hands, a method for shrinking long chronologies proved a two-edged sword. It could threaten the long lives of biblical patriarchs as well as those of Egyptian kings. Augustine—unlike his Renaissance commentator—declared his lack of faith in such expedients (*De civitate Dei*, 12.10). And Lactantius treated the whole idea as a pagan effort, for which Varro was responsible, to throw doubt on the long life spans of the patriarchs described in the *Sibylline Oracles* (*Divinae institutiones*, 2.12). Hence,

---

[42] Giuliano Gliozzi, *Adamo e il nuovo mondo*, Florence, 1977; see also P. Vidal-Naquet, *La Démocratie grecque vue d'ailleurs*, Paris, 1990, ch. 6.

[43] Augustine, *De civitate Dei*, ed. J. L. Vives, Basel, 1522, p. 370, on 12.10: 'In numerandis tamen annis mira apud veteres libertas et liberalitas... "Perhibentur enim Aegyptii quondam" Et hi non pauca de annis suis sunt mentiti. Plato ex narratione Aegyptii sacerdotis res gestas Sais Aegyptiis octo milia annorum literis esse mandatas inquit...Plinius libro septimo [7.55] annum menstruum Aegyptiis fuisse ait...'

[44] Montaigne, *Essais*, 2.12 in M. Montaigne, *Oeuvres complètes*, ed. R. Barral, Paris, 1967, p. 238. For the source see the translation in *The Essays of Michel de Montaigne*, ed. and transl. J. Zeitlin, II, New York, 1935, p. 549.

those who reduced Plato's chronology did so in the teeth of authoritative
exegetical traditions. They saved the Bible and the classics, but only at the cost
of jettisoning the Fathers.

In fact, those who tacked on the course Bruno criticized when the chill wind
of biblical authority blew against them were often chiefly inspired by a pagan, not
a Christian, source. The historian of Peru Agustin de Zárate explained the point
most fully. Plato's story of Atlantis, he insisted, was a history, not an allegory,
and 'what he says about the 9,000 years is not an argument in favor of its being
fabulous'. After all, as Ficino and Eudoxus had pointed out, 'those years are to
be understood, by the Egyptian computation, as lunar, not solar; thus they were
9,000 months, which make 750 years'. This was exactly the notion that Bruno
attacked: that one could save Plato's veracity by reducing his chronology. Zárate,
moreover, helpfully identified the source of his thesis: Ficino's commentaries on
the *Timaeus* and *Critias*.[45] Ficino there insisted that the tale of Atlantis was
history and that anyone who 'listened to Eudoxus stating that the 9,000 years of
the Egyptians were not solar, but lunar', who realised that 'Eudoxus counted the
9,000 years as 9,000 months', would not find anything disturbing in its dating.[46]
Bruno directed his dialogue against Ficino as well as the many later humanists
and historians, from Fracastoro to Las Casas, who accepted his explanation.

Ficino's reference to Eudoxus is especially revealing. For it identifies what
neither Bruno nor Gliozzi mentions: the ultimate source of the theory Bruno
attacked. The argument Ficino describes is attributed to Eudoxus in a text on
which Ficino drew quite heavily: 'If', says Proclus in his commentary on the
Timaeus, 'what Eudoxus says is true, that the Egyptians called the month a year,
then the sum of all these many years would not be at all surprising'.[47] Eudoxus,
a member in good standing of the Academy, the deft mathematician who created

[45] Agustin de Zárate, *Historia del descubrimiento y conquista de la provincia del Perú* (1555), in
Historiadores primitivos de las Indias, ed. Enrique de Vedia, II, Madrid, 1853, p. 461: 'Esta historia dicen todos
los que escriben sobre Platon que fué cierta y verdadera, en tal manera que los mas dellos, especialmente
Marsilio Ficino y Platino, no quieren admitir que tenga sentido alegórico, aunque algunos se lo dan, como lo
refiere el mismo Marsilio en las *Anotaciones sobre el Timeo*, y no es argumento para ser fabuloso lo que allí
dice de los nueve mil años; porque, segun Eudoxo, aquellos años se entendian, segun la cuenta de los egipcios,
lunares, y no solares; por manera que eran nueve mil meses, que son setecientos y cincuenta años.'

[46] M. Ficino, *Opera omnia*, Basel, 1576; repr. Turin, 1959, II, p. 1439 (on the *Timaeus*): 'Hic iterum te
admoneo, ut memineris novem annorum millia ab Eudoxo millia mensium computari. Item Phaethontem Solis
filium fulminatum exusisse terra, significare apud quosdam vastam cometam natura solarem tandem dissolutam
intolerabiles aestus concitasse.' On the *Critias* Ficino writes:'Quod vero huic historiae deest, potest summatim
ex Timaei prooemio resarciri. Est autem historia de rebus gestis ante diluvium. Post vero diluvium narraturus,
ut arbitror, erat Hermocrates. Neque te turbabunt novem illa annorum millia, si Eudoxum audieris dicentem
annos illos Aegyptiorum non solares fuisse, sed lunares'.

[47] Eudoxus, fr. 302: *Die Fragmente des Eudoxos von Knidos*, ed. and transl. F. Lasserre, Berlin, 1966, p.
111 [Proclus, *In Platonis Timaeum commentaria*, ed. E. Diehl, I, Leipzig, 1903, p. 102]: 'Ει δὲ καὶ ὅ φησιν
Εὔδοξος ἀληθές, ὅτι Αἰγύπτιοι τὸν μῆνα ἐνιαυτὸν ἐκάλουν, οὐκ ἂν ἡ τῶν πολλῶν τούτων ἐνιαυτὸν
ἀπαρίθμησις ἔχοι τι θαυμαστόν.'

a homocentric astronomy, apparently devised the argument that let Christian readers have faith in the historicity of Atlantis.

The passage in question seems almost certainly genuine. Proclus had excellent sources for the early history of Greek mathematics; the short survey of the pre-history of Euclid's *Elements* that adorns his commentary on book 1 of that text rests on very solid foundations, some of them laid by Eudemus.[48] And Eudoxus's method for reducing long chronologies to more sober short ones occurs in several other pagan writers, some of whom could well have drawn indirectly on Eudoxus's work.[49] Evidently, then, the study of chronology already formed part of the mathematical sciences in Plato's Academy.

A second Eudoxan fragment—which scholars have not usually connected with the first one—suggests a purpose for this activity. In his Γῆς περίοδος Eudoxus notoriously dated Zoroaster to 6,000 years before Plato's death.[50] The passage in Pliny and a related text in Diogenes Laertius that record his view have spawned a large and contentious body of literature. They have inspired revised dates for Eudoxus's own life (which supposedly ended before Plato's), speculations about Zoroastrian millenarian chronology in Greek dress, and fascinating arguments about the impact of Eastern thought on the Academy. But none of these deep points requires attention here.[51] What matters for now is simply that the two arguments, the one about Egypt and the one about Persia, give one another a motivation and a context. Both define the antiquity of Eastern traditions; both reflect a profound concern with the genealogy of wisdom. Taken together, they suggest that Eudoxus reduced the antiquity of the Egyptian tradition for one simple reason: he wanted to prove the superior age and profundity of the Persian. The device that he chose, the reduction of years to months, would have a long life; it recurs in patristic, Byzantine and early modern chronology. But the original connection between the dating of Egyptian and Persian sages and the debate about the origins of wisdom seems as evident to me as it did to Pletho—who accepted the 9,000 years of Egyptian history that he found in the *Timaeus* as well as the 6,000 years from Zoroaster to Plato (oddly, for one who preferred Persian to Egyptian revelations, he did not seek to reduce Plato's Egyptian

---

[48] See T. L. Heath, *A History of Greek Mathematics*, Oxford, 1921.

[49] See e.g. Diodorus, 1.26.3; Plutarch, *Numa,* 18.4; Censorinus, 19.4, and—above all—Varro, as cited in Lactantius, *Divinae institutiones*, 2.12.

[50] Eudoxus, fr. 342 (see n. 47 above), p. 119 = J. Bidez and F. Cumont, *Les Mages hellénisés...*, II, Paris, 1938, fr. B 2 (Pliny, *Naturalis historia*, 30.3): 'Eudoxus, qui inter sapientiae sectas clarissimam utilissimamque eam [sc. magicam] intelligi voluit, Zoroastren hunc sex milibus annorum ante Platonis mortem fuisse prodidit; sic et Aristoteles'.

[51] A classic account is W. Jaeger, *Aristotle*, tr. R. Robinson, 2nd edn., Oxford, 1948, pp. 131–8; more recent discussions are listed in H. Herter, 'Von Xanthos dem Lyder zu Aineias aus Gaza: Tylon und andere Auf-erweckte', *Rheinisches Museum für Philologie*, N.F. 108, 1965, pp. 203–4 n. 81 and in Lasserre's note *ad loc.*

chronology).[52]

Comparative, polemical chronology, which deals with more than one nation and uses, in a primitive way, the reckonings of astronomers, is usually treated as a characteristically Hellenistic genre, one partly created by non-Greeks and soon appropriated by Christians. In fact it came into being in classical Athens, probably as part of that general effort to criticize and rationalize the inherited myths to which parts of the *Timaeus* attest.[53] No wonder that Isocrates, in his more or less contemporary Egyptian idyll, the *Busiris*, could make fun of another rhetorician who had committed an error in accommodating Egyptian chronology to Greek (8, 36–38). The subject must have been as fashionable as it was novel—at least in the precise, comparative form in which the Academy pursued it, as opposed to the more general form that went back to Herodotus and Hecataeus.[54] Formally precise but substantively speculative long-period intervals, reckoned backwards from the date when the modern text is composed, occur at the start of the best-preserved document of Hellenistic chronology, the *Marmor Parium*. They may well descend directly from the lost works of Eudoxus and his fellows.

Chronology often serves as a synonym for triviality. Its supposed Hellenistic origin and clear late antique vogue enable it to be defined—and dismissed—as a study that classical Greeks would have found sterile and trivial. What gripped Diogenes Laertius could hardly have interested Plato. In fact, however, it appears that chronology was almost as Greek, though not as ancient, as Pramnian wine with goat's cheese grated on it. Chronology mattered to Plato and Eudoxus as well as to Eratosthenes; the genealogies of wisdom that it could supply were needed in Athens as well as Alexandria. Bruno's sacrifice thus opens our minds, exactly as the nineteenth-century free-thinkers who erected his statue hoped that it might. And chronology itself emerges as a coherent set of strands within the

---

[52] See G. G. Pletho, *Traité des lois*, ed. C. Alexandre, tr. A. Pellissier, Paris, 1858; repr. Amsterdam, 1966, 3.43, pp. 252–3, partly repr. in Bidez and Cumont, *Mages* (n. 50 above), fr. O 113 (cf. fr. O 109b); see also his reply to Scholarius, *Traité*, p. 297 (= Bidez and Cumont, *Mages*, fr. O 114), and his commentary on the *Oracula Chaldaica* (Bidez and Cumont, *Mages*, fr. O 109a). Pletho cites Plutarch, *De Iside et Osiride*, 369E, as his authority for dating Zoroaster 5,000 years before the Trojan War (which puts him roughly 6,000 years before Plato); but he also dates him to 5,000 years before the return of the Heraclidae, perhaps an effort to make the interval longer; see Bidez and Cumont, *Mages*, p. 258 n. 2. As to Menes, the founder of Egypt, Pletho dates him 3,000 years before Zoroaster (apparently taking the 9,000-year duration of the Egyptians' historical memory, as described in *Timaeus*, 23e, rather than the 8,000 years of their records, as the length of their history). But he challenges the claim that Menes was a sapient legislator. Pletho's argument for the priority of Zoroaster, in short, was conceptual, not chronological. Cf. M. Anastos, 'Pletho's Calendar and Liturgy', *Dumbarton Oaks Papers*, 4, 1948, pp. 279–99.

[53] See the brilliant discussion of M. Detienne, *The Creation of Mythology*, tr. M. Cook, Chicago and London, 1986.

[54] See T. S. Brown, 'The Greek Sense of Time in History as Suggested by their Accounts of Egypt', *Historia*, 11, 1962, pp. 257–70.

western tradition—not a mere annoyance to the scholar in search of more profound subjects, but one of the many implements devised by the Greek creators of critical reason in their brave, if perhaps misguided, efforts to open windows into traditions that they had begun to find opaque. I hope that Momigliano, to whom both critical reason and chronology mattered, would have approved.

Naissance d'un aspect de la recherche antiquaire. Les premiers travaux sur les lois romaines: de l'*Epistula ad Cornelium* de Filelfo à l'*Historia iuris ciuilis* d'Aymar du Rivail

JEAN-LOUIS FERRARY

Comme l'a noté A. Momigliano dans son étude sur 'Ancient History and the Antiquarian', si la recherche antiquaire trouve ses origines dans l'humanisme du quinzième siècle:

> the word *antiquitates* meant in the book-titles of the fifteenth century either simply history (*Antiquitates Vicecomitum* by G. Merula, 1486) or ruins of monuments (*Antiquitates urbis* by Pomponio Leto): the original Varronian meaning of a survey of the whole life of a nation was perhaps first reintroduced as a title of a book by J. Rossfeld, called Rosinus, in *Antiquitatum Romanarum Corpus Absolutissimum* (1583).[1]

Un projet antérieur d'*Antiquitates Romanæ* (au sens varronien du terme) avait cependant été conçu par Paolo Manuzio dès les années 1540: il était prévu en dix livres, comme celui de Rosinus, mais seul fut publié du vivant de l'auteur le *liber de legibus* (1557), qui aurait dû être le sixième, et les trois qui le furent après sa mort, présentent un évident caractère d'inachèvement.[2] Rosinus à son tour consacrera aux lois le huitième livre de son ouvrage, mais je ne reviendrai pas ici sur cette période des années 1540–1580, dont j'ai eu l'occasion de traiter dans une étude sur le *De legibus* d'Antonio Agustín.[3] Pour rendre hommage aux travaux pionniers d'A. Momigliano sur historiens et antiquaires, ce sont les toutes premières recherches des humanistes sur les lois romaines que je me propose d'étudier.

I

Dans les *Antiquitates* de Rosinus, Pomponio Leto ouvre la liste de ceux qui ont traité des lois romaines, et dans les années 1540 déjà il est le plus ancien

---

[1] A. Momigliano, in the *Journal of the Warburg and Courtauld Institutes*, 13, 1950, pp. 285–315 and reprinted in *Contributo alla storia degli studi classici*, Rome, 1955, pp. 67–106 (quotation at p. 73).

[2] Le livre 4, *De senatu*, fut publié en 1581; les livres 2, *De ciuitate Romana*, et 5, *De comitiis*, le furent en 1585. Le *De legibus* annonçait aussi un premier livre *De urbe*, un troisième *De religione* (ch. 1), et, sans précision quant à leur place dans l'ensemble du projet, un livre *De iudiciis* (ch. 8) ainsi que, semble-t-il, un *De ludis* (ch. 3). La dédicace au cardinal Hippolyte d'Este du même *De legibus* précise que ce projet avait été conçu plus de dix ans auparavant, sous les auspices de Bembo et de Bernardino Maffei. La mort de Bembo fournit le *terminus ante quem* de 1547.

[3] 'La Genèse du *De legibus et senatus consultis*' dans *Antonio Agustín between Renaissance and Counter-Reform*, Warburg Institute Surveys and Texts, 25, Londres, 1993, pp. 31–55.

prédécesseur que mentionnent Johann Ulrich Zasius et Antonio Agustín dans leurs recueils de lois romaines. Son *De Romanis magistratibus, sacerdotibus, iurisperitis et legibus ad M. Pantagathum libellus*, écrit avant 1483,[4] avait été imprimé au moins deux fois de son vivant à Venise, et connut un succès dont témoignent de nombreuses réimpressions, de Rome à Bâle.[5] Les chapitres concernant les magistrats et les prêtres s'inspirent très largement du *De potestatibus Romanorum* écrit vers 1425 par Andrea di Domenico Fiocchi, une œuvre qui connut elle aussi une grande diffusion, sous une fausse attribution à l'érudit d'époque tibérienne Fenestella, et qu'on trouve souvent imprimée en même temps que celle de Pomponio Leto.[6] Le développement concernant les juristes, de son côté, dérive directement du long extrait de l'*Enchiridion* de Pomponius conservé dans le titre 1, 2 du *Digeste*. Reste le chapitre sur les lois, quarante-trois brèves notices rangées dans un ordre alphabétique[7] et dépourvues de toute indication sur les sources utilisées: 'questo catalogo sommario', écrivait V. Zabughin, 'è attinto ad una o più fonti postclassiche, ribelli alle più accurate ricerche, e non ha legami diretti coi testi giuridici.'[8]

A. G. Luciani, dans un récent article,[9] a attiré l'attention sur une autre liste: quarante-six notices concernant des lois romaines, copiées sur les folios 48–9 du manuscrit Ottobonianus Latinus 1256. Il a souligné les similitudes existant entre cette liste et celle de Pomponio Leto, même si l'ordre du manuscrit Ottoboni n'est pas alphabétique, si ses notices sont dans l'ensemble plus longues que celles de Pomponius, si enfin on y trouve (dans les notices 31, 40 et 44) des mots grecs absents du *libellus* de Pomponius. Luciani a noté d'autre part que le commentaire aux discours de Cicéron d'Asconius ou du Pseudo-Asconius[10] était la source principale de la liste Ottoboni, dix-sept notices s'en inspirant, souvent presque mot pour mot; pour les autres notices, en revanche, il n'a guère poussé la recherche, parlant seulement d''una fonte diversa da Asconio o pseudo-Asconio,

---

[4] Le Pantagathus dédicataire du traité était Gian-Battista Capranica, évêque de Fermo, qui mourut en 1483.

[5] Premières éditions vénitiennes parues du vivant de Pomponio Leto: Maximus de Butricis, s.d. [1491–1492]; Joannes Tacuinus de Tridino, 1493. Une édition romaine fut ensuite donnée par Mazochius, s.d. [1510], une édition parisienne par Ascensius, 1511, une édition bâloise par Valentinus Curio, 1523. Toutes ces éditions sont plus ou moins fautives, la plus incorrecte étant l'édition romaine de 1510.

[6] Sur Fiocchi, voir G. Mercati, *Ultimi contributi alla storia degli umanisti*, I. *Traversariana*, Cité du Vatican, 1939, pp. 97–131. Il faudra attendre 1561 pour que l'ouvrage soit publié sous son véritable titre, attribué à son véritable auteur et précédé de la dédicace au cardinal Branca da Castiglione.

[7] Seules exceptions, deux des lois Clodiæ sont regroupées avec les lois Ælia et Fufia; d'autre part la loi Hortensia est rangée à la lettre O, bien que l'auteur en soit d'ailleurs appelé L. Hortensius jusqu'à l'édition bâloise de 1523. Sur l'ordre des notices, voir la concordance donnée dans l'appendice I.

[8] V. Zabughin, *Giulio Pomponio Leto*, Rome–Grottaferrata, 1909–12, II, p. 202. Sur les autres chapitres du *libellus*, pp. 195–207.

[9] A. G. Luciani, 'Il Codice Ottobonianus Latinus 1256 fra il commento asconiano a Cicerone e il *De legibus* di Pomponio Leto', *Studia et documenta historiae iuris*, 48, 1982, pp. 395–412.

[10] Rappelons qu'on appelle Pseudo-Asconius un commentaire partiel aux *Verrines*, qui ne peut être attribué à Asconius lui-même, mais qui suit le texte d'Asconius dans les copies du manuscrit perdu de St-Gall.

forse "reliquiæ" asconiane non meglio identificate'.[11] La liste du manuscrit Ottoboni, en tout cas, serait un précieux témoin d'une phase préparatoire du *libellus* de Pomponio Leto.[12]

Luciani a malheureusement ignoré l'existence, signalée pourtant par L. Gaddi et G. Rotondi,[13] d'un texte de Filelfo qui est le plus ancien recueil de lois romaines compilé par un humaniste. Il ne fut imprimé qu'après la mort de Filelfo, à la fin de 1483, dans le recueil des *Orationes et nonnulla opera*,[14] mais il y est présenté comme une lettre envoyée de Bologne, en 1439, à Fredericus Cornelius, un patricien vénitien de la famille des Corner ou Cornaro,[15] et rien, nous le verrons, n'amène à contester cette date pour l'essentiel du texte. Cette lettre n'avait pas été incluse dans les trente-sept livres d'*Epistulæ* envoyés pour impression à Venise en 1473,[16] mais elle le fut, avec indication de la même date, dans un second recueil resté largement inédit, l'actuel manuscrit 873 de la Biblioteca Trivulziana de Milan,[17] qui provient de la bibliothèque personnelle de

---

[11] Luciani, 'Il Codice Ottobonianus Latinus 1256' (n. 9 supra), p. 396.

[12] Luciani, 'Il Codice Ottobonianus Latinus 1256' (n. 9 supra), p. 398, envisage deux hypothèses: 'una fase preparatoria del *De legibus*, un appunto di matrice asconiana, da riconoscere nel testo fornito dall'Ottobonianus; un *excerptum* ricavato…mentre il *De legibus* era allo stato di "work in progress" ed erano in corso letture asconiane in vista della sua edizione'.

[13] L. Gaddi, 'Cronologia delle leggi comiziali romane' dans le tome 2 des *Fonti del diritto romano* de P. Cogliolo, Turin, 1887, p. 503; G. Rotondi, *Leges publicæ populi Romani*, Milan, 1912, p. 175 n. 1.

[14] *Francesci Philelphi equitis aurati laureatique poetæ et oratoris ac philosophi clarissimi orationes et nonnulla opera in quibus omne bene dicendi genus omnesque artis rhetoricæ partes ac diuinæ philosophorum et theologorum sententiæ comperiuntur.* Le recueil est précédé d'une dédicace à Ludovico Maria Sforza, datée de Milan le 27 mai 1481, mais le départ puis la mort de Filelfo en retardèrent l'impression: le privilège ducal ne fut accordé que le 15 mars 1483, et la première édition, sans doute de peu postérieure à novembre 1483, doit être celle, s.l.n.d., qui peut être attribuée à Pachel et Scinzenzeler (cf. E. Motta, 'Di Filippo di Lavagna e di alcuni altri tipografi-editori del '400', *Archivio storico lombardo*, ser. 3, 10, 1898, pp. 51–2; L. A. Scheppard, *A Fifteenth-Century Humanist, Francesco Filelfo*, Londres, 1935, pp. 23–4), et dont j'ai consulté l'exemplaire de la Biblioteca Trivulziana de Milan. J'ai pu vérifier que le MS Paris. Lat. 7810, provenant de la bibliothèque du roi Ferdinand I de Naples (G. Mazzatinti, *La biblioteca dei re d'Aragona in Napoli*, Rocca San Casciano, 1897, pp. 96–9, no. 239) n'est qu'une luxueuse copie, faite par Pier Ippolito Lunense, de l'édition de 1483. Les *Orationes* de Filelfo furent ensuite réimprimées à Brescia en 1488 (J. Britannicus), à Venise en 1491 (B. de Zanis) et 1492 (P. de Pinzis), à Bâle avant 1498 (J. Amerbach), à Paris enfin en 1502 (Ascensius).

[15] Deux autres lettres de l'édition de 1502 lui sont adressées (f. 3^r: Venise, 27 décembre 1427; ff. 18^v–19^r: Pavie, 15 octobre 1439, à l'occasion de son mariage avec une Contarini), ainsi qu'une lettre inédite du manuscrit Trivulce 873 (ff. 16^v–17^r: Florence, 1er septembre 1430). Il est aussi le dédicataire des satires 2, 10 et 3, 5, et d'une troisième satire encore inédite (Florence, 13 novembre 1430; K. Wagner, 'Un Manuscrit autographe inconnu de Francesco Filelfo', *Scriptorium*, 31, 1977, pp. 70–82 (75)).

[16] Les seize premiers livres furent seuls imprimés dès 1473, par Wendelinus de Spira, l'ensemble des trente-sept ne l'étant qu'en 1502, par Johannes et Gregorius de Gregoriis.

[17] Description de ce manuscrit, et notamment des onze livres supplémentaires contenant les lettres écrites de juillet 1473 à mai 1477, dans A. Calderini, 'I codici milanesi delle opere di Francesco Filelfo', *Archivio storico lombardo*, ser. 5, 2, 1915, pp. 355–77; C. Santoro, *I codici medioevali della Biblioteca Trivulziana*, Milan, 1965, pp. 222–8. Les lettres latines inédites, déjà abondamment utilisées par C. de' Rosmini (*Vita di Francesco Filelfo da Tolentino*, Milan, 1808), doivent être publiées par V. Giustiniani; les lettres grecques l'ont été par E. Legrand, *Cent-dix lettres grecques de François Philelphe*, Paris, 1892.

Filelfo léguée à la Bibliothèque capitulaire de Milan. Le texte du manuscrit Trivulce (ff. 41ᵛ–43ʳ), pourtant, n'est pas de la main de Filelfo et n'a été qu'imparfaitement corrigé, de même que les mots grecs n'y ont été que partiellement ajoutés. A deux reprises inférieur au texte imprimé, il permet de le corriger en trois autres endroits, cependant que des fautes communes laissent supposer l'utilisation dans les deux cas d'une même copie déjà défectueuse et non corrigée.[18]

Une confrontation des deux textes ne permet pas de douter que le recueil de lois du manuscrit Ottoboni dérive de celui de Filelfo. Le texte des notices est le même,[19] à quelques variantes près (modifications de l'ordre des mots, substitution d'une tournure passive à une tournure active, ou inversement); le seul cas où apparaisse une différence significative est celui de la loi Falcidia, mais le texte de Filelfo, tant dans le manuscrit Trivulce que dans l'édition de 1483, est manifestement corrompu.[20] L'ordre des notices est aussi le même, et cette

---

[18] Le grec a été ajouté dans la notice sur la loi Cornelia (49), mais il manque pour la loi Scantinia (36) et la loi Fabia (45). Les seules corrections sont 'FLAVIA' pour 'FAVIA' (45) et 'simia' pour 'similia' (48). Le texte du manuscrit Trivulce est meilleur que celui de l'édition imprimée en trois endroits: 'celebriores' au lieu de 'crebriores' (lettre à Cornelius), 'annonianam' au lieu de 'annoniam' (17), βέλος au lieu de belws (49); en revanche, 'tenerentur' (28) est erroné face au 'tuerentur' du texte imprimé, comme 'temporum' (44) face à 'ipsorum', et dans la notice 'lex Othonis' (35) les mots 'in gradu quatuordecim' ont par erreur été copiés deux fois dans le manuscrit, après 'libertis' et après 'liceret'. Une semblable duplication, commune cette fois au manuscrit et à l'édition imprimée, se trouve dans la notice 'lex Aurelii Cottæ' (31): 'Aurelius Cotta legem dedit, **cum** Sylla ad diminuendam plebis potentiam multos **cum** ei magistratus ademisset, ut plebi liceret interceptos magistratus capere' (on notera que Pier Ippolito Lunense a vu la nécessité de supprimer le second 'cum' dans sa copie du Paris. Lat. 7810). Autre erreur commune, dont il est difficile de dire si elle remonte à Filelfo lui-même ou à une copie intermédiaire: 'ut quidam etiam ex ipsa lege' dans la notice sur la loi Plotia (33), au lieu de 'et quidam etiam ex ipsa plebe' (Asconius, p. 61, ed. Stangl); notons qu'on trouve 'et quidam etiam ex ipsa lege' dans les listes de Guarnerio d'Artegna et Mariano de Préneste. Voir aussi n. 33 infra.

[19] Signalons deux erreurs dans la transcription de Luciani: on trouve dans le MS Ottoboni, comme dans le texte de Filelfo, 'Papius ciuis Ro.' et non 'Papius Caius Ro.' (no. 10, Papia), 'annoniana' et non 'annonaria' (no. 12, Clodia).

[20] MS Trivulce et édition de 1483: 'Falcidius legem tulit qua cauetur ne plus legare liceat quam lege Clodia: ut emptorum bonorum est uncias nouem: idque ipsorum [éd; temporum: MS] testatorum gratia prouisum est ob id quod plerumque intestati moriebantur, recusantibus scriptis heredibus pro nullo aut minimo lucro hereditatis'; MS Ottoboni: 'lata est a Falcido [*sic*] lex qua cauetur ne plus legare liceret quam dodrantem totorum bonorum, uncias nouem, idque ipsorum testatorum gratia prouisum est ob id: plerumque intestati morebantur [*sic*] recusantibus scripsit [*sic*] heredibus qui nullo aut minimo lucro hæreditates adhire [*sic*]'; Pomponio Leto: 'lege Falcidia a Falcidio lata cauetur ne plus dodrante legare liceret propterea quod multi hereditatem recusabant'. La source de Filelfo est *Institutiones*, 2, 22, pr.: 'idque ipsorum testatorum gratia prouisum est ob id quod plerumque intestati moriebantur, recusantibus scriptis heredibus pro nullo aut minimo lucro hereditates adire... Lex Falcidia qua cauetur ne plus legare liceat quam dodrantem totorum bonorum', avec la glose accursienne 'dodrantem, id est nouem uncias totius hereditatis' (voir également Priscianus, *Grammatici latini*, III, p. 408). Il y a manifestement eu corruption de 'dodrantem totorum' en '[cl]od[i]a [u]t emto[to]rum' ('quam Clodia ut emptorum', nous le verrons, est le texte copié par Guarnerio d'Artegna: n. 31), puis en 'lege Clodia ut emptorum', mais le problème est de savoir si cette corruption remonte à un manuscrit aberrant des *Institutiones* dont Filelfo aurait adopté la leçon, ou seulement à une copie fautive et non corrigée de la lettre à Cornelius (ou de sa minute), qui serait la source commune du MS Trivulce et de l'édition de 1483 (voir n. 18). L'ampleur de

similitude est d'autant plus significative qu'il s'agit d'un ordre apparemment incohérent: on note seulement, par rapport au recueil de Filelfo, l'absence de cinq notices et le déplacement de deux autres.[21] Le manuscrit Ottob. Lat. 1256 contient les notes prises par un certain Mariano de Préneste lors de cours donnés à l'université de Rome par Martino de Filettino (Filetico) sur les satires de Perse, de Juvénal et d'Horace.[22] Le catalogue de lois a été noté sur des pages restées blanches d'un cahier du cours sur Juvénal, et on est tenté de penser avec Mercati que 'sono appunti senza relazione col resto, per non lasciar vane delle pagine bianche'.[23] Comme le cours sur Juvénal date de l'année universitaire 1469–1470,[24] il n'y aurait aucun obstacle à supposer que les notices sur les lois aient été ajoutées en 1475/6, lorsque Filelfo, à son tour, professa à Rome sur l'invitation du pape Sixte IV.[25]

Une autre hypothèse pourrait être suggérée par la présence, dans le cours de Filetico sur Juvénal, de commentaires sur la loi Julia *de adulteriis* et la loi Scantinia qui sont trop proches des notices 36 et 37 de Filelfo pour que ce puisse être un hasard (voir n. 59): il faut, ou bien que Filelfo et Filetico se soient inspirés d'une source commune, qui devrait être en ce cas un commentaire humaniste antérieur à 1444, ou bien que Filetico ait connu et utilisé dès 1469/1470 l'opuscule de Filelfo.[26] La liste de lois, d'autre part, n'a pas été notée par Mariano de Préneste alors qu'il suivait un cours de Filetico ou de Filelfo lui-

la corruption, qui s'explique sans doute mieux si elle se fit en plusieurs étapes, favoriserait plutôt la première hypothèse, mais l'existence d'une glose sur 'dodrantem' aurait dû éviter dans la tradition manuscrite des *Institutiones* pareille corruption (dont l'apparat le plus complet, celui de Schrader, 1832, ne fait pas mention), et la notice de Filelfo telle qu'elle est transmise par le manuscrit Trivulce et par l'édition n'est pas seulement inexacte: elle n'a pas de sens. Le manuscrit Ottoboni en tout cas, ou plutôt le texte dont le manuscrit Ottoboni nous a conservé une copie très défectueuse, doit s'expliquer par une correction du texte (originel ou corrompu) de Filelfo (cf. n. 31 infra).

[21] Manquent les notices 2, 8, 9, 50 et 51 de Filelfo, tandis que les notices 7 et 10 de Filelfo sont placées après la notice 49 (voir la concordance de l'appendice I).

[22] G. Mercati, 'Tre dettati universitari dell' umanista Martino Filetico sopra Persio, Giovenale ed Orazio', *Opere minori*, VI, Vatican, 1984, pp. 13–24.

[23] Ibid., p. 13 n. 4.

[24] E. M. Sanford, dans *Catalogus translationum et commentariorum*, ed. P. O. Kristeller, I, Washington, 1960, pp. 210–2.

[25] Filelfo fut à Rome de décembre 1474 à juin 1475, puis de janvier à avril 1476.

[26] Sur Filetico, voir B. Pecci, 'Contributo per la storia degli umanisti nel Lazio', *Archivio della R. Società romana di storia patria*, 13, 1890, pp. 468–526; R. Sabbadini, *Epistolario di Guarino Veronese*, III, Milan, 1919, pp. 474–6; D. R. Robathan, 'A Postscript on Martino Filetico', *Medievalia et Humanistica*, 8, 1954, pp. 56–61; C. Dionisotti, '*Lauinia uenit litora*. Polemica virgiliana di M. Filetico', *Italia medioevale e umanistica*, 1, 1958, pp. 283–315; E. Lee, *Sixtus IV and Men of Letters*, Rome, 1978, pp. 175–7. L'admiration de Filetico pour Filelfo est bien attestée (Dionisotti, p. 308), mais les lettres de Filelfo (y compris les lettres inédites du manuscrit Trivulce) ne mentionnent jamais son nom, et Pecci (p. 473) n'a aucune preuve lorsqu'il prétend que Filetico pendant ses années de formation séjourna à Milan et y connut Filelfo. On ne sait rien de lui avant 1454, où il se trouve à Urbin, si ce n'est qu'il fut élève de Guarino à Ferrare, et qu'il étudia non seulement en Italie, mais aussi en Grèce. S'il naquit en 1423 (Dionisotti) plutôt que vers 1430 (Pecci), ce sont les trente premières années de sa vie qui restent dans l'ombre.

même: un certain nombre d'erreurs montrent clairement qu'elle a été copiée sur un texte souvent mal déchiffré, et non prise sous la dictée d'un professeur.[27] Mais il faut surtout la rapprocher d'une autre liste, copiée dans le Frioul, entre 1461 et 1466, par Guarnerio d'Artegna.[28] Quatre des quarante-huit notices qu'elle contient ne proviennent pas de l'opuscule de Filelfo,[29] mais les quarante-quatre autres, qui dérivent de Filelfo, ont manifestement une même source intermédiaire que la liste du manuscrit Ottoboni: elles sont dans le même ordre, qui est celui de Filelfo avec une commune omission des notices 2, 7 à 10 et 50–51 (voir l'appendice I),[30] et, si chaque copie a ses fautes propres, le texte des notices, à de rarissimes exceptions près, présente les mêmes variantes stylistiques par rapport à celui du texte imprimé et du manuscrit Trivulce de Filelfo.[31]

---

[27] Voir l'apparat de Luciani, 'Il Codice Ottobonianus Latinus 1256' (n. 9 supra; e.g. notices no. 2: 'desecta eorum' pour 'de sectatorum', et 'cognitiorum' pour 'comitiorum'; no. 7: 'et ædem' pour 'hæredem'; no. 8: 'prætor' pour 'præter', etc.). Particulièrement significatives sont deux erreurs de copie que n'a pas relevées A. G. Luciani, mais que rend évidentes la comparaison avec le texte de Filelfo: 'et uir cons.' pour 'et iur. cons.' (no. 20, Licinia Mucia); 'in ionium mare' pour 'in uicinum mare' (no. 43, Pompeia de parricidiis; cf. 'in murinum mare' dans la liste de Guarnerio d'Artegna).

[28] Guarnerio, de la maison des seigneurs d'Artegna, vicaire général du cardinal Ludovico Scarampo patriarche d'Aquilée, mourut en 1466 et légua sa riche bibliothèque au couvent de San Michele Archangelo à San Daniele del Friuli. Ces manuscrits sont restés dans la Bibliothèque communale de San Daniele, et un catalogue très détaillé vient d'en être publié par L. Casarsa, M. D'Angelo et C. Scalon, La libreria di Guarnerio d'Artegna, Udine, 1992. Le manuscrit 87, qui contient notamment des traductions de Plutarque par Filelfo et Guarino de Vérone, y est décrit (pp. 306–7); la liste de lois, copiée de la main même de Guarnerio, y occupe les folios 71–4. Je remercie la Professoressa Laura Casarsa, auteur de la notice identifiant le texte ('Franciscus Philelphus (?), De legibus') de m'en avoir obligeamment fourni une reproduction photographique.

[29] Entre les lois Cornelia de falsis et Pompeia de parricidiis (no. 47 et 48 Filelfo): 'Lex Titia est qua antiquitus cauetur ne quis ob causam orandam pecuniam donumue accipiat' (d'après Tacite, Annales, 11, 5, utilisé par Filelfo pour sa notice no. 5 [Lex Cinthia] et, d'après lui, dans la notice no. 4 de Guarnerio; la leçon Titiam utilisée dans cette notice est celle de manuscrits deteriores: voir n. 50 infra). Après la loi Cornelia de sicariis (no. 49 de Filelfo) et en fin de liste, trois notices, dont les deux premières: ('Lex Curriata. Curius legem tulit ut imperatores proconsules aut prætores succedere in prouinciis non possent nisi eas consules sortiti fuissent. – Lex Cornelia. Cornelius legem tulit ut senatus contra legem curriatam, hoc est sine sorte, prouincias ciuibus [corr. in marg.: ciuilibus] magistratui [sic] assignare posset' proviennent d'un commentaire à Cicéron, Ad familiares, 1, 9, 25; celui d'Ubertino da Crescentino, écrit dans les années 1470, fournit un rapprochement intéressant ('lex curiata non a Curio latore, sed a curiatis comitiis...dicta est, ...quæ lex prohibebat prouinciam cuiquam designari sine sorte, hoc est ne prætores aut proconsules aut imperatores succedere in prouinciis possent, nisi eas prius inter se sortiti fuissent. Huic contraria erat lex Cornelia, qua permittebatur ut prouinciæ etiam sine sorte designari possent sine senatu [sic]. L'origine de la dernière notice ('Lex Plautitia præcipiebat si aliquando coniuratio r. pu. immineret uel si aliquis r. pu. aggredi machinaretur, deberent eligi tres præstantissimi uiri ex ordine senatorio qui de hac re iudicarent') reste pour moi mystérieuse: s'agirait-il de la loi Plautia, avec une utilisation particulièrement déconcertante d'Asconius, p. 61, ed. Stangl, mêlant loi Plautia et loi Varia de maiestate, et faisant une confusion entre tribus et tres? Je ne propose cette hypothèse qu'avec la plus grande prudence.

[30] La liste de Mariano de Préneste avait d'abord omis les lois 7 à 10 de Filelfo, mais les lois 7 et 10 se retrouvent à la fin, après la loi 49. L'omission des mêmes lois 7 à 10 dans la liste de Guarnerio rend improbable l'hypothèse que les lois 7 et 10 aient figuré à leur place dans le texte copié par Mariano, été omises par celui-ci au moment de la copie, puis ajoutées après que cet oubli eut été constaté.

[31] Il n'y a aucun accord significatif entre les textes de Filelfo et de Mariano contre celui de Guarnerio. Les

Il n'est pas douteux que l'opuscule de Filelfo a connu, avant d'être imprimé, une diffusion manuscrite non négligeable, ce qui confirme l'hypothèse de son utilisation par Filetico lorsque ce dernier commenta Juvénal en 1469/1470. Je ne pense pas, d'autre part, que les listes copiées par Guarnerio d'Artegna et Mariano de Préneste nous conservent la trace d'une version primitive de l'opuscule de Filelfo, tandis que le manuscrit Trivulce et l'édition imprimée nous en donne-raient un texte augmenté et partiellement réécrit: la notice de la loi Pompeia (no. 8 de Filelfo), absente des listes de Mariano et de Guarnerio, est à sa place, nous le verrons, dans l'ordre des textes d'Asconius dont elle provient, entre les lois Aurelia (no. 6 de Filelfo) et Calpurnia (no. 13 de Filelfo). La solution la plus économique, la plus vraisemblable, est que les deux listes copiées par Guarnerio et Mariano aient utilisé un modèle commun, lui-même dérivé de l'opuscule de Filelfo avec plusieurs omissions et une certaine liberté dans la formulation des notices; ce modèle commun a pu être augmenté après collation avec une autre copie de l'opuscule de Filelfo: deux au moins des lois de Filelfo qui avaient été omises se trouvaient à la fin de la liste copiée par Mariano;[32] il a pu aussi être enrichi de notices dont rien ne prouve que l'origine soit Filelfo: c'est le cas de la liste copiée par Guarnerio. Il n'est pas impossible, enfin, mais nullement certain ni nécessaire, que le texte des listes copiées par Guarnerio et Mariano soit plus fidèle à l'original de Filelfo dans des cas où il est plus complet ou plus exact que celui du manuscrit Trivulce et de l'édition imprimée:[33] nous avons observé

deux seuls accords significatifs entre les textes de Filelfo et de Guarnerio contre celui de Mariano (loi Junia [Filelfo, no. 26]: 'M. Junius Silvius', Filelfo, Guarnerio [et Pomponio Leto], 'Silanus', Mariano; loi Falcidia [Filelfo, no. 44]: 'quam lege [ce mot chez Filelfo seul] Clodia ut emptorum bonorum est', Filelfo et Guarnerio, 'quam dodrantem bonorum' Mariano [et Pomponio Leto]) viennent de corrections apportées au texte de Filelfo dans la liste copiée par Mariano. En revanche, les cas sont nombreux d'accord entre Guarnerio et Mariano contre Filelfo, qu'il s'agisse de différences de formulation, de modifications dans l'ordre des mots, d'omissions etc. (voir lois no. 3, 13, 16, 17, 18, 19, 20, 22, 23, 24, 29, 33, 42, 43, 44, 47). L'exemple de la loi no. 3 suffira: 'Fabius adiecit pœnam iis qui non certo numero ut ante fuerant definiti deducerent et sectarentur candidatos in campum comitiorum tempore', Filelfo; 'qui deducant et sectentur candidatos [om. M.] in campum comitiorum [cognitiorum: M.] tempore numero definiuntur [diff-: G.] a Fabio, adiecta pœna', Guarnerio et Mariano.

[32] Deux au moins, car le texte du manuscrit Ottoboni semble incomplet, se terminant avec 'Lex Aquilia de iustitia' (Filelfo, no. 10) sans la notice ainsi annoncée. On notera que la notice 'lex Oppia' (Filelfo, no. 7), placée dans la liste de Mariano entre la loi Cornelia *de sicariis* (Filelfo, no. 49) et la loi Aquilia, reprend presque mot pour mot leur source commune, Tite-Live, 34, 1, 3, que Filelfo avait beaucoup plus librement adaptée. Cela va dans le même sens que les deux corrections signalées dans la note précédente.

[33] Dans les notices sur les lois Clodiæ *de collegiis* et *de censoribus* (Filelfo, no. 18 et 19), on trouve dans les listes de Guarnerio et de Mariano les mots 'nouisque instituendis' et 'qui apud eos accusatus et' qui figurent chez Asconius (p. 16, ed. Stangl) et manquent dans le texte imprimé de Filelfo comme dans le manuscrit Trivulce. De même, dans la notice sur la loi Licinia Mucia (Filelfo, no. 25), on a chez Guarnerio et Mariano comme chez Asconius (p. 54, ed. Stangl) 'cupiditate ciuitatis Romanæ', dans le texte imprimé de Filelfo et le manuscrit Trivulce 'cupiditate urbis Romæ'. Dans la notice sur la loi Falcidia (Filelfo, no. 44), le texte imprimé de Filelfo et le manuscrit Trivulce ont 'recusantibus scriptis heredibus pro nullo aut minimo lucro hereditatis'; Guarnerio et Mariano ont 'recusantibus scriptis [scripsit: M.] heredibus pro [qui: M.] nullo aut minimo lucro hereditates adire', ce qui est le texte d'*Institutiones*, 2, 22, *pr.* Dans la notice sur la loi Cornelia *de falsis* (Filelfo, no. 47), Guarnerio et Mariano ont 'testamentum uel aliud instrumentum falsum', comme *Institutiones*, 4, 18,

que ces derniers devaient eux-mêmes remonter à une copie fautive et imparfaitement corrigée de la lettre à Cornelius, mais la liste copiée par Mariano, en
d'autres endroits déjà, nous a paru corriger l'opuscule de Filelfo en suivant de
plus près, ou plus exactement, le texte des sources utilisées (voir notes 31 et 32).

Pour ce qui est des ressemblances notées par Luciani entre le texte du
manuscrit Ottoboni et le *libellus* de Pomponio Leto, elles sont incontestables,
mais elles prouvent seulement que le *libellus* dépend lui aussi, quoiqu'un peu plus
librement, du recueil de Filelfo. Six des notices de Filelfo manquent chez
Pomponio,[34] les omissions n'étant d'ailleurs pas toutes les mêmes que dans les
listes copiées par Guarnerio et Mariano, et cela confirme encore l'importance et
la complexité de la diffusion manuscrite de l'opuscule de Filelfo. Il n'y a pas,
entre les notices de Pomponio et celles de Filelfo, de différences significatives sur
le fond (la seule exception concernant, cette fois encore, la loi Falcidia, pour
laquelle le texte de Pomponio est plus proche de la notice Ottoboni: voir la note
20). Les notices de Pomponio sont souvent plus brèves, la seule véritable addition
étant, à propos de la loi Acilia, la phrase: 'L. Piso primus legem tulit de pecuniis
repetundis'.[35] La disparition de tout mot grec, enfin, s'inscrit dans le cadre plus
général de la retombée de l'hellénisme qu'a notée C. Dionisotti dans la seconde
moitié du quinzième siècle:[36] à la différence, on le sait, d'un Filelfo ou d'un
Filetico, Pomponio n'eut qu'une connaissance tardive et rudimentaire du grec.[37]
A confronter les deux textes, il apparaît que le *libellus* de Pomponio dépend
encore plus de Filelfo pour les lois que de Fiocchi pour les magistrats et les
sacerdoces: il n'a guère fait, en réalité, que résumer et classer dans un ordre
alphabétique la quasi-totalité des notices de son prédécesseur. On ne peut dire
avec certitude quand Pomponio connut le texte de Filelfo: ce ne fut pas
nécessairement en 1475/6, quand Filelfo lui-même vint à Rome, car il faut tenir
compte de la diffusion manuscrite de l'opuscule. Mais, à supposer même que le
libellus ait été écrit dans les années 1477–83, après le séjour de Filelfo à Rome,[38]
et malgré la parution en 1477 à Venise de l'*editio princeps* d'Asconius, on ne

---

7, alors que le texte imprimé de Filelfo et le manuscrit Trivulce ont 'testamentum uel alias tabulas falsas'.

[34] Il s'agit des notices 2, 18, 28, 31, 47 et 51 de Filelfo (voir l'appendice I). En revanche, et contrairement
à ce qu'écrit A. G. Luciani, Pomponio a bien, dès l'édition de 1491, des notices correspondant aux notices 17,
30 et 33 de Filelfo. M. H. Crawford a bien voulu consulter pour moi l'exemplaire de cette édition que possède
la British Library.

[35] D'après Cicéron, *In Verrem*, 2, 3, 195 et 4, 56; *Brutus*, 106.

[36] Dionisotti, 'Lavinia' (n. 26 supra), p. 310.

[37] V. Zabughin, *Pomponio* (n. 8 supra), II, pp. 8–10 et 46–7.

[38] Pendant ce temps, Pomponio ne dut quitter Rome que du printemps à octobre 1480, pour son voyage
en Allemagne et en 'Scythie', puis dans l'hiver 1482–3, pour une brève mission auprès de Frédéric III: W.
Bracke, 'The MS Ottob. Lat. 1982. A Contribution to the Biography of Pomponio Leto', *Rinascimento*, 29,
1989, pp. 293–9. En ce qui concerne ses relations avec Filelfo, on notera que ce dernier lui fait transmettre son
salut à la fin de deux lettres envoyées à Papinius Hipponicus, le 13 août 1475 et le 26 juillet 1476 (MS Triv.
873, ff. 497ᵛ et 521ʳ).

saurait douter de l'utilisation de Filelfo par Pomponio: comment expliquer, sinon, que toutes les notices de Pomponio ne fassent que reprendre ou résumer des notices de Filelfo, même quand la source ultime n'en est pas Asconius, et qu'elles reprennent dans des notices d'origine asconienne des erreurs de Filelfo? L'*epistula* de Filelfo a ensuite été occultée par le *libellus* de Pomponio, et même ceux qui n'ont pas ignoré l'existence de la première ne paraissent guère avoir vu ce que le second lui devait.[39] Sans doute est-ce une des raisons pour lesquelles ce texte a finalement suscité si peu d'intérêt.[40]

Il faut partir d'abord de la brève lettre à Cornelius introduisant les notices sur les lois:

> Quod multarum legum mentionem factam inuenias et apud M. Tullium Ciceronem et apud T. Liuium aliosque ueteres scriptores, neque quid legibus illis contineretur aut quam ob causam latæ fuerint satis intelligas, ob eamque rem quid ipse habeam certi scire cupias, non teneo diutius te suspensum. Itaque leges eas quas celebriores[41] sunt magisque necessarie quo facilius et clarius ueterum oratorum atque historicorum et ipsorum quoque iureconsultorum scripta locis suis comprehendantur, hisce litteris subieci.

Mais il est certain qu'on ne saurait se satisfaire de cette déclaration d'intentions, et qu'une appréciation de la signification et de l'intérêt de l'opuscule de Filelfo passe par une analyse de la nature de ses notices et une identification de ses sources.

Luciani, s'il n'a pas été le premier à en prendre conscience,[42] a eu le mérite de souligner l'importance de l'utilisation d'Asconius dans le *libellus* de Pomponio Leto. Cette observation doit bien sûr être reportée de Pomponio sur Filelfo, mais

---

[39] Ainsi L. Gaddi, 'Cronologia' (n. 13 supra), qui porte un jugement sévère sur l'opuscule de Filelfo (pp. 503–4), et beaucoup plus favorable, presque enthousiaste, sur celui de Pomponio (p. 505).

[40] La bibliographie, en fait, se réduit pratiquement à deux pages de V. Fera 'Itinerari filologici di Francesco Filelfo' dans *Francesco Filelfo nel quinto centenario della morte. Atti del XVII convegno di studi maceratesi (27–30 sett. 1981)*, Padoue, 1986, pp. 110–12: 'pure senza un' adeguata prospettiva storica', écrit-il notamment, 'questo opusculo resta un esempio notevole dell' approccio di un grammatico e di un retore del primo quattrocento al diritto romano. Certamente forte di questa esperienza del lavoro..., nel giugno 1441 l'umanista polemizzerà, in una lettera indirizzata a Catone Sacco, contro quei giuristi "qui Bartolum modo Baldumque legerint"... L'opuscolo dunque intendeva sollecitare un diretto aggancio con gli *auctores*, oltre i tramiti d'informazione medievali: nella pur povera messa a punto di *leges* romane si configura, perciò, come un' operazione di spiccato senso umanistico'. La lettre à Cornelius, en effet, n'est que de six ans postérieure à la très violente diatribe de Lorenzo Valla contre les Bartolistes, diatribe que Valla avait d'abord pensé dédier à Catone Sacco, un juriste de Pavie qui s'intéressait aux humanités, et qui fut l'ami de Filelfo comme de Valla. Cette polémique des humanistes contre les juristes traditionnels, si elle ne doit jamais être perdue de vue, n'apparaît pourtant que marginalement dans la lettre à Cornelius, lorsque Filelfo prétend éclairer non seulement les textes des orateurs et des historiens anciens, mais aussi ceux des juristes.

[41] Leçon du MS Trivulce, préférable à celle des éditions imprimées ('crebriores').

[42] Comme il le note lui-même ('Codice' [n. 9 supra], p. 398 n. 14), le philologue hollandais P. Scriverius en avait déjà fait la remarque lorsqu'il inclut en 1626 le *Libellus* de Pomponius dans son recueil *Respublica Romana*.

l'utilisation d'Asconius ne pouvait avoir en 1439 la même signification que vers 1480. Sur les cinquante et une notices de Filelfo, vingt-trois ont comme source sûre Asconius ou le Pseudo-Asconius, qui est souvent cité presque littéralement: la proportion, on le voit, est tout à fait considérable.[43] La discordance, d'autre part, est évidente entre nombre de ces notices et les intentions affichées dans la lettre à Cornelius, ces lois étant souvent loin d'être les plus célèbres ou les plus utiles à la compréhension des textes anciens.[44] L'intérêt de ces notices, en revanche, tenait à la faible diffusion d'Asconius jusqu'à l'*editio princeps* vénitienne de 1477: la découverte de ce texte au monastère de St-Gall, par Poggio Bracciolini et Bartolomeo Aragazzi de Montepulciano, ne remontait qu'à 1416, et le 15 juin 1471 encore, donnant à Giampietro Arrivabene une interprétation (fausse d'ailleurs) de 'collybus' dans *In Verrem*, 2, 3, 181, Filelfo ajoutait:

> Hæc mihi quæ ad te scriberem occurrerunt. Tu, si quid melius inueneris, eo utere. Moneo tamen ut uideas Q. Asconium Pædianum, qui in Verrinas orationes commentatus est, et quantum ad historiam attinet permulta narrat utilia. Is Mediolani nusquam est, quem ego et Florentiæ et Senæ uidisse memini.[45]

Outre la difficulté de se procurer Asconius en Italie du Nord avant 1477, on déduira de ce texte que Filelfo n'en possédait pas une copie (qui lui aurait permis de vérifier que le commentaire du Pseudo-Asconius s'arrête en *In Verrem*, 2, 2, 35), mais qu'il en avait consulté deux, à Florence (entre 1429 et 1434) puis à Sienne (entre 1434 et 1439). La seconde ne peut être identifiée, mais la première doit être celle de Poggio lui-même, l'actuel manuscrit Matritensis 8514, qui en décembre 1429 était encore entre les mains de Niccolò Niccoli,[46] et que Filelfo put donc voir avant de se brouiller avec les deux hommes. Qu'il n'ait fait que prendre à deux reprises un certain nombre de notes, sur des copies d'Asconius consultées à Florence puis à Sienne, est une indication importante: elle permet de mieux comprendre que telle notice de l'*Epistula* résulte de la fusion malheureuse de deux *excerpta* asconiens;[47] elle explique surtout que les notices empruntées à

---

[43] Voir le tableau de l'appendice I. Asconius est sensiblement résumé dans les notices 14 et 26; la fin de la notice 28 est une libre addition de Filelfo, comme le titre de consul attribué au Cornelius auteur des lois 22–24. Luciani a curieusement ignoré l'origine asconienne d'un certain nombre de notices du MS Ottoboni (les notices 11, 20, 22, 23, 24, 25 et 28 de Filelfo).

[44] Asconius est notre source unique pour quatre de ces lois (notices 8, 26, 30 et 33 de Filelfo); il le reste presque pour quatre autres (notice 1: outre Asconius, Pline, *Naturalis historia*, 3, 138, d'ailleurs peu clair; notices 22–24: outre Asconius, Cassius Dio, 36, 38–40).

[45] MS Trivulce, f. 393ᵛ; édition de 1502, f. 232ʳ.

[46] Voir A. C. Clark, p. xvi de son édition d'Asconius, *Orationum Ciceronis quinque ennaratio*, Oxford, 1907.

[47] Ainsi la notice 20: 'lex iudiciaria Aurelia. Aurelius Cotta iudiciariam legem tulit cum esset prætor, qua communicata sunt iudicia senatui et equitibus Romanis et tribunis ærariis, ut ex iis tribus ordinibus lecti iudices res iudicarent'; cf. Asconius, p. 21, ed. Stangl: 'legem iudiciariam ante aliquot annos quibus temporibus accusatus Verres a Cicerone tulit Aurelius Cotta prætor, qua communicata sunt iudicia senatui et equitibus Romanis et tribunis ærariis. Rursus deinde Pompeius in consulatu secundo, quo hæc oratio dicta est, promulgauit

Asconius s'ordonnent clairement en deux séries distinctes, suivant chacune avec une régularité presque absolue l'ordre du manuscrit, et qui doivent correspondre aux deux séries de notes prises à Florence puis à Sienne.[48]

D'autres notices entrent dans la même catégorie que celles qui proviennent d'Asconius. L'une (no. 3) concerne la loi Fabia *de numero sectatorum*, qui ne nous est connue que par Cicéron, *Pro Murena*, 71. C'est le seul cas où l'on soit sûr que la source d'une notice est un discours de Cicéron, mais le *Pro Murena*, comme Asconius, faisait partie des découvertes récentes, n'ayant été retrouvé qu'en 1415, toujours par Poggio, dans la bibliothèque de l'abbaye de Cluny.[49] La notice no. 5, concernant la loi Cincia, a pour source Tacite, *Annales*, 11, 5.[50] Il est vrai que le texte de Tacite contribuait à éclairer la formule 'de donis et muneribus' des textes de Cicéron (*De oratore*, 2, 286; *Cato maior*, 10; *Ad Atticum*, 1, 20, 7) et de Tite-Live (34, 4), mais il faut aussi rappeler que les livres 11 à 16 des *Annales* et les livres conservés des *Histoires* n'ont été transmis que par un seul manuscrit médiéval, écrit vers 1050 à Monte Cassino, et passé, dans des conditions assez suspectes, dans les mains de Boccace puis de Niccolò Niccoli.[51] Ce manuscrit n'ayant guère été copié avant la mort de Niccoli en 1437,

---

ut amplissimo ex censu ex centuriis aliter quam antea lecti iudices, æque tamen ex illis tribus ordinibus, res iudicarent'. Un autre exemple est fourni par la notice 31: 'Aurelius Cotta legem dedit cum Sylla ad diminuendam plebis potentiam multos [cum] ei magistratus ademisset, ut plebi liceret interceptos magistratus capere et communicata sunt iudicia senatui et equitibus Romanis et tribunis ærariis'; cf. Asconius, p. 61, ed. Stangl: 'hic Cotta…legem tulit ut tribunis plebis liceret postea alios magistratus capere, quod lege Sullæ eis erat ademptum… Aurelia lege communicata esse iudicia inter senatores et equestrem ordinem et tribunos ærarios…'

[48] Première série: notices 1 (p. 12, ed. Stangl); 4 (pp. 15–6); 6 (p. 21); 8 (p. 35); 11 (p. 221); 12 (pp. 247–8); 13 (p. 55); 14 (p. 57). Les deux notices mal ordonnées, 11 et 12, proviennent du Pseudo-Asconius, qui se trouve ainsi inséré entre les commentaires au *Pro Milone* et au *Pro Cornelio*. Deuxième série: notices 17–19 (pp. 15–6); 20 (p. 21); 21 (p. 24); 22–24 (pp. 47–8); 25 (p. 54); 26 (p. 54); 27 (p. 53); 28 (p. 60); 29–33 (p. 61). On notera la complémentarité, pour les lois Clodiæ (pp. 15–6), des notices 4 et 17–19; en revanche, les notices 6 et 20 font doublon (d'après la p. 21, outre la notice 31 empruntée à la p. 61). On notera surtout que la continuité de la seconde série contraste avec la discontinuité de la première.

[49] A. C. Clark, *The Vetus Cluniacensis of Poggio*, Oxford, 1905. Il est vrai qu'à Padoue Sicco Polenton (mort en 1447) put ajouter de sa main le texte du *Pro Murena* à un recueil de discours de Cicéron copié en 1413 (MS Palat. Lat. 1478), mais il était en correspondance avec Niccoli depuis 1414, et connut aussi dès avant 1420 le Tacite du même Niccoli.

[50] 'Cinthius legem tulit qua cauetur antiquitus ne quis ob causam orandam donum pecuniamue acciperet'; cf. Tacite, *Annales*, 11, 5: 'patres legem Cinciam flagitant, qua cauetur antiquitus ne quis ob causam orandam pecuniam donumue acciperet'. Filelfo a même conservé 'antiquitus', qui n'a de sens que par rapport à un débat sénatorial de l'époque impériale. On notera que la bonne leçon, 'Cinciam', conservée dans l'*editio princeps* de Tacite donnée à Venise par Jo. Vendelin de Spire (ca. 1470), sera corrigée à tort en 'Titiam' à partir de l'édition de Puteolanus (ca. 1487) jusqu'à ce qu'elle soit rétablie par J. Lipse (1574), si bien qu'Alciat, et Agustín encore dans la première version de son *De legibus*, ne rapporteront pas ce texte à la loi Cincia. Sur une notice 'Lex Titia' dans la liste copiée dans les années 1461–1466 par Guarnerio d'Artegna, voir n. 29 supra.

[51] Filelfo dut voir le MS Laur. LXVIII.2 au début de son séjour à Florence, quand ses rapports avec Niccoli étaient encore bons, à moins qu'il n'ait consulté un manuscrit conservé encore à S. Spirito en 1451, sans doute une copie qu'en avait fait faire Boccace: *Mostra di manoscritti, documenti ed edizioni. VI centenario della morte di Giovanni Boccaccio, Firenze, Bibl. Medicea Laurenziana, 23 maggio-31 agosto 1975*, I, pp. 129–31, no. 105; *Texts and Transmission: A Survey of the Latin Classics*, ed. L. D. Reynolds, Oxford, 1983, p. 408.

le texte cité par Filelfo n'était encore connu que par un petit nombre en 1439. Peut-être faudrait-il enfin associer à ce groupe les notices no. 40 et 43, dont la source est Aulu-Gelle.[52] Une lettre à Pietro Perleone du 13 août 1437 montre en effet que Filelfo pensait avoir vu en Toscane les meilleurs manuscrits de cet auteur, supérieurs en tout cas à ceux que son correspondant pouvait consulter à Venise:

> Quod autem mones dictitare istic quosdam non 'lachryma' esse apud A. Gellium sed 'latrina', et ita quodam in codice legisse te, profecto codex iste latrinarius quispiam est. Nam hi omnes, quotquot in Tuscia sunt, Gelli codices habent 'lachryma' non 'latrina', qui et emendatissimi sunt et istorum omnium, ut ita dixerim, parentes.[53]

A côté de textes encore rares, Filelfo a pu vouloir utiliser d'autres textes, pour lesquels il pensait avoir eu l'occasion de connaître les manuscrits les plus corrects et les plus anciens.

Une lettre à Lodrisio Crivelli du 7 septembre 1444 présente pour la genèse du *De legibus* un intérêt particulier:

> Miror quid tibi in mentem uenerit, ut ex Papia litteras ad me dederis, quibus petis habeamne quicquam exploratum ac certum cuiusmodi legem tulisset Otho imperator de consessu ordinis equestris in theatro, et quæ item fuerit lex Julia, et quæ Scatinia. Quid enim te non mirer, qui cum habeas istic iureconsultorum Homerum, Catonem Saccum, non ex isto potius quam ex Filelfo quæsieris de istiusmodi legibus. Ceterum, ut tibi morem geram, non Otho Cæsar Imperator, sed M. Otho tribunus plebis legem tulit ne quis in ordine equestri spectaturus sederet nisi sestertia quadraginta millia possideret. Quod cui contingeret, quisquis is tandem esset, siue ingenuus siue libertus, ei liceret in gradu quatuordecimo inter equites spectaculo interesse. Ad quadraginta autem subintelligi oportet millia, antiquo more... Legem uero Juliam sanxit G. Julius Cæsar, qua cauebatur ne liceret adulterium perpetrare, sed depræhensi qui fuissent in adulterio, ii supplicio dederentur. Quod uero loco ultimo abs te petitur, lex Scatinia a Scatinio lata est, contra puerorum concubitores qui uocantur ἀρσενοκοῖται, arsenocœtæ. Hos enim graui supplicio afficiebat. Nos tum pædicatores, tum pædicones appellamus istiusmodi homines flagitiosos et impuros ac plane sceleratos. Vale cum Catone nostro.[54]

---

[52] Loi Hortensia, d'après Aulu-Gelle, 15, 27, 4 (les autres témoignages sont Tite-Live, *Periochae*, 11; Diodore de Sicile, 21, 18, 2; Pline, *Naturalis historia*, 16, 37; Dion Cassius, fr. 37, 2; *Digesta*, 1, 2, 2, 8). Loi Aternia d'après Aulu-Gelle, 11, 1, 2 (l'unique autre témoignage étant Denys d'Helicarnasse, 10, 50).

[53] MS Trivulce, f. 34ʳ; édition de 1502, f. 14ʳ. La discussion portait sur Aulu-Gelle, 2, 3, 3 (l'édition vénitienne de 1472 ayant 'lachrymas', mais les éditions romaines de 1467 et 1472 'latrinas'). Comme le note E. K. Marshall, 'the story of Gellius in the fifteenth century has yet to be written': *Texts and Transmission* (n. 51 supra), p. 179 n. 17. Du moins sait-on que Niccoli, en 1431 ou juste avant, copia un manuscrit ancien des livres 9–20 (ceux à qui sont empruntées les notices 40 et 43). Filelfo aurait-il pu le consulter, en même temps que ceux d'Asconius et de Tacite?

[54] MS Trivulce, f. 72ʳ; édition de 1502, f. 34ʳ (avec deux fautes mineures). Sur Lodrisio Crivelli, voir F.

Cette lettre doit être rapprochée des notices no. 35, 36 et 37:

> Lex Othonis. Otho tr. pl. legem tulit ne quis in ordine equestri spectaturus sederet nisi sestertia quadraginta millia possideret. Quodsi contingeret, quisquis esset siue ingenuus siue libertus, inter equites spectare ei liceret in gradu XIIII.

> Lex Scatinia. Scatinius legem tulit qua puerorum concubitores graui supplicio afficerentur, quos ἀρσενοκοῖτας, arsenocœtas uocant.

> Lex Julia. C. Julius Cæsar lege sanxit ne adulteri forent, deprehensi autem supplicio dederentur.

Il n'y a, on le voit, que deux possibilités: ou bien Filelfo en 1444 a repris presque mot pour mot ce qu'il avait déjà écrit en 1439 dans sa lettre à Cornelius; ou bien les notices 35–37 ont été insérées après 1444 dans la collection déjà constituée en 1439. Le manuscrit Trivulce pourrait nous inciter à favoriser la première hypothèse, puisqu'on y trouve à la fois la lettre à Crivelli et la lettre à Cornelius, suivie de toutes les notices de l'édition de 1483. Mais le regroupement des trois notices 35 à 37, et surtout leur succession dans le même ordre que dans la lettre à Crivelli, ne permettent guère de douter, selon moi, que la bonne hypothèse soit plutôt la seconde. On peut d'ailleurs produire un autre argument en ce sens. La question de Crivelli sur la 'lex Othonis' était de toute évidence provoquée par la lecture de Juvénal (3, 153–159 et 14, 322–326), de même que son intérêt pour les lois Julia et Scantinia (2, 36–45). Or Filelfo avait expliqué Juvénal à Sienne, peu avant d'écrire la lettre à Cornelius, et nous conservons des notes de cours sur les *Satires,* I–IV, 48:[55] non seulement on n'y trouve rien sur la loi Julia et la loi Roscia, ce qui pourrait suggérer seulement que ces notes sont incomplètes, mais surtout le commentaire sur la loi Scantinia n'y est pas encore formulé de la même façon que dans la lettre de 1444 et dans le *De legibus.*[56] Les notices 35–37 ont donc probablement été ajoutées après 1444.

Le travail de réflexion et d'élaboration y est plus important que dans les notices qui reprennent presque mot pour mot le commentaire d'Asconius. Il est

---

Gabotto, 'Ricerche intorno allo storiografo quattrocentista Crivelli', *Archivio storico italiano,* ser. V, 7, 1891, pp. 267–98; F. Petrucci, *Dizionario biografico degli Italiani,* 31, 1985, pp. 141–52. On notera que Crivelli avait eu une formation de juriste avant de recevoir une culture humaniste auprès de Filelfo, qu'il enseigna même les *Décrétales* à Pavie en 1443–4, à Milan en 1448, à Ferrare de 1449 à 1452. L'ironie légère des premières lignes de la lettre n'en prend que plus de saveur.

[55] Sanford, dans *Catalogus translationum* (n. 24 supra), I, pp. 214–5. Ces notes (MS Barb. Lat. 134, ff. 69–72) ont été publiées par G. Vignuolo, 'Note inedite di Francesco Filelfo a Giovenale', *Studia Picena,* 42, 1975, pp. 96–125. Elles avaient été prises, comme celles d'autres leçons de Filelfo recueillies dans le MS Chigi H.IV.99, ff. 133–9, par le notaire siennois Antonius Michaelis Ventura: R. Bianchi, 'Note di Francesco Filelfo al *De natura deorum,* al *De oratore,* all' *Eneide* negli appunti di un notaio senese' dans *Francesco Filelfo* (n. 40 supra), pp. 365–8. On notera que Filelfo avait déjà commenté Juvénal à Florence, pendant l'année 1429–30, mais que seule a été conservée la leçon inaugurale: L. G. Rosa, dans *Francesco Filelfo* (n. 40 supra), pp. 286–7.

[56] Ad *Satiram,* 2, 44: 'Scatinius ipse condidit leges contra illos qui patiuntur muliebria; Scatinia est lex quæ contra alienas artes exercentes loquitur, et qua pœna puniuntur.'

vrai que le texte de Juvénal n'avait cessé d'être glosé et commenté depuis
l'Antiquité tardive, mais Filelfo ne paraît pas dépendre des commentaires
médiévaux[57] quand il définit le contenu de la loi Scantinia, profitant d'ailleurs de
l'occasion pour introduire et interpréter un mot grec, ou lorsqu'il précise
qu'Othon n'est pas l'empereur, mais un tribun de la plèbe.[58] Certaines similitudes
avec le commentaire de Filetico[59] posent en revanche le problème de savoir si
tous deux s'inspirent d'un même commentaire humaniste, antérieur à 1444,[60] ou
s'il faut supposer une utilisation de Filelfo par Filetico: cette dernière hypothèse,
nous l'avons déjà dit, n'aurait rien d'invraisemblable. On notera d'autre part que
Filelfo avait déjà consacré une autre notice à la loi Roscia (no. 32): 'L. Roscius
Otho cos. legem tulit ut in theatro equitibus Romanis ordines quattuordecim
spectandi gratia darentur'; d'après Asconius (p. 61, ed. Stangl): 'L. Roscius Otho
biennio ante cons. firmauit in theatro ut equitibus Romanis XIIII ordines spectandi gratia darentur.'

Le texte d'Asconius tel qu'il était transmis par le manuscrit de St-Gall faisait
de Roscius Otho un consul et non un tribun,[61] si bien que la juxtaposition des
notices 32 et 35 est moins surprenante que celle des notices 6 et 20 pour la loi
Aurelia. Notons qu'on la trouvera encore chez Pomponio Leto, alors pourtant que
Domizio Calderini, son collègue et rival à la Sapienza, avait surmonté la difficulté
dès son commentaire de 1474, en corrigeant implicitement le texte d'Asconius.[62]

---

[57] Telle est du moins l'impression qui ressort des sondages auxquels j'ai procédé parmi les manuscrits de
la Bibliothèque nationale de Paris.

[58] Par inadvertance, cependant, Filelfo attribue au tribun le prénom de l'empereur.

[59] Le cours de Filetico nous est connu par trois manuscrits (Florence, Biblioteca Riccardiana 1190; Paris,
Bibliothèque Mazarine 3857; Vatican, MS Ottob. Lat. 1256), dont j'ai consulté les deux derniers. 'Lex Julia
quam C. Julius Cæsar sanxit, ut adulteri non forent, deprehensi autem graui supplicio dederentur' (Maz., f. 14ʳ;
Ottob., f. 6ʳ); 'Scantinia lex est quam Scantinius ciuis Romanus tulit. Ex ea puerorum concubitores (Maz.:
concubinatores) graui supplicio afficiebantur, quos Græci arsenochitas (Maz.: arxenochitas) dixerunt'. Pour la
loi Roscia (ad *Satiram*, 3, 15), Filetico reprend la définition d'Asconius, p. 61, ed. Stangl, mais on notera que
l'ordre des mots est exactement celui de la notice 32 de Filelfo: 'legem Rosciam (Maz.: Rosiam) dicit quam
Lutius (om. Maz.) Roscius (Maz.: Rosius) Otho tulit, ut in theatro equitibus Romanis ordines quatuordecim
spectandi gratia darentur' (Maz., f. 24ʳ; Ottob., f. 10ʳ; Asconius: 'in theatro ut et XIIII ordines'), et que la glose
se termine sur une distinction entre le tribun et l'empereur: 'nec hic intellegendum est de Othone illo qui post
mortem Neronis et Galbe imperator fuit'.

[60] On pense bien sûr à Guarino de Vérone, maître de Filetico et ami de Filelfo depuis 1418–9 (pour un
exemple d'utilisation par Filelfo d'un commentaire de Guarino, voir A. T. Grafton et L. Jardine, 'Humanism
and the School of Guarino...', *Past and Present*, 96, 1982, pp. 72–3). Mais la seule indication chronologique
que nous ayons d'un cours de Guarino sur Juvénal se rapporte à l'année 1449, cf. Sanford, *Catalogus* (n. 24
supra), pp. 205–8, et surtout rien de semblable aux textes de Filelfo et de Filetico ne semble se trouver dans les
manuscrits que l'on peut rapporter au commentaire de Guarino sur Juvénal. J'ai consulté le MS Paris. Lat.
16696, et J.-Y. Tilliette a bien voulu examiner pour moi le MS Ottob. Lat. 1146; je doute qu'une consultation
des MS Ambr. A 121 inf. et Marc. Lat. XII.19 donnerait des résultats sensiblement différents.

[61] La corruption du texte d'Asconius ne fut explicitement signalée qu'en 1547 par P. Manuzio, et la
correction 'confirmauit' ne fut proposée qu'en 1559 par Sigonio.

[62] 'De ordine sedendi in theatro Lucius Roscius Otho tribunus plebis, ut scribunt Pedianus, Liuius,
Porphyrio, multis ante annis legem tulerat, ut scilicet quattuordecim proximi gradus equitibus assignarentur' (*ad*

Même si, comme je le crois, les notices 35–37 datent de 1444, il ne faudrait pas en déduire que toutes celles qui suivent sont également des additions à la liste originelle de 1439. Les notices 34 et 38 ont toutes deux pour source le *Bellum Jugurthinum* de Salluste, un texte que Filelfo avait expliqué à Florence en 1432.[63] On pourrait envisager l'hypothèse que la liste originelle ait pris fin avec la notice 33, la dernière qui provient d'Asconius, mais une addition des seules notices 35–37 me paraît mieux rendre compte de la disjonction des notices 34 et 38. Ces dernières méritent quelque intérêt, ne serait-ce qu'en raison du succès qu'elles ont connu. La notice no. 34: 'Satyra lex est quæ uno rogatu multa simul et uaria comprehendit, ut uultisne iubetisne ut cum Jugurtha bellum componatur, elephantos tradat omnis, transfugas reddat uniuersos', a pour source Salluste, *Bellum Jugurthinum*, 29, 5:

> Rex..., pauca præsenti consilio locutus...uti in deditionem acciperetur, reliqua cum Bestia et Scauro secreto transigit; dein postero die, quasi per saturam sententiis exquisitis, in deditionem accipit. Sed, uti pro consilio imperatum erat, elephanti triginta, pecus atque equi multi cum paruo argenti pondere quæstori traduntur.

interprété à la lumière de Diomède (*Grammatici latini*, I, 486):

> Alii autem (saturam) dictam putant a lege satura, quæ uno rogatu multa simul comprehendit. Cuius saturæ legis Lucilius meminit in primo..., et Sallustius in Jugurtha: deinde quasi per saturam sententiis exquisitis in deditionem accipitur.

On notera d'ailleurs que, sous l'influence sans doute du texte de Diomède, le mot 'legem' s'était glissé après 'quasi per saturam' dans la tradition manuscrite de Salluste, dès le treizième siècle au moins, et qu'il se trouve dans la plupart des *recentiores* puis dans les premières éditions.[64] On notera aussi que 'saturam legem' est assez fréquemment glosé dans les manuscrits, et on peut donc se demander si Filelfo ne s'est pas inspiré d'une telle glose. Cette hypothèse me paraît cependant peu probable: Filelfo commence par reprendre mot pour mot (avec la seule addition de 'et uaria') la définition de Diomède, puis donne un

3, 153–159). Domizio Calderini (1446–1478) était depuis 1470/1 le collègue de Pomponio Leto à l'Université de Rome; son commentaire à Juvénal, écrit en 1474, fut publié à Venise et Brescia en 1475: voir A. Perosa, *Dizionario biografico degli Italiani*, 16, 1973, pp. 597–605; E. Lee, *Sixtus IV* (n. 26 supra), pp. 179–82. Filelfo en 1444 ne pouvait connaître qu'Asconius et Tite-Live, *Periocha*, 99; le commentaire de Porphyrion à Horace (*Épodes*, 4, 15) ne fut introduit en Italie qu'en 1455 par Énoch d'Ascoli.

[63] Ne nous est malheureusement parvenu que le texte de la leçon inaugurale: Fera, 'Itinerari' (n. 40 supra), p. 92.

[64] La consultation de manuscrits plus anciens, la constatation aussi que le mot ne figure pas dans le texte tel qu'il est cité par Festus (ed. Lindsay, p. 416) et par Diomède lui-même, n'entraînèrent que progressivement son expulsion: voir le commentaire de Rivius (1539) et les scholies d'Alde le Jeune (1563).

exemple qui est pour l'essentiel une espèce de centon sallustien,[65] mais ne paraît pas avoir de précédent dans les gloses médiévales.[66] Quant à la notice no. 38:

> Mamilius tr. pl. legem tulit ut quando res a nobilibus aduerse gestæ fuerant, etiam ii ad magistratus gerendos admitterentur quorum maiores in romana republica magistratus non exercuissent. Huiusmodi autem homines noui appellantur.

elle est une interprétation erronée de *Bellum Jugurthinum*, 65, 5: 'simul ea tempestate plebs nobilitate fusa per legem Mamiliam nouos extollebat'.

Écrit en 1470 à Vérone ou Padoue, imprimé à Brescia en 1495 et souvent reproduit par la suite, le commentaire de Giovanni Crisostomo Soldo[67] interprète le chapitre 29 à la lumière d'une conception différente et totalement erronée de 'lex satura', que l'on trouvait déjà dans certaines gloses médiévales;[68] mais figure aussi dans l'édition imprimée, faisant irruption au milieu d'une phrase dont elle interrompt le mouvement naturel, une autre définition, qui est dérivée de Diomède et très proche de Filelfo.[69] Je ne crois pas que Filelfo et Soldo aient utilisé une source commune, mais plutôt que les mots interpolés s'inspirent de la notice de Filelfo: il s'agit en ce cas d'une addition de Soldo lui-même en 1470 (la lettre à Cornelius pouvait être connue en Vénétie), ou plus probablement d'une note portée en marge du manuscrit de Soldo après l'édition des *Orationes* en 1483 (ou sa réimpression à Brescia même en 1488). Pour le chapitre 65, en revanche, Soldo donnait dès 1470 la bonne solution, qui avait échappé à Filelfo.[70] Mais un

---

[65] 'Bellum componere' vient de *Bellum Jugurthinum*, 97, 2 et 103, 3; 'elephantos...transfugasque' doit s'inspirer de *Bellum Jugurthinum*, 32, 3 et 40, 1. Intéressante est d'autre part l'utilisation de la formule 'uultisne iubetisne' (à l'indicatif il est vrai): des souvenirs de Cicéron, Tite-Live, ou Aulu-Gelle servent à donner à cette reconstitution un aspect plus authentique.

[66] Telle est à nouveau l'impression qui ressort des sondages auxquels j'ai procédé parmi les manuscrits de la Bibliothèque nationale de Paris.

[67] Sur Soldo, on trouve quelques rares renseignements dans L. Cozzando, *Libreria bresciana*, Brescia, 1694, II, p. 261. Il aurait été dominicain, mais ne figure pas parmi les *Scriptores Ordinis Prædicatorum* de J. Quétif et J. Échard, Paris, 1719-21. La date du commentaire est fournie par deux lettres de l'auteur à son frère, envoyées de Vérone le 28 décembre 1469 et de Padoue le 18 juin 1470, pour annoncer le début et l'achèvement de l'entreprise. Le manuscrit fut alors envoyé à Brescia, et c'est dans cette ville qu'il fut publié pour la première fois en 1495 par Angelo et Jacopo Britannici. M. H. Crawford a bien voulu consulter pour moi l'exemplaire de cette édition que possède la British Library.

[68] 'Legem satyram...que iubebat, dux et imperator exercitus sententias exquireret totius consilii cum graue aliquid deliberandum esset, præsertim cum deditio facienda uel suscipienda esset'. Cf., e.g., MS Paris. Lat. 6088 (13ème siècle): 'satura lex præcipiebat ut nullus qui sic offendisset senatum in deditionem acciperetur nisi communi consensu'.

[69] 'Nam consul simulabat se nihil facere uelle nisi de consensu consilii cum [lex satyra est que uno rogatu plura continet. Hoc modo placet cum Jugurthe [*sic*] fœdus feriatur, in deditionem Jugurtha recipiatur, elephantos tradat omnes transfugas] tamen parua et pauca ad consilium referret, magna autem et multa secreto cum Scauro perageret' (les crochets droits, bien sûr, sont de moi). Dès l'édition vénitienne de 1497, 'cum' a été corrigé en 'ut'; la notice de Filelfo a 'placet ut cum Jugurtha'.

[70] 'Nobilitas post legem Mamiliam uires amiserat. Multi enim damnati sunt per eam legem et omnes perculsi... Per legem Mamiliam, quia Mamilius tr. pl. tulit, ut supra uisum est'. Le lien entre *Bellum Jugurthinum*, 40 et 65, 5 est ce que n'avait pas vu Filelfo, de même que la nécessité de rapporter 'per legem

autre commentaire souvent réimprimé, celui de Josse Bade (Ascensius), paru à Paris en 1504, s'inspirera étroitement de Filelfo, pour la 'lex satyra' comme pour la 'lex Man(i)lia':[71] Bade avait d'ailleurs réimprimé les *Orationes* de Filelfo quelques mois plus tôt seulement.[72] La même interprétation de la loi Mamilia se retrouvera ensuite parmi de brèves notes marginales attribuées à Melanchton dans des éditions données en 1536 à Cologne (Gymnicus) et Lyon (Gryphius), et qui figurent, anonymes bien sûr, jusque dans la dernière édition aldine de 1588.[73] Quant à la 'lex satyra', on lit jusque dans le *Lexicon* de Forcellini revu par De Vit (1858–60): 'per saturam latæ legis exemplum esto: uelitis iubeatisne cum Jugurtha pacem componi, fœdus feriri, elephantos tradi itemque profugas omnes etc.'. Le relais en ce cas a probablement été l'une des rééditions du *Thesaurus eruditionis scholasticæ* de Basilius Faber.[74]

Les notices no. 44–49 constituent un autre groupe homogène: les *Institutiones* en sont très clairement la source unique, même si le texte en est plus ou moins remanié, et dans l'ensemble abrégé. De ce que ce groupe n'inclut pas la loi Julia *de adulteriis*, dont la notice (no. 37) ne dérive pas des *Institutiones* (4, 18, 4), on ne saurait déduire qu'il fut nécessairement ajouté après celui des notices no. 35–37: manquent tout aussi bien les lois Juliæ *de maiestate* (*Institutiones*, 4, 18, 3) et *de ui* (4, 18, 8). De même constatons-nous que Filelfo a utilisé les *Institutiones* (2, 22) pour la loi Falcidia (no. 44), mais non pour la loi Aquilia (no. 10), qu'il a, nous le verrons, si mal interprétée. La part d'intervention personnelle apparaît dans la loi Cornelia *de sicariis* où, résumant fortement le texte des *Institutiones*, il privilégie tout ce qui est consacré aux étymologies grecques, et surtout dans la loi Fabia *de plagiariis*, où il introduit une étymologie absente de sa source:

Flauius inter iudicia publica constituit de plagiariis, cum quis πλαγίοις, plagiois, i.e. obliquis et insidiosis pollicitationibus seruum a domino uel filium a patre subtrahit uel etiam pecus.

Mamiliam' à 'nobilitate fusa', et non à 'nouos extollebat'.

[71] 'Quæ uno rogatu priusquam respondeatur multa simul et uaria comprehendit, ut uultisne iubetisne cum Jugurtha bellum componatur, elephantos tradat etc.'; 'quam Manlius seu Manilius tr. pl. constituit ut, re male gesta a nobilibus, noui ad magistratus admitterentur.'

[72] L'épître dédicatoire de l'édition commentée de Salluste est du 31 octobre 1504, celle des *Orationes* de Filelfo du 10 mars 1503 (= 1504 n.s.).

[73] 'Qua lege cautum erat ut re male gesta a nobilitate mandarentur nouis hominibus magistratus.'

[74] La phrase reprise par Forcellini ne semble figurer dans aucune édition ni de Calepinus ni d'Estienne. Parmi les rééditions du *Thesaurus* de Faber, elle n'apparaît pas dans celle de 1587 (je n'ai pu consulter l'édition originale de 1571), mais figure dans celle de 1686, due à Christoph Cellarius. Il doit donc s'agir d'une addition de Cellarius lui-même ou de son prédécesseur August Buchner, faite en tout cas dans le courant du 17ème siècle.

Alors que l'étymologie courante faisait venir 'plagiarius' de 'plaga', la connaissance du grec qu'avait Filelfo lui a permis de proposer la bonne interprétation, et Alciat ne manquera pas de lui rendre hommage sur ce point.[75]

L'origine de plusieurs autres notices peut être identifiée de façon presque certaine: le résumé de Festus par Paul Diacre (p. 25, ed. Lindsay) pour la loi 'annaria' (no. 41); Tite-Live, 34, 1 pour la loi Oppia (no. 7) mais à 'iuncto uehiculo' Filelfo substitue 'pilentis' (sans doute d'après Tite-Live, 5, 25, 9), ce qui lui donne l'occasion de gloser ce mot rare ('i.e. redis pensilibus'). Le *De officiis* surtout est la source de plusieurs notices: la loi Papia (no. 15, cf. 3, 47), la loi Latoria (no. 16, cf. 3, 61), la loi Aquilia aussi (no. 10), où la confusion est évidente entre la loi Aquilia *de damno* et les 'formulæ de dolo malo' introduites par C. Aquillius Gallus (*De officiis*, 3, 60–61; également *De natura deorum*, 3, 74), comme si Filelfo avait cru trouver une occasion de corriger les textes juridiques à l'aide de Cicéron;[76] enfin l'aberrante notice no. 50: 'Latorius ciuis Romanus legem condidit qua cautum est ut si quis pupillorum bona diriperet, acerrimas pœnas lueret' qui dérive peut-être elle aussi d'un souvenir inexact de Cicéron, *De officiis*, 3, 61, déjà utilisé pour la notice no. 16: 'ut tutela XII tabulis, circumscriptio adulescentium lege Latoria (sc. uindicatur)'. Ne restent que cinq notices dont je suis incapable de préciser les sources, et que Filelfo a pu écrire d'après des réminiscences cicéroniennes ou liviennes diverses, celles qui concernent les lois Porcia (no. 2), Valeria (no. 9), Sempronia (no. 39), Ælia et Fufia (no. 42), Appuleia (no. 51):

Portia lege non licebat interfici ciuem Romanum uerum [*sic*] uirgis uerberari. Hoc autem significatur: quod ea re tolleretur dignitas ciuilis et redigeretur in seruum, quia tandem faciebat seruum.

Valerius Publicola legem tulit ut nulli magistratui liceret corpus Romani ciuis indicta causa condemnare, liceretque damnatis ad populum prouocare.

Sempronius Gracchus legem tulit qua frumentum e publico distribueretur populo Romano, quæ frumentaria dicta est.

Ælius et Fufius tr. pl. sua auctoritate legem tulerunt ne quis per eos dies quibus cum populo agi liceret non nisi de cælo seruasset quippiam ageret.

---

[75] Alciat, *Parerga*, liv. I (1538), ch. 47: 'uidendum est unde plagiarii dicantur, et uulgo creditur a plaga, i.e. dolore quo ille officitur qui surreptus est. Sed huic sententiæ plurima aduersantur, et in primis ratio syllabæ, quæ in plaga producitur, in plagio uel plagiario corripitur... Verius est igitur quod Philelphus scripsit, ἀπὸ τοῦ πλαγίου, i.e. ab obliquo dici, quia obliquis quibusdam artibus et dolis in seruitutem trahebant.'

[76] Cette confusion sera dénoncée par Agustín, qui l'attribuera au seul Pomponio Leto, dans la première version de son *De legibus* (MS Vat. Lat. 6231).

Apuleius legem tulit qua cauebatur, si quis publicam maiestatem minuisset, capitalis esset.

Il apparaît donc que le recueil de Filelfo est un ensemble relativement hétérogène, où des doublons peuvent être indicatifs de strates successives, dont trois notices au moins ont été introduites après 1444, mais qui, pour l'essentiel, remonte bien à 1439. La lettre à Cornelius, d'autre part, ne doit pas être prise au pied de la lettre: si un certain nombre de notices correspondent bien au programme affiché, Filelfo a largement privilégié des textes récemment découverts et encore peu connus en Vénétie. Néanmoins, en 1439 comme en 1444, le point de départ est l'explication des grands auteurs (Cicéron et Tite-Live; Juvénal). Un groupe de notices dérive des *Institutiones*, mais à aucun moment il ne paraît y avoir utilisation du *Digeste*, et un juriste comme Agustín aura beau jeu de railler la confusion entre loi Aquilia et *exceptio* Aquilia, alors que les seules *Institutiones* fournissaient de la loi une définition claire, et même plusieurs citations. Filelfo pouvait critiquer l'enseignement traditionnel du droit, et tirer satisfaction d'être consulté par des juristes comme Crivelli ou même Catone Sacco; mais ce sont des juristes qui, quelques décennies plus tard, parviendront le mieux à réaliser une fructueuse synthèse entre culture humaniste et connaissance profonde des textes juridiques. L'œuvre de Filelfo révèle d'autres faiblesses: confusions dans une seule notice d'indications d'Asconius relatives à deux lois distinctes (no. 20 et 31); attribution à un consul des lois Corneliæ de 67 (no. 22–24); interprétations erronées de Salluste (no. 34 et 38) etc. Surtout, rares sont les notices réunissant des informations d'origine diverse: la plupart s'inspirent d'un seul texte, et ne lui apportent que quelques modifications formelles. Enfin, lorsque l'*Epistola* fut imprimée en 1483, elle avait perdu une partie de son intérêt puisque les textes les plus rares avaient déjà été publiés (*Pro Murena*: 1471; Tacite: 1472–1473; Asconius: 1477). Malgré tout, sans doute parce qu'elle était le premier recueil de lois romaines qu'on ait songé à constituer, et parce qu'elle avait su réunir des notices empruntées aux sources les plus diverses (Cicéron et ses commentateurs, historiens, grammairiens antiquaires, textes juridiques), elle connut pendant plusieurs décennies un succès et une influence incontestables. En témoignent le *Libellus* de Pomponio Leto et l'*Historia iuris ciuilis* d'Aymar du Rivail.

II

Nous avons vu déjà que le *Libellus* de Pomponio Leto, datable des années 1477–1483, n'est pratiquement, pour les lois, qu'une mise en ordre alphabétique des notices de Filelfo. Pomponio ne fit même aucun usage de la *Roma triumphans* de Biondo Flavio, le premier grand ouvrage humaniste traitant des antiquités romaines dans leur ensemble, qui avait pourtant été composé à Rome entre 1453 et 1459,[77] et où il aurait pu trouver, comme le fera plus tard Aymar du Rivail, la matière de nouvelles notices. L'intérêt du *Libellus* tient au fait qu'il réunit un traité sur les magistratures et les sacerdoces dont l'idée revenait à Andrea di Domenico Fiocchi et un recueil de notices sur les lois dont l'idée revenait à Filelfo. On notera que Pomponio Leto inverse l'ordre du *De potestatibus* de Fiocchi, où l'étude des sacerdoces précédait celle des magistratures, et surtout qu'il adjoint au livre sur les magistatures de brèves notices sur les jurisconsultes. L'*Enchiridion* de Pomponius, source évidente de ces notices, l'est également de l'idée d'associer dans un même livre l'histoire des magistratures et celle des jurisconsultes. Son influence devait être plus décisive encore sur l'*Historia iuris ciuilis* d'Aymar du Rivail, à laquelle sera consacrée la dernière partie de mon étude.

III

Du Rivail fut, sinon le premier historien du droit,[78] du moins le premier qui, à l'époque moderne, entreprit d'écrire une histoire des sources du droit romain et, dans une bien moindre mesure, du droit pontifical. Cette *Historia iuris ciuilis et pontificii* fut publiée pour la première fois à Valence en 1515, et connut ensuite d'assez nombreuses rééditions en France et en Allemagne;[79] mais le projet en a été conçu et, semble-t-il, réalisé pour l'essentiel, au cours d'un séjour d'études en Italie qui prit fin en 1512 et commença au plus tard en 1509: 'Italiam peragrando coniungere quinque libris ius et historiam Romanorum primo enixus sum'.[80] Le contemporain d'Alciat qu'était Du Rivail appartient à une génération de juristes profondément marqués par la lecture des grands humanistes italiens: en dehors des auteurs anciens, parmi lesquels est inclus le Pseudo-Fenestella, les sources utilisées dans l'*Historia iuris* sont, bien sûr Filelfo et Pomponio Leto (le *Libellus* et les *Cæsares*), mais aussi Biondo Flavio (la *Roma triumphans* et les *Decades*),

---

[77] A. Mazzocco, 'Some Philological Aspects of Biondo Flavio's *Roma Triumphans*', *Humanistica Lovanensia*, 28, 1979, pp. 2–4.

[78] La seule étude qui lui ait été consacrée, celle d'E. von Möller, est intitulée *Aymar du Rivail, der erste Rechtshistoriker*, Historische Studien, 56, Berlin, 1907. On ne peut guère signaler depuis que quelques remarques de P.-F. Girard ('Les Préliminaires de la Renaissance du droit romain', *Nouvelle revue historique de droit français et étranger*, 1922, p. 38) et de D. Maffei (*Gli inizi dell' umanesimo giuridico*, Milan, 1956, pp. 138–9, et 'Les Débuts de l'activité de Budé, Alciat et Zase ainsi que quelques remarques sur Aymar du Rivail' dans *Pédagogues et juristes*, Paris, 1963, p. 29).

[79] L'édition de Valence est s.d., mais le privilège accordé à l'imprimeur Olivelli est daté du 8 août 1515. L'ouvrage fut ensuite réédité à Paris, s.d. [c. 1516: B. Moreau, *Inventaire chronologique des éditions parisiennes du XVIe siècle*, II, Paris, 1977, p. 367, no. 1338]; Mayence, 1527, 1530, 1533, 1539; Lyon, 1551. Il fut repris une dernière fois dans le premier tome des *Tractatuum celeberrimorum in utraque tum Pontificii tum Cæsarei iuris facultate iurisconsultorum* de Ziletti (Venise, 1584.)

[80] F. 2. Sur la chronologie du séjour de Du Rivail en Italie et de la rédaction de l'*Historia iuris*, voir l'appendice II.

Valla, Platina, Poliziano, Crinito, le grammairien Curio Lancellotto Pasi, et même l'édition de Virgile par Benedetto Ricardini, qui venait d'être imprimée à Florence en 1510 par Filippo Giunta.[81] Le texte célèbre d'Aulu-Gelle (16, 10) où l'on voit le poète Julius Paulus expliquer un terme des XII Tables après qu'un juriste s'était révélé incapable de le faire, est l'occasion pour Du Rivail de fustiger ceux des juristes de son temps qui ignorent et méprisent une formation plus large que l'enseignement traditionnel,[82] mais il ne néglige pas non plus l'occasion de souligner ailleurs la nécessité de posséder des connaissances juridiques pour comprendre un texte de Virgile.[83] Après son *Historia iuris*, Du Rivail persistera dans son activité historiographique en écrivant, entre 1530 et 1532, une histoire des Allobroges qu'il renoncera finalement à publier.[84] Il n'était pas le premier juriste français à exalter le passé de sa province ou de sa cité, et il suffira de mentionner deux ouvrages comptant parmi les sources du *De Allobrogibus*: le *De Tholosanorum gestis* (1515) de Nicolas Bertrand, avocat au parlement de Toulouse, et les *Annales d'Aquitaine* (1524) de Jean Bouchet, procureur à Poitiers. On trouve dans tous ces textes le même patriotisme outrancier, la même confiance aveugle dans les 'fragments' édités par Annio de Viterbe, les mêmes erreurs chronologiques graves. Mais l'ouvrage de Du Rivail ne se distingue pas seulement par son premier livre, une description du Dauphiné et des pays limitrophes d'intérêt comparable à celle que donnera vingt ans plus tard de la Franche-Comté l'humaniste Gilbert Cousin.[85] S'il s'inscrit essentielle-ment dans la tradition historiographique des chroniques, le *De Allobrogibus* manifeste également un intérêt pour les documents qui le rapproche de la tradition antiquaire qui se constitue à partir du 15ème siècle: d'assez nombreuses inscriptions latines sont signalées, souvent transcrites, et parfois commentées, presque toutes dans le premier livre; et pour la période médiévale, Du Rivail

---

[81] Dans sa notice sur Modestin, Du Rivail signale que les résumés décastiques des chants de l'*Énéide* traditionnellement attribués à Ovide le sont à Modestin, sur la foi d'un manuscrit très ancien, par 'Benedictus Philogius [*sic*] Florentinus' (f. 126 de l'édition de 1515). L'intérêt de Du Rivail pour cette information est éclairé par la notice qu'il consacre au juriste 'Arrianus' (*sic*, en fait Arrius Menander), qu'il est tenté d'identifier avec l'historien d'Alexandre: 'quod nullus ideo improbare potest, quod iureconsulti ius, non historiam scribant, si aliud non afferat. Nam Celius Antipater et plures alii iureconsulti historias conscripserunt, sed et carmina Modestinus edidit' (f. 123).

[82] 'Hoc tamen in compluribus nostræ ætatis iurisperitis euenire solet, qui multa legum uocabula ignorant, uimque legum et intelligentiam non habent, nec mirum est, cum inferiores disciplinas negligant, immo uero eas callentes irrideant et contemnant' (f. 61). Et Du Rivail célèbre, au contraire, toujours d'après Aulu-Gelle, Ateius Capito, l'auteur des *Coniectanea*.

[83] 'Hoc et aliis locis probatur satis Maronem sine pontificio iure...non posse intelligi. Discant igitur hasce leges qui Virgilium habere cupiunt, et pœtarum fateantur studiosi iuris noticiam non officere pœmati' (ff. 22–23).

[84] *Aymardi Rivallii Delphinatis de Allobrogibus libri nouem*, ed. A. de Terrebasse, Vienne, 1844. Sur la date de rédaction de cet ouvrage, voir l'appendice II.

[85] G. Cousin (Cognatus), *Breuis ac dilucida Superioris Burgundiæ quæ Comitatus nomine censetur descriptio*, Bâle, 1552. De larges parties du livre I de Du Rivail furent d'ailleurs dès 1852 traduites en français par A. Macé, de même que la *Descriptio* de Cousin le fut en 1863 par A. Chérau, puis en 1907 par E. Monot.

utilise volontiers les monuments funéraires, qu'il décrit et dont il copie les épitaphes, ainsi que des chartes anciennes que ses fonctions et missions lui ont
donné l'occasion d'examiner. Cet aspect de l'œuvre mérite d'être souligné, même
si la critique des documents et leur intégration dans le cadre d'un récit traditionnel ne sont pas toujours satisfaisants, loin de là. Il apparaissait déjà, plus discrètement, dans l'*Historia iuris*, où inscriptions et monnaies sont parfois utilisées pour
compléter une documentation essentiellement tirée des textes littéraires et juridiques.[86]

Le modèle principal d'une *Historia iuris* ne pouvait être que le long texte de
Pomponius repris dans le titre *De origine iuris et omnium magistratuum et
successione prudentium* du *Digeste*: un texte que les glossateurs avaient négligé,
mais qui suscitait un intérêt nouveau au moment où Du Rivail composa son
œuvre.[87] Alors que, pour Savigny, l'*Historia iuris* suivait l'ordre du fragment de
Pomponius, von Möller a soutenu que le plan de Du Rivail était original.[88] De
fait, on y peut retrouver trois influences, celles de Pomponius, des *Institutiones*
et d'Aristote, mais dans un mélange très inégal. Si Aristote est le point de départ
affiché des deux développements ('IVSTITIA' et 'TRES REI PVBLICÆ
SPECIES') qui servent en quelque sorte de préface à l'ouvrage proprement dit,
il est en fait bien vite abandonné. La distinction aristotélicienne entre justice
légale et justice particulière ne sert qu'à introduire des définitions et des
distinctions dont les sources sont *Digeste*, 1, 1 et surtout *Institutiones*, 1, 1 et 2.[89]

[86] Inscriptions: f. 11 (deux funéraires de Valence et de Lyon, *Corpus inscriptionum latinarum*, XIII, 2132
et XII, 1749); f. 94 (versions 4 et 2 du faux s.c. du Rubicon, *Corpus inscriptionum latinarum*, XI, 30*); f. 124
(versions C et A de la fausse inscription funéraire de Papinien, *Corpus inscriptionum latinarum*, VI, 5, 11*);
f. 38 (tribunat militaire dans des cursus); f. 51 (questure dans des cursus); f. 119 (abréviations AVG. et CÆS.).-
Monnaies: f. 6 (remarques diverses sur les représentations monétaires); f. 94 (S.C. sur des monnaies d'époque
impériale, confirmant la permanence du rôle du Sénat); f. 99 (consulats multiples des empereurs); f. 100
(titulature des triumvirs); f. 118 (légende d'une monnaie de Justinien acquise par Du Rivail lui-même); f. 119
(abréviations AVG. et CÆS.).

[87] Pomponio Leto, nous l'avons déjà dit, doit à Pomponius toute la partie de son *Libellus* consacrée aux
jurisconsultes. Le commentaire d'Antonius Garro, un disciple de Pomponio Leto, dut être écrit dans les dernières
années du 15ème siècle, mais il ne fut publié qu'en 1543 par Gilbert Cousin, et ne semble guère avoir circulé
sous forme manuscrite. Celui d'Ulrich Zasius parut pour la première fois à Bâle en 1518 dans ses *Lucubrationes
aliquot* (voir, sur ce texte, C. Ghisalberti, 'Il Commentario dello Zasio al *Dig.* 1.2.2', *La parola del passato*, 21,
1966, pp. 81–110, et S. Rowan, *Ulrich Zasius*, Francfort, 1987, pp. 92–104). Les premières *Annotationes in
Pandectas* de Budé contenaient des éléments de commentaire à *Digesta*, 1, 2, 2 (ff. 14–31), et elles avaient été
publiées en 1508, mais rien ne prouve que Du Rivail, dont la bibliographie paraît tout entière italienne, les ait
connues lorsqu'il écrivit l'*Historia iuris*.

[88] F. C. von Savigny, *Geschichte des römischen Rechts im Mittelalter*, VI, 2nd edn, Heidelberg, 1850, p.
451; von Möller, *Aymar du Rivail* (n. 72 supra), pp. 43–50 (comparant le plan de l'*Historia iuris* avec celui du
texte complet de Pomponius, et non, comme il eût fallu le faire, avec les seuls paragraphes 1–12).

[89] Le texte auquel se réfère Du Rivail (f. 3) est l'*Ethique à Nicomaque*, V, 1129 a 26 sqq., mais, de la
justice particulière, il omet la justice corrective et ne retient que la justice distributive, et la définition qu'il en
donne ('per hanc enim mortalis homo ius suum unicuique tribuit') est pratiquement celle d' Ulpien (*Digesta*,
1, 1, 10, *pr.*), reproduite au tout début des *Institutiones* ('iustitia est constans et perpetua uoluntas ius suum

De la même façon, la théorie aristotélicienne des trois types de régime ('regia respublica', 'aristocratia', 'timocratia')[90] et de leurs formes perverties ('tyrannis', 'oligarchia', 'democratia') ne sert qu'à introduire un schéma historique qui est celui des douze premiers paragraphes de Pomponius. Au tableau donné par von Möller:[91]

Liber	Rei publicæ species	Juris ciuilis species
I	1 – Regia respublica	1 – Leges a) regiæ
II	2 – Timocratia	b) populi
		2 – Plebiscita
III	3 – Aristocratia	3 – Senatusconsulta
		4 – Prætorum edicta
IV	4 – Principatus	5 – Decreta principum
V		6 – Responsa prudentium

cuique tribuens' —1, 1, *pr.*). Les divisions qui viennent ensuite reprennent dans l'ordre celles des *Institutiones*, 1, 2: 'ius naturale', 'ius gentium' et 'ius ciuile'; à l'intérieur du 'ius ciuile', 'ius ex scripto' et 'ex non scripto'; à l'intérieur du 'ius scriptum', 'lex', 'plebis scita', 'senatus consulta', 'principum placita', 'magistratuum edicta', 'responsa prudentium'. Les *Institutiones* sont la véritable source du texte dans son ensemble, même si Du Rivail ne se réfère explicitement qu'à Ulpien (*Digesta*, 1, 1, 1, 4), pour la définition du 'ius gentium', et à Papinien (*Digesta*, 1, 1, 7), pour les sources du 'ius scriptum' (mais Papinien énumérait les sources d'un 'ius ciuile' opposé au 'ius honorarium', et Du Rivail doit donc ajouter les 'magistratuum edicta' à la liste de Papinien, retrouvant ainsi, avec des différences minimes d'ordre et de terminologie, la liste des *Institutiones*).

[90] Curieusement, alors qu'il se réfère au troisième livre de la *Politique*, Du Rivail adopte la terminologie d'*E.N.*, VIII, 12, 1160 a 32, où la troisième forme simple non pervertie est appelée à la fois 'timocratia' et 'politeia', alors que dans *Pol.* III il n'est question que de 'politeia'. On retrouve 'timocratia' au sens de 'régime républicain' dans quelques lignes du *De Allobrogibus* consacrées aux Burgondes: 'et illic [sc. citra Rhenum] sine rege duodequadraginta annis in timocratia usque ad a. C. 414 uixerunt' (p. 329). Plus généralement se pose le problème de savoir d'où Du Rivail tire sa connaissance d'Aristote, alors que rien ne permet de supposer qu'il ait appris le grec: ni les traductions de la *Politique* par Guillaume de Mœrbeke et Leonardo Bruni, ni celle de l'*E.N.* par Jean Argyropoulos, ni enfin les résumés des ouvrages d'Aristote par Volaterranus (Raffaello Maffei) dans le livre 36 de ses *Commentaria urbana* ne rendent compte de la terminologie utilisée par Du Rivail dans cette page de l'*Historia iuris*.

[91] Von Möller, *Aymar du Rivail* (n. 78 supra), p. 49.

on peut en adjoindre un second, comparant le plan de Du Rivail avec *Digesta*, 1, 2, 2, 1–12 et *Institutiones*, 1, 2, 4–8:

Pomponius		*Institutiones*	Du Rivail
§2	1. leges regiæ	1. lex	1. leges regiæ
§4 *deinde*	2. leges (XII Tab.)		2. leges populi
	ius ciuile (= prudentes)		
§6 *eodem fere tempore*	legis actiones		
§8 *deinde*	3. plebiscita	2. plebiscita	plebiscita
§9 *deinde*	4. senatusconsulta	3. senatusconsulta	3. senatusconsulta
§10 *eodem tempore*	edicta prætorum		edicta
§11 ***nouissime***	5. constitutiones	4. principum	4. decreta
	principum	placita	principum
		5. magistratuum	
		edicta	
		6. responsa	5. responsa
		prudentium	prudentium

Les 'reipublicæ species' aristotéliciennes, on le voit, n'ont guère d'autre fonction que d'être plaquées sur les étapes distinguées par Pomponius. C'est de ce dernier que Du Rivail reprend l'idée d'un pouvoir passant par nécessité du peuple au Sénat puis au Prince en raison de l'accroissement de la cité et de l'empire,[92] à ce dernier aussi qu'il emprunte l'idée de regrouper dans une même période 'senatus consulta' et 'edicta'. Il ne se sépare finalement de Pomponius que sur deux points. L'équivalence des *plebis scita* et des lois ne constitue pas chez lui une étape nouvelle: le schéma aristotélicien aurait pourtant pu être utilisé de ce point de vue, en considérant que la loi Hortensia marquait un passage de la 'timocratia' à la 'democratia'. Plus remarquable est la différence concernant les 'responsa prudentium': alors que Pomponius en fait remonter l'importance au lendemain même de la promulgation des XII Tables, Du Rivail les cantonne à l'époque du Principat, faisant commencer son livre V avec les jurisconsultes 'qui imperatorum authoritate responderunt'.[93] Le texte de Pomponius ne manquait pas de signaler

---

[92] *Digesta*, 1, 2, 2, 9: 'deinde quia difficile plebs conuenire cœpit, populus certe multo difficilius in tanta turba hominum, necessitas ipsa curam rei publicæ ad senatum deduxit', et 11 'nouissime sicut ad pauciores iuris constituendi uias transisse ipsis rebus dictantibus uidebatur per partes, euenit ut necesse esset rei publicæ per unum consuli (nam senatus non perinde omnes prouincias probe gerere poterat').

[93] F. 121. La décision, malgré tout, de ne pas commencer avec Sabinus, mais déjà avec Capito et Labeo est significative de l'intérêt que la lecture d'Aulu-Gelle suscita chez Du Rivail pour ces deux modèles de juristes

l'institution du 'ius respondendi' (§§48–50), mais je décèlerais volontiers ici, une nouvelle fois, une influence des *Institutiones*, non seulement parce que les 'responsa prudentium' y sont, comme chez Du Rivail, la dernière des sources du droit, mais surtout parce qu'y est particulièrement souligné le lien entre la valeur des 'responsa prudentium' comme source du droit et la concession par les empereurs du 'ius respondendi'.[94] Le plan adopté est donc bien, pour l'essentiel, emprunté aux douze premiers paragraphes de Pomponius, avec une importante modification que les *Institutiones* durent contribuer à inspirer, et un placage aristotélicien sans réelle importance, n'amenant pas en tout cas Du Rivail à remettre en cause le schéma de Pomponius, dont il n'ignore pourtant pas totalement le caractère artificiel.[95] C'est chez le grand Ulrich Zasius qu'on trouvera une utilisation plus intéressante d'Aristote, avec l'idée que la Rome républicaine entrait davantage dans la catégorie de la constitution mixte.[96] Notons que Zasius, de toute évidence, ne connaissait pas plus que Du Rivail le livre VI de Polybe, et que l'un et l'autre pourtant auraient pu trouver quelques lignes résumant les théories de Polybe dans le commentaire de Lefèvre d'Étaples à la *Politique* d'Aristote publié en 1506:

> species quas hic enumerat simplices sunt. Volunt autem eas in ciuitates componi, ut in Laconica et Romana republica secundum Polybium. Nam qui aspicit ad imperatores belli, regia uidetur, qui ad senatum, optimatum, qui illic ad ephoros, hic autem ad tribunitios, censupotestatum. Verum Laconicam non recte illa continere, et in multis aberrare et labi, monstrauit Aristoteles cap. VII præcedentis. De Romana autem republica qualis ipsa fuerit, non est impresentiarum disserendum (f. 42ʳ).

C'est, à ma connaissance, la plus ancienne référence imprimée qui soit faite au livre VI, et on doit la mettre en relation avec le séjour en France de Janus Lascaris.[97]

---

antiquaires.

[94] *Institutiones*, 1, 2, 8: 'responsa prudentium sunt sententiæ et opiniones eorum quibus permissum erat iura condere. Nam antiquitus institutum erat, ut essent qui iura publice interpretarentur, quibus a Cæsare ius respondendi datum est, qui iuris consulti appellabantur. Quorum omnium sententiæ et opiniones eam auctoritatem tenent, ut iudici recedere a responso eorum non liceat, ut est constitutum'.

[95] Ainsi cette remarque à propos des 'senatusconsulta': 'neque senatui iuris constituendi potestatem lex deinde regia in principes transferens imperium abstulit, ut argumento sunt multa... Fere quæcumque senatus consulta in libris digestorum quinquaginta leguntur imperatorum temporibus facta fuerunt, quod magna est probatio aduentum Augustorum senatus potestatem non extinxisse' (ff. 93–4).

[96] Après 509, 'porro et Romanis nec pura fuit popularis gubernatio, cuius tamen plures enumerantur species per Philosophum lib. IIII Polit. Mixtam potius receperim, cum et pauci gubernarint et tamen populo eligendorum magistratuum facultas remanserit': *Lucubrationes*, p. 9 (= *Opera omnia*, Lyon, 1550, I, col. 279), avec une référence évidente à la 'politeia' comme mélange d'éléments oligarchiques et démocratiques dans Arist., *Pol.*, IV, 8–9.

[97] Sur la redécouverte de Polybe, et notamment du livre VI, voir A. Momigliano, 'Polybius' Reappearance in Western Europe' dans *Polybe*, Entretiens sur l'Antiquité Classique, 20, Vandœuvres–Genève, 1974, pp. 347–72 (= *Sesto contributo*, Rome, 1980, pp. 103–23) et *Polybius between the English and the Turks*, Oxford,

L'*Historia iuris* souffre par ailleurs d'un évident déséquilibre, qui révèle une espèce de dualité de l'ouvrage: le livre II, consacré aux lois et plébiscites, occupe 84 folios sur un total de 130, et, à l'intérieur même du livre II, 69 folios, plus de la moitié de l'ouvrage dans son ensemble, sont consacrés aux XII Tables. Il s'agissait donc à la fois de la première histoire du droit romain et de la première tentative de palingénésie des XII Tables, et les réimpressions parues à Mayence à partir de 1527 n'ont pas manqué de le souligner, en adoptant le titre: *Ciuilis historiæ iuris, siue in XII Tabularum leges commentariorum libri quinque.* Une première partie de ce commentaire des XII Tables est consacrée aux lois de Solon. La tradition voulait en effet que, juste avant la rédaction des XII Tables, une ambassade ait été envoyée en Grèce, notamment à Athènes, pour y prendre connaissance des lois en vigueur, et que plusieurs des lois décemvirales se soient inspirées de celles de Solon,[98] mais Du Rivail n'hésite pas à donner en capitales, comme fragments des XII Tables, toutes les lois de Solon connues grâce à Plutarque, y compris celles dont rien absolument ne suggère qu'elles aient jamais été en usage à Rome. Il est conscient, d'ailleurs, du caractère conjectural de cette démarche,[99] et son utilisation de la *Vie de Solon* de Plutarque est de ce point de vue assez comparable à celle qu'il fera des livres 2 et 3 du *De legibus* de Cicéron. Il n'hésite pas non plus à prétendre que l'ambassade envoyée en Grèce avant la rédaction des XII Tables serait également allée à Sparte, en sorte que le droit non écrit des Lacédémoniens serait une autre source des XII Tables.[100] Il se fonde pour cela sur un texte des *Institutiones* qui voit dans Athènes et Lacédémone les sources des deux grandes divisions du droit civil, le droit écrit et le droit non écrit,[101] mais les *Institutiones* ne font pas particulièrement mention des XII Tables,

---

1974 (= *Sesto contributo*, pp. 125–41); A. C. Dionisotti, 'Polybius and the Royal Professor' dans *Tria Corda. Scritti in onore di Arnaldo Momigliano*, Côme, 1983, pp. 179–99. Janus Lascaris séjourna en France de 1494 à 1509, et il possédait, sans doute depuis son voyage en Orient de 1490–1, un manuscrit contenant les fragments conservés du livre 6 de Polybe (Dionisotti, op. cit, p. 188n).

[98] Ambassade à Athènes: Tite-Live, 3, 31, 8 et 33, 5; Denys de Halicarnasse, *Antiquitates Romanae*, 10, 51 et 54. Pomponius (*Digesta*, 1, 2, 2, 4) rapporte deux traditions sur les origines grecques des lois décemvirales, mais aucune d'entre elles ne souligne le rôle d'Athènes comme le font les historiens. Rapprochements faits par les Anciens eux-mêmes entre les lois décemvirales et les lois de Solon: *Digesta*, 10, 1, 13; Cicéron, *De legibus*, 2, 59 et 64.

[99] Ff. 9–10: 'utrum autem lex Solonis de seditione ciuium in XII tabulis relata fuerit non satis constat, sicut neque de aliis compluribus Solonis legibus, nisi ex coniectura, qua magis quam authore aliquo fretus, multas Atheniensium leges in XII tabulas fuisse translatas et descriptas paulo ante affirmaui. Nam cum teste Liuio populus Romanus, legatis Athenas missis, Solonis describere et aliarum Græciæ ciuitatum instituta, mores iuraque noscere iusserit, sitque hæc lex, utpote ciuium seditionem coercens, una e dignioribus quas Athenienses habuerint, necnon illæ quas supra retuli, uerisimile est Xuiros eas in XII tabulas retulisse'.

[100] F. 14: 'hæ sunt leges quas ab Atheniensibus Romani habuere. A Lacedæmoniis autem tres legati Postumius, Camerinus et Manlius non ius scriptum ut ab Atheniensibus, sed mores et consuetudines habuerunt. Unde non immerito in duas species, ius scriptum et non scriptum, ius ciuile Romanorum distributum est, ut Justinianus affirmat'.

[101] *Institutiones*, 1, 2, 10: 'et non ineleganter in duas species ius ciuile distributum uidetur. Nam origo eius ab institutis duarum ciuitatum, Athenarum scilicet et Lacedæmonis, fluxisse uidetur: in his enim ciuitatibus ita

et aucun des textes anciens parlant de l'envoi de l'ambassade ne précise qu'elle soit allée à Sparte. Le thème des droits écrit et non écrit trouvant leur origine à Athènes et à Sparte sera repris à la fin du livre V:[102] il apparaît alors, comme dans les *Institutiones*, pour réintroduire assez artificiellement le 'ius ex non scripto' après que les 'responsa prudentium' ont été analysés comme la sixième et dernière source du 'ius ex scripto'.[103] Ce doublon me paraît caractéristique de l'ambiguïté des XII Tables dans l'ouvrage de Du Rivail, puisqu'elles y sont à la fois une étape dans le développement de l'une des sources du droit romain (la loi), et une expression de la totalité du 'ius ciuile', où doivent donc converger le droit écrit venu d'Athènes et le droit non écrit venu de Sparte. La même ambiguïté apparaît dans la deuxième partie du traitement consacré aux XII Tables. Le plan y est cette fois thématique, abordant successivement le droit sacré, le droit public et le droit privé, mais les deux premières parties, qui occupent 42 folios, plus de la moitié du développement sur les XII Tables, près du tiers de l'œuvre dans son ensemble, ne sont qu'un commentaire aux 'lois' des livres 2 et 3 du *De legibus* de Cicéron qui, à quelques dispositions près, n'ont rien à voir avec les lois décemvirales. C'est bien entendu sur ce point que Du Rivail fut le plus violemment critiqué, depuis Agustín et Baudouin au 16ème siècle, jusqu'à Dirksen en 1824. Ces critiques ont parfois durci l'opinion de Du Rivail, et von Möller a pu citer plusieurs passages montrant qu'il était bien conscient de ce qu'une partie des textes cicéroniens ne pouvaient remonter aux XII Tables.[104] Le texte le plus éclairant est sans doute celui qui conclut, précisément, le commentaire aux 'lois' cicéroniennes (f. 57):

satis de religione et magistratibus Romanorum dixerimus, si hoc intellexeris, M. scilicet Ciceronem sensisse, has omnis constitutiones relatas non fuisse <in> XII tabul. leges, nam relatis religionis constitutionibus, postea de eadem re aliquot XII tab. leges subiungit [*De legibus*, 2, 58–68], præterea duas leges e XII tabulis ad magistratuum sanctionem fuisse translatas scribit [*De legibus*, 3, 44]. Inuenit ergo alias magistratuum leges non fuisse in XII tab. Nihilominus boni autores has XII tab. leges sæpenumero appellant. Et forte his uerbis Cicero discrimen inter leges priuati iuris et publici, quod in sacris, sacerdotibus et magistratibus consistit

agi solitum erat, ut Lacedæmonii quidem magis ea quæ pro legibus obseruarent memoriæ mandarent, Athenienses uero ea quæ in legibus scripta reprehendissent custodirent'.

[102] F. 127: 'De altera parte iuris ciuilis, quæ ius non scriptum appellatur, dicere non est animus, propterea quod in origine parum difficultatis habeat. Nam diuturni mores consensu utentium comprobati id ius constituunt, legesque imitantur, tollunt aut interpretantur. Et non immerito in duas species ius ciuile Romanorum sicut in principio libelli nostri diximus, distributum est, quoniam eius origo ab Atheniensibus et Lacedæmoniis authore Justiniano fluxisse uidetur, et Athenienses legibus scriptis rempublicam magis gubernabant, Lacedæmonii autem tamen ab usu iuris scripti abfuerunt'.

[103] Pour Pomponius, le 'ius sine scripto' était celui des 'prudentes' (*Digesta*, 1, 2, 2, 5).

[104] F. 39: 'omnia tamen hæc, origo scilicet ædilium curulium et alia quæ diximus post XII tabulas fuerunt, ut e Liuio apparet'; f. 40: 'Livius censuræ initium post XII tab. M. Geganio et Q. Capitolino coss. fuisse refert'; f. 41: 'prætoris inuentio post XII tabulas fuit, ut e Liuio et aliis didicimus'.

[*Digesta*, 1, 1, 1, 2], facere uoluit, licet iisdem tabulis descriptæ essent. Sed qualescumque prædictæ leges fuerint, non paruam iuris et hystoriæ cognitionem afferunt. Nam luculenter religionem et magistratus Romanorum, et sic publicum ius explicant, et ideo non ab re huic loco eas leges accommodauimus.

Du Rivail, on le voit, est hésitant. Certaines observations le troublent, et il sent le besoin de se justifier. Les 'boni autores' derrière lesquels il se réfugie sont une évidente allusion à Crinito, et beaucoup moins sûrement à Budé, dont je ne suis pas sûr qu'il l'ait lu[105] Mais j'ai l'impression que la principale raison du choix adopté est dans les toutes dernières lignes: l'influence de l'humanisme favorisait, en même temps que l'association du droit et de l'histoire, un essor des études concernant le droit public, et les 'lois' cicéroniennes fournissaient à Du Rivail une occasion, qu'il s'est empressé de saisir même s'il fallait pour cela reléguer au second plan les préoccupations chronologiques, de traiter du droit public dans tous ses aspects. Il me paraît significatif que, de toutes les divisions établies au début des *Institutiones* d'Ulpien (*Digesta*, 1, 1, 1 et 6) et de Justinien (1, 1–2), la seule que ne reprenne pas Du Rivail au début de son propre ouvrage soit la distinction première faite entre 'ius publicum' et 'ius priuatum': alors que, dans les texte d'Ulpien et de Justinien, le 'ius ciuile' n'apparaît que comme l'une des trois composantes du 'ius priuatum', le 'ius publicum' n'étant en quelque sorte mentionné que pour être aussitôt exclu, Du Rivail peut au contraire introduire la distinction entre 'ius publicum' et 'ius priuatum' à l'intérieur d'une *Historia iuris ciuilis*, retrouvant d'ailleurs ainsi la conception livienne des XII Tables comme 'fons omnis publici priuatique iuris' (3, 34, 6).

En ce qui concerne les lois autres que les XII Tables et les *plebiscita*, point de départ de mon intérêt pour l'*Historia iuris ciuilis.*, le projet de Du Rivail impliquait qu'il pût distinguer nettement lois et plébiscites, et ranger les unes et les autres dans un ordre chronologique. On ne saurait s'étonner qu'il n'y soit parvenu que pour la période couverte par la première décade de Tite-Live. Par la suite, la tâche était irréalisable dans l'état de la documentation dont il disposait: nombre de *plebiscita* sont dans nos sources appelés 'leges', et les premières recherches sur les fastes consulaires ne pourront commencer qu'après la publication par Sichard, en 1529, de la *Chronique* de Cassiodore. Il reste cependant que certaines erreurs chronologiques sont difficilement explicables,[106]

---

[105] Pietro Crinito, disciple de Poliziano, dans son *De honesta disciplina* paru à Florence en 1504, commentait plusieurs textes des 'lois' cicéroniennes en les qualifiant d' 'antiqu(issim)æ leges' (VIII, 13; XIV, 5; XXV, 12) ou même de 'Xuirales leges' (II, 5 et XVII, 7). Commentant *Digesta*, 1, 2, 2, 46 ('Tubero...sermone etiam antiquo usus affectauit scribere'), et proposant de corriger 'usus' en 'uersus', Budé écrit (ff. 30–1): 'uersus autem intelligendi XII tabul. Huiusmodi enim uersibus compositæ erant', et l'exemple qu'il donne est Cicéron, *De legibus*, 3, 8 ('iuris disceptator...tot sunt') ; un peu plus loin, il ajoute: 'huiusmodi autem uersus nonnulli erant obscuri propter uerborum antiquitatem, ut ille: mulieres genas ne radunto neue lessum funeris ergo habento' (authentique fragment des XII Tables cité par Cicéron dans *De legibus*, 2, 59).

[106] Ainsi la loi Pompeia *de Transpadanis* et la loi Fabia *de sectatoribus* sont-elles placées juste après les

et que Du Rivail surtout n'a pas pris conscience de l'inadéquation qui existait entre ce qu'il prétendait et ce qu'il pouvait faire. L'échec de l'*Historia iuris ciuilis* entraîna généralement un retour à l'ordre alphabétique de Pomponio Leto: ce fut la solution retenue notamment par Zasius et par Agustín dans les années 1540,[107] par Hotman en 1557, et en 1567 par Prateius, qui ne fournit d'ailleurs qu'une compilation avouée de notices empruntées à Zasius et Hotman,[108] tandis que Manuce (1557) et Rosinus (1583) préféraient adopter un ordre thématique convenant davantage à leurs projets d'*Antiquitates*. Celui d'une *Historia iuris ciuilis* ne devait être repris qu'en 1565 par Forster, sans grand succès d'ailleurs, bien qu'on y trouve inévitablement un reflet des considérables progrès accomplis depuis 1515 en matière de chronologie romaine.[109]

---

lois tirées de la première décade de Tite-Live et la loi Porcia *de prouocatione*, peut-être parce que les trois premières notices de Filelfo étaient consacrées aux lois Pompeia, Porcia et Fabia, et bien que Du Rivail ajoute au texte de Filelfo la précision que l'auteur de la loi Pompeia était 'Magni Pompei pater'. Inversement, le *plebis scitum* Ogulnien est un des derniers de la liste, bien que la source de Du Rivail soit Tite-Live, 10, 6–9.

[107] Joannes Udalricus Zasius, auteur du *Catalogus legum antiquarum una cum adiuncta summaria interpretatione*, publié en 1551 à Strasbourg par les soins de Jean Sturm, et republié à Paris en 1554 et 1578 avec des additions de Loys Le Caron (Charondas), n'est pas le grand Zasius, dont j'ai eu l'occasion de mentionner le commentaire à Pomponius, ni même son fils, comme on l'a dit souvent, mais un homonyme, mort jeune en 1547. Pour la lente genèse du *De legibus et senatus consultis* d'Agustín, je renvoie à mon étude dans *Antonio Agustín between Renaissance and Counter-Reform* (n. 3 supra). La conception de l'ouvrage de Manuzio remonte également aux années 1540, alors que celui de Hotman ne fut commencé qu'en 1556 (voir la préface à l'édition du *Legum Romanarum index* publié séparément à Bâle en 1558).

[108] L'ordre alphabétique convenait tout particulièrement à des ouvrages comme le *Lexicon iuris* de Prateius ou le *Commentarius uerborum iuris* de Hotman. Mais le cas de Hotman est plus complexe: le catalogue des lois parut d'abord seul, en 1557, sous le titre *Liber de legibus*, mais ce n'était qu'une partie d'un ouvrage qui sera publié en 1558, sous le titre complet *Commentarius uerborum iuris, antiquitatum Romanarum elementis amplificatus, de magistratibus, de legibus, de iurisconsultis, de senatu et senatusconsultis, de formulis, de comitiis*. On aimerait savoir ce que ces 'antiquitatum Romanarum elementa' doivent à l'influence du projet de Manuzio, dont Hotman avait eu connaissance en 1556. Il est en tout cas significatif que, dans le *De legibus*, le catalogue des lois dans l'ordre alphabétique soit précédé d'un résumé de la partie du traité de Manuzio consacrée à la procédure d'élaboration des lois. En 1558, les 'antiquitatum elementa' sont encore insérés dans l'ordre alphabétique général (par exemple le *De legibus* sous la lettre L), mais dans le *Nouus commentarius* de 1563 ils sont regroupés en fin de volume, et dans l'édition posthume des *Opera* (1600) ils deviendront le premier livre d'un recueil, à vrai dire assez artificiel, d'*Antiquitatum Romanarum libri V*. Cette évolution, tout comme la compilation de Rosinus publiée en 1583, est significative de l'émergence du genre des *Antiquitates*.

[109] *Valentini Forsteri I.C. de historia iuris ciuilis Romani libri tres, in quibus traditur ortus Romani imperii, subiiciuntur mutationes insignes magistratuum in republica Romana et caussæ, initia et progressus iuris ciuilis nec non secundum seriem annorum catalogus legum tam ad publicum quam ad priuatum statum pertinentium, denique uitæ ueterum I.C. a Papyrio inde usque ad Justinianum, item recentiorum I.C. qui restituta per Lotharium Saxonem iuris professione celebritatem scribendo, consulendo et docendo ad ætatem nostram consecuti sunt*, Bâle, 1565. Les loi sont rangées en fonction de leur date *ab urbe condita*, entreprise qui n'avait pas de précédent. Mais cela se fait aux dépens du nombre des notices: 180 seulement alors que la troisième édition de Hotman, parue en 1563, ne cataloguait pas moins de 288 lois; et on pourrait donner bien des exemples d'erreurs chronologiques graves ou de manque de cohérence (la loi Atia, par exemple, fait l'objet de trois notices, en 499 *a.u.c.* [254 av. J.-C], 689 [64] et 690 [63]). Le résultat général est d'une incontestable médiocrité.

Une autre raison de la déception que suscite l'œuvre de Du Rivail en ce domaine est l'influence déterminante que continuent d'exercer sur lui les travaux de Filelfo et de Pomponio Leto.[110] Si l'on met à part les notices tirées de la première décade de Tite-Live, on constate que 22 notices de lois sur 27 et 10 notices de *plebis scita* sur 18 ont comme point de départ une notice existant déjà chez Filelfo ou Pomponio, et que le texte de Filelfo ou de Pomponio est généralement conservé, même si Du Rivail ajoute ensuite des indication nouvelles, voire contradictoires. Exemplaire est le cas de la loi Julia *de adulteriis* (f. 72):

> C. Julius Cæsar lege sanxit ne adulteri forent, deprehensi autem supplicio dederentur [texte de Filelfo]. Vlpianus tamen de adulteriis a diuo Augusto hanc legem fuisse latam scribit, cui Tranquillus in uita Augusti astipulatur. [Suivent des références au *Digeste*, à Aulu-Gelle et à Juvénal].

Seules ont été totalement remaniées les notices consacrées à la loi Oppia, à la loi Man(i)lia de 66, et surtout, parce que Du Rivail était bien meilleur juriste que ses prédécesseurs, à la loi Falcidia et la loi Aquillia.[111] Les progrès, par rapport à Filelfo et Pomponio Leto, ne se font guère que par addition et juxtaposition, ce qui n'empêche pas qu'ils soient considérables. Outre les lois et *plebiscita* trouvés dans la première décade de Tite-Live, outre les lois mentionnées un peu en vrac à l'occasion d'une réflexion sur les modification apportées aux XII Tables (ff. 74–75), ou à la fin du développement sur les lois (ff. 82–83),[112] outre treize notices nouvelles empruntées (directement ou par l'intermédiaire de Biondo Flavio) à Aulu-Gelle, Macrobe, Valère-Maxime ou Plutarque, d'assez nombreuses lois sont rattachées à une loi d'objet identique ou analogue qui figurait déjà dans les catalogues de Filelfo et Pomponio Leto: ainsi la loi Julia *de repetundis* est-elle rattachée à la loi Acilia, la loi Julia *de maiestate* à la loi Appuleia etc. Des éléments de regroupement thématique interfèrent avec l'ordre chronologique, comme ils interféreront avec l'ordre alphabétique dans le *Catalogus* de Zasius.[113]

---

[110] Étrangement, si l'on pense à l'extrême dépendance de Pomponio envers Filelfo et au fait que l'un et l'autre avaient réuni sans distinction lois et *plebiscita*, Du Rivail a choisi de mentionner Filelfo seul au début des pages qu'il a consacrées aux lois postérieures aux XII Tables, et Pomponio Leto seul au début des pages qu'il a consacrées aux *plebiscita*.

[111] On retrouve en revanche chez Du Rivail un certain nombre des erreurs les plus graves de Filelfo: distinction entre une lex Roscia consulaire et un plébiscite Othonien; confusion entre les lois Aureliæ de 75 et de 70; interprétation de la loi Mamilia fondée sur une interprétation erronée de Salluste. Je signale également un texte étonnant, dont je n'ai pu identifier l'origine: 'Apuleius Saturninus plebis tribunus legem tulit, ut nemini præter decretum populi in regione esse liceret. Quatuor enim regiones, id est maiores in urbe partes erant, ut Varro et alii tradunt... Et licet hoc plebiscitum non haberet necessitatem, tamen senatores id iureiurando confirmare Saturninus cœgit.'

[112] En particulier des lois que Du Rivail a jugé inutile de commenter parce que le contenu en était assez éclairé par les textes du *Corpus iuris ciuilis*: 'has leges ultimas consulto perstringimus, eo quod iurisperiti illas diligenter commemorant' (f. 83).

[113] Zasius, *Catalogus legum antiquarum* (n. 107 supra), f. A4ᵛ: 'leges iuxta latinarum literarum progressum recensebimus, nisi ubi coniunctarum materiarum ratio auelli eas a se inuicem non patitur'. Les lois de même

Ce sont en tout 116 lois et *plebiscita* qui font l'objet d'une notice ou sont du moins signalés, plus du double de ce que l'on trouvait chez Filelfo,[114] plus de la moitié de ce que réuniront dans les années 1540 Manuce, Zasius et Agustín.[115]

Dernier fait nouveau et important, mention est généralement faite des sources utilisées dans les suppléments aux notices reprises de Filelfo ou Pomponio (voir l'exemple de la loi Julia *de adulteriis* citée supra) ainsi que dans les notices nouvelles: on peut ainsi constater l'ampleur des lectures de Du Rivail, qu'il s'agisse des textes juridiques ou des textes littéraires (historiens, grammairiens, corpus cicéronien avec le commentaire d'Asconius).

L'*Historia iuris ciuilis* est une œuvre de jeunesse, et l'œuvre d'un auteur qui n'avait pas les moyens de ses ambitions, qui avait plus d'aptitude à compiler qu'à trier avec esprit critique le matériel qu'il avait rassemblé: nous avons déjà vu l'usage qu'il fit des 'lois' de Cicéron; non moins significative est l'absence de toute discussion du texte des sources invoquées. Malgré ses défauts, il s'agit pourtant d'une œuvre pionnière dans le domaine de l'histoire des sources du droit romain et de la palingénésie des textes, qui commença au seizième siècle par celle des XII Tables.[116] Pour ce qui est des lois, en revanche, et compte tenu de l'existence de travaux antérieurs, il s'agit plutôt d'une œuvre charnière, annonçant les livres des décennies suivantes par l'accroissement du nombre des lois recensées et l'indication des sources utilisées, mais dépendant encore dans une large mesure de l'*Epistula* de Filelfo. C'est seulement dans les années 1540, un siècle donc après la rédaction de la lettre à Cornelius, soixante ans après son impression, que l'influence du texte de Filelfo apparaît véritablement révolue: non seulement Zasius et Agustín ne mentionnent plus son nom, ne faisant référence qu'à Pomponio Leto, mais surtout, dans leurs notices tout comme dans celles de

---

objet sont alors rangées derrière la plus ancienne (*e.g.* 'lex Cassia agraria et reliquæ leges agrariæ') ou derrière celle à qui est consacré un titre du *Digeste* (*e.g.* toutes les lois *de repetundis* derrière la loi Julia).

[114] Comme Filelfo, d'ailleurs, Du Rivail ne prétend pas être exhaustif, mais inclure seulement dans son ouvrage les lois le plus fréquemment mentionnées chez les auteurs anciens: 'non omnes leges enumerare proponimus, sed eas tantum quarum uetusti scriptores crebrius meminerunt' (f. 75).

[115] 188 lois dans la première édition du *De legibus* de Manuzio, 195 dans le *Catalogus* de Zasius, 196 dans la première rédaction du *De legibus et senatusconsultis* d'Agustín. La première édition du *De legibus* de Hotman en cataloguera 237.

[116] Alessandro d'Alessandro, dans ses *Genialium dierum libri sex* publiés pour la première fois à Rome en 1522, devait consacrer aux fragments des XII Tables une analyse supérieure à celle de Du Rivail, ne mêlant aux fragments authentiques ni les 'lois' cicéroniennes ni les lois de la *Vie de Solon* de Plutarque: liv. 6, ch. 10; voir D. Maffei, *Alessandro d'Alessandro giureconsulto umanista (1461–1523)*, Milan, 1956, pp. 160–74. L'influence de Du Rivail devait cependant l'emporter quelque temps, comme en témoignent les *Leges XII Tabularum* d'Oldendorp (1539) et de Le Sueur (1547), ce dernier d'ailleurs ne faisant que reprendre les fragments dans l'ordre où les avait regroupés Oldendorp, et sans le moindre commentaire: les 'lois' cicéroniennes ne seront expulsées que dans le très long développement sur les XII Tables contenu dans le *De legibus et senatus consultis* d'Agustín dès sa première rédaction de 1544–5, mais resté inédit jusqu'en 1583, et dans les *Libri duo ad leges Romuli regis, ad leges XII Tabularum* de F. Baudouin, Lyon, 1550.

Manuce, on ne retrouve pratiquement plus rien qui rappelle celles de Filelfo.[117] Une période nouvelle s'ouvrait, et la multiplication des ouvrages sur les lois fut telle, dans les années 1550, que Hotman faillit renoncer à son projet en apprenant la prochaine parution du livre de Manuce, et qu'Agustín interrompit ses travaux après la publication de ceux de Manuce et de Hotman.

Appendice I

Concordance des recueils de Filelfo, du Manuscrit Ottoboni et de Pomponio Leto

FILELFO	OTTOBONI	POMPONIUS	SOURCE
1 Pompeia (de Transpadanis)	1	32	Asc., 12, St.
2 Portia (de prouocatione)			?
3 Fabia (de numero sectatorum)	2	18	Cic., *Mur.*,71
4 Clodia (de obnuntiatione)	3	2	Asc., 15–16
5 Cinthia (sc. Cincia)	4	10	Tac., *Ann.*, 11,5
6 Aurelia (iudiciaria)	5	4	Asc., 21
7 Oppia	45	30	Liv., 34,1
8 Pompeia (de quæst. extr.)		33	Asc., 35
9 Valeria (de prouocatione)		43	?
10 Aquilia	46	9	Cic., *off.*, 3,60–61
11 Acilia	6	5	Ps.-Asc., 221
12 Voconia	7	42	Ps.-Asc., 247–8
13 Calphurnia (de ambitu)	8	11	Asc., 55
14 Gabinia	9	22	Asc., 57
15 Papia	10	35	Cic., *off.*, 3,47
16 Latoria (sc.Plætoria)	11	26	Cic., *off.*, 3,61
17 Clodia (frumentaria)	12	6 (annonia)	Asc., 15–16
18 Clodia (de collegiis)	13		Asc., 15–16
19 Clodia (de censoribus)	14	3	Asc., 15–16
20 Judiciaria Aurelia	15	4	Asc., 21
21 Varia	16	41	Asc., 24

---

[117] On trouve pourtant dans un paragraphe du *De legibus* d'Agustín (p. 153 de l'édition romaine de 1583) un dernier écho, sceptique, d'une notice de Filelfo: 'Manilia siue Manlia... VI–Addunt quidam eumdem tulisse ut nouis hominibus magistratus decernerentur. Quod a ueteribus nescio an memoriæ traditum sit.'

22 Cornelia (de ære alieno)	17	12	Asc., 47–48
23 Cornelia (de legibus soluendis)	18	13	Asc., 47–48
24 Cornelia (de edicto)	19	14	Asc., 47–48
25 Licinia et Mucia	20	27	Asc., 54
26 Junia	21	23	Asc., 54
27 Manilia	22		Asc., 53
28 sacratæ	23		Asc., 60
29 Cassia (tabellaria)	24	16	Asc., 61
30 Cassia (de damnatis)	25	17	Asc., 61
31 Aurelii Cottæ	26		Asc., 61
32 Roscia (theatralis)	27	37	Asc., 61
33 Plotia (iudiciaria)	28	36	Asc., 61
34 satyra	29	38	Sall., *B.J.*, 29,5
35 Othonis (sc. Roscia)	30	29	Juv., 3,153–9
36 Scatinia	31	39	Juv., 2,36–45
37 Julia (de adulteriis)	32	24	Juv., 2,36–45
38 Mamillia	33	28	Sall., *B.J.*, 65,5
39 Sempronia (frumentaria)	34	19 (frumentaria)	?
40 Hortensia	35	31	Gell., 15,27,4
41 annaria (sc. annalis)	36	7	Paul, 25 L.
42 Ælia et Fusia (sc. Fufia)	37	1	?
43 Aterina (sc. Æternia)	38	8	Gell., 11,1,2
44 Falcidia	39	20	*Inst.*, 2,22,pr.
45 Flauia (sc. Fabia de plagiariis)	40	21	*Inst.*, 4,18,10
46 Julia (de peculatu)	41	25	*Inst.*, 4,18,9
47 Cornelia (de falsis)	42		*Inst.*, 4,18,7
48 Pompeia (de parricidiis)	43	34	*Inst.*, 4,18,6
49 Cornelia (de sicariis)	44	15	*Inst.*, 4,18,5
50 Latoria		40 (tutelaris)	? Cic., *off.*, 3,61
51 Appuleia (de maiestate)			?

L'ordre des notices du manuscrit de Guarnerio d'Artegna est le même que celui du manuscrit Ottoboni de 1 à 42 (Cornelia, de falsis). L'insertion d'une notice 'Lex Titia' fait que les notices 43 et 44 du manuscrit Ottoboni sont les notices 44 et 45 de Guarnerio; quant aux notices 46 à 48 de Guarnerio (note 29), elles ne proviennent pas de l'opuscule de Filelfo.

Appendice II

Note biographique sur Aymar du Rivail

Quelques précisions ou corrections peuvent être apportées aux études déjà consacrées à la biographie d'Aymar du Rivail.[118] Il appartenait à une famille noble du Dauphiné, exerçant à la fois charges militaires et judiciaires (son grand-père fut bailli de Vienne et Valence, son père, vice-bailli de Saint Marcellin, l'un de ses frères aînés, official de l'archevêque d'Embrun). Sa date de naissance peut être fixée entre 1485 et 1490. La seule indication précise figure dans la notice de l'*Historia iuris ciuilis* consacrée à Papinien, lorsque Du Rivail regrette de ne pas encore s'être illustré dans le domaine juridique: 'annum enim quintum et uigesimum gero, et consultores nullos adhuc admisi, proh dolor, nec responsis humanam societatem iuui' (f. 124). Cette phrase, selon qu'elle appartenait au texte primitif ou qu'elle fut ajoutée au moment de remettre le manuscrit à l'imprimeur, put être écrite entre 1509 environ (date fournie, nous le verrons, par la notice sur Paul) et 1515. Je ne pense pas qu'on puisse tirer une plus grande précision de l'indication du *De Allobrogibus* selon laquelle Du Rivail était 'ipsum in adolescentia' lorsqu'il fut question, en 1513–14, qu'il devienne précepteur de Renée de France:[119] on sait avec quelle marge d'incertitude peut être utilisé un mot comme 'adolescentia', surtout dans un contexte où l'auteur cherche à rehausser ses mérites en soulignant le contraste entre son jeune âge et la charge qu'on a malgré tout failli lui confier. Rappelons que Savigny encore datait d'avant 1461 la naissance de Du Rivail, et le comptait donc au nombre des précurseurs de la 'nouvelle école'. Il n'est en fait que de quelques années l'aîné d'Alciat (1492–1550), étudia à Pavie sous les mêmes maîtres que lui, et dédia en 1515 son *Historia* au même chancelier Duprat à qui Alciat, en 1518, allait dédier ses *Paradoxa*.

Le jeune Du Rivail apprit la grammaire, la rhétorique et la dialectique à l'Académie de Romans,[120] puis fit pendant trois ans des études de droit à

---

[118] A. de Terrebasse, dans son édition du *De Allobrogibus libri nouem*, Vienne, 1844, pp. II–XX; M. Giraud, *Aymar du Rivail et sa famille*, Lyon, 1849; J.-J.-A. Pilot, 'Aymar du Rivail', *Bulletin de la Société de statistique de l'Isère*, 1860, pp. 269–321; E. von Möller, *Aymar du Rivail* (n. 78 supra), pp. 12–29; F. Vindry, *Les Parlementaires français au XVIème siècle*, I, Paris, 1909, pp. 101–20.

[119] *De Allobrogibus*, p. 557. Moins précise encore, quoi que paraissent prétendre Terrebasse, Giraud et Vindry, est la remarque: 'et hoc ego adhuc puer uidi', à propos de l'expédition du duc Louis d'Orléans contre Novare en 1495 (*De Allobrogibus*, p. 536). Ces mots ont d'ailleurs été rayés et remplacés par: 'nec liberos adhuc ad bellum aptos propter iuuentutem habebat [sc. pater meus]' (MS Paris. Lat. 6014, f. 324ᵛ), et le texte confirme seulement qu'en 1495 ni Aymar ni ses frères n'avaient l'âge de porter les armes.

[120] *De Allobrogibus*, pp. 35 et 168 (avec la précision 'tener annis').

l'Université d'Avignon.[121] Ce n'est pourtant pas là, mais sans doute à l'occasion de son séjour en Italie, qu'il reçut son titre de docteur.[122] On sait, par le *De Allobrogibus*, qu'il était en 1512 à Pavie, y suivant l'enseignement de Jason de Mayno et Filippo Decio, mais que le développement d'un sentiment antifrançais le contraignit, en décembre de la même année, à se replier sur Casales.[123] L'*Historia iuris* fut conçue pendant un séjour à travers l'Italie ('Italiam peragrando coniungere quinque libris ius et historiam Romanorum primo enixus sum', f. 2), qu'E. von Möller date de 1514–15, en ajoutant que la guerre entre le roi de France et l'Empereur aurait alors empêché Du Rivail de visiter Padoue.[124] L'erreur est sur ce point évidente, car, dans sa notice sur Paul, Du Rivail écrit: 'Patauinus fuit, eiusque statua, ut audio, adhuc extat in patria, quam tanti uiri doctrina et amore captus uiserem, nisi Cæsaris et Gallici regis milites Patauium obsiderent' (f. 125). Il n'est donc pas question de guerre entre l'Empereur et le roi de France, mais d'un siège de Padoue par les deux souverains coalisés, ce qui se produisit en 1509 pendant la guerre contre Venise. On en déduira donc que Du Rivail parcourut l'Italie dans les années qui précédèrent 1512, au moins depuis 1509, et qu'il n'y revint probablement qu'en 1515 avec l'armée de François I, assistant alors, comme il le précise lui-même, à la bataille de Marignan et à l'entrée du roi dans Pavie.[125] C'est sans doute pendant ces années 1509–1512 qu'il obtint son doctorat en droit, peut-être à Pavie,[126] et qu'il écrivit pour l'essentiel l'*Historia iuris*,[127] bien que d'ultimes compléments aient été ajoutés après le retour en France[128] et que le privilège pour l'impression n'ait été sollicité qu'en 1515. Entre temps, il avait été question de Du Rivail comme précepteur de Renée de France, mais la mort d'Anne de Bretagne le 9 janvier 1514 avait ruiné ce

---

[121] *De Allobrogibus*, p. 110.

[122] Le nom de Du Rivail ne figure pas dans la *Chronologie des docteurs en droit civil d l'Université d'Avignon (1303–1797)*, publiée par E. de Teule (Paris, 1887).

[123] *De Allobrogibus*, p. 553.

[124] Von Möller, *Aymar du Rivail* (n. 78 supra), p. 17.

[125] *De Allobrogibus*, pp. 561–2.

[126] On ne trouve qu'une fort médiocre notice sur Du Rivail dans E. Picot, *Les Professeurs et les étudiants de langue française à l'Université de Pavie au XVème et au XVIème siècles*, Paris, 1916, p. 48, no. 109. Mais de toute façon les matricules n'existent plus pour cette période.

[127] 'Viserem' (et non 'uisissem') semble bien impliquer que la notice sur Paul fut écrite en 1509, et le plus récent ouvrage mentionné par Du Rivail dans l'*Historia* fut, nous l'avons vu, imprimé à Florence en 1510. La notice 'Leges triumphandi' contient une allusion à la campagne de 1512 ('nostri ergo milites Gallici triumphare possent, qui primum Hispanos Bononia raptis aliquot uexillis repulerunt, mox quattuor et uiginti milia Brixiensium occiderunt propterea quod a Galliarum rege desciscentes Venetis se dederant, postremo in campum Bononiensem celeriter reuersi apud Rauennam Hispanos Pontificisque Julii et Venetorum milites ad unum fere occiderunt': liv. II, f. 89), très probablement une addition au texte primitif.

[128] Une phrase comme 'nisi imperitia aliqui senatores aliorum sequi opinionem cogerentur, quo superioribus mensibus euenit: quidam enim primum sententiam rogatus se censere dixit quod eius amicus statim dicturus erat' (lib. III, f. 96) n'a pu être écrite que par un Du Rivail rentré en France et sans doute établi déjà à Grenoble, siège du parlement du Dauphiné. Au vu des listes établies par F. Vindry, l'anecdote doit dater de 1513, quand furent installés deux nouveaux conseillers.

projet.[129] En 1515, la publication de l'*Historia*, dédiée au chancelier Duprat, et la présence de Du Rivail dans l'armée royale, avaient peut-être pour but d'obtenir quelque charge auprès de la Cour, mais ses efforts, en ce cas, furent vains.

Vindry signale une délibération des consuls de Grenoble en date du 10 avril 1521 indiquant que Du Rivail était alors official du diocèse, mais rejette cette information comme invraisemblable bien que d'autres pièces établissent qu'il exerçait des fonctions auprès de l'évêque de Grenoble.[130] Le témoignage de Du Rivail lui-même ne laisse pourtant aucun doute à ce sujet: 'et ut ei [sc. Laurent II Alleman] complacerem, ex amicitia in teneris annis contracta, aliquando diœcesis Gratianopolitanæ uicariatum et officialatum gessi.'[131] Du Rivail avait pu appartenir déjà à l'entourage de Laurent I Alleman, oncle et prédécesseur de Laurent II.[132] Il dut, en tout cas, entrer dans l'entourage de Laurent II dès que celui-ci devint évêque de Grenoble, en 1518. C'est ainsi qu'il l'accompagna en 1520 quand, après la mort de son oncle, il alla à Toulouse prendre possession de son abbaye de Saint-Sernin: ce voyage est daté par la rencontre qu'ils firent alors de Philibert de Chalon, qui lui-même se rendait en Espagne auprès de Charles-Quint.[133] Une indication fournie par le *De Allobrogibus* ('et Viennæ aliquot annis militiam sub diuo Mauricio militaui')[134] me paraît également se rapporter aux années 1515–21. Giraud,[135] suivi par Vindry, en voulait déduire qu'il aurait été envoyé à Vienne vers 1500, âgé d'environ dix ans, pour s'y préparer à l'état ecclésiastique, mais que ce projet aurait rapidement été abandonné, tandis que von Möller supposait une activité proprement militaire, par exemple contre les Vaudois, qu'il plaçait entre 1515 et 1521.[136] Cette dernière datation me paraît juste, mais je ne doute pas que 'militiam...militare' ait dans ce texte un sens métaphorique, d'ailleurs usuel, et signifie seulement que Du Rivail fit quelque temps partie du chapitre de la cathédrale Saint Maurice de Vienne. Aymar II, le second fils de notre historien, fournit un excellent parallèle: il est qualifié dans le testament de 1557 de docteur en droit, chanoine de Saint Apollinaire de Valence et official de Grenoble, mais il n'est pas encore *in sacris*,[137] et il sera reçu en

---

[129] *De Allobrogibus*, p. 557.

[130] Vindry, *Parlementaires* (n. 118 supra), p. 107.

[131] *De Allobrogibus*, p. 44. De Terrebasse, développant mal une abréviation, a édité par erreur 'aliquem' au lieu de 'aliquando': MS Paris Lat. 6014, f. 23ʳ.

[132] Cf. *De Allobrogibus*, pp. 529–30. Les liens étaient anciens: le parrain de Du Rivail était un Alleman, Barrachin, appartenant il est vrai à une autre branche que les évêques de Grenoble (*De Allobrogibus*, p. 537); son oncle maternel Pierre de Maubec avait aidé Laurent I en conflit avec Louis XI (p. 529).

[133] *De Allobrogibus*, p. 94. Vindry, *Parlementaires* (n. 118 supra), p. 110, date à tort ce voyage de 1526. Voir U. Robert, *Philibert de Chalon*, Paris, 1902, p. 41.

[134] *De Allobrogibus*, p. 25.

[135] Giraud, *Aymar du Rivail* (n. 118 supra), p. 16.

[136] Von Möller, *Aymar du Rivail* (n. 78 supra), p. 19.

[137] Le testament d'Aymar du Rivail daté de 1557 a été publié par Giraud, *Aymar du Rivail* (n. 118 supra), pp. 77–100.

1560 au parlement de Grenoble comme conseiller-lai. Du Rivail, qui avait été official de Grenoble avant d'entrer au parlement en 1521, avait pu de la même façon recevoir en bénéfice un canonicat à Vienne sans être *in sacris*. On objectera qu'il était déjà marié lorsqu'il écrivit l'*Historia iuris*, puisqu'il commente ainsi la mesure des XII Tables interdisant les unions entre patriciens et plébéiens: 'horum [sc. Allobrogum patriciorum] morem secutus sum, dum quamdam uirginem nobili genere ortam me arctissimo gradu coniungentem matrimonio iampridem collocaremus.'[138] Mais ce premier mariage, dont il n'est plus jamais question et qui fut sans postérité, dut être bientôt rompu par la mort de la jeune femme. Veuf, Du Rivail pouvait envisager une carrière ecclésiastique, et un canonicat à Vienne dans les années où il fut official de Grenoble me paraît une hypothèse plus vraisemblable que celles de Giraud et von Möller. On aimerait savoir si Du Rivail écrivit le commentaire au concordat de 1516 que lui attribuent Chacón et König,[139] mais dont aucune trace ne paraît avoir été conservée. Il semble bien, en tout cas, avoir alors envisagé une carrière semblable à celle de son frère Guigue, qui avait été vicaire et official du cardinal de Fiesque, archevêque d'Embrun.[140] Mais l'occasion se présenta de viser plus haut.

La création, le 1er septembre 1521, de quatre nouvelles charges au parlement de Grenoble lui permit d'en acquérir une.[141] Il la résignera en faveur de son fils Philippe le 24 septembre 1548,[142] tout en continuant de siéger jusqu'en 1556,[143] et à ces fonctions de conseiller s'ajouteront un certain nombre de missions confiées par les rois François I et Henri II.[144] C'est alors qu'il écrivit son second

---

[138] *Historia*, liv. II, f. 67ᵛ.

[139] A. Ciaconius (mort en 1599), *Bibliotheca libros et scriptores ferme cunctos ab initio mundi ad a. 1583 ...complectens*, Paris, 1731, col. 326; G. M. König, *Bibliotheca uetus et noua*, Altdorf, 1678, p. 694. Von Möller, *Aymar du Rivail* (n. 78 supra), p. 27, note que l'occasion d'un tel ouvrage aurait pu être aussi l'ordre donné par François I au parlement de Grenoble, en 1530 seulement, d'enregistrer le concordat.

[140] *De Allobrogibus*, p. 145.

[141] Terrebasse, *De Allobrogibus* (n. 118 supra), p. XI; Vindry, *Aymar du Rivail* (n. 118 supra), p. 108.

[142] *Catalogue des actes de Henri II*, II, Paris, 1986, 09.24².

[143] Pilot, 'Aymar du Rivail' (n. 118 supra), pp. 282–3; Vindry, *Parlementaires* (n. 118 supra), p. 108 n. 1.

[144] C'est au cours d'une mission royale ('aliquid negotii a Regia Maiestate commissione Auenione peragentes', *De Allobrogibus*, pp. 135–6) qu'il connut sa seconde épouse, la belle Marguerite Girard: leur fils aîné Laurent étant mort en août 1531 âgé de six ans et demi, le mariage, ainsi que la mission à Avignon, peut être daté de 1524 (Giraud, *Aymar du Rivail* [n. 118 supra], p. 19), ou 1523 (Vindry, *Parlementaires* [n. 118 supra], p. 82). En 1529, il fut l'un des deux conseillers au parlement de Grenoble envoyés par François I pour protester auprès du duc de Savoie après la prise de Château-Dauphin par des Piémontais (*Catalogue des actes de François I*, VI, Paris, 1894, p. 175, no. 19787; cf. *De Allobrogibus*, pp. 21 et 152). Une mission intéressante, bien que les précédents biographes n'en fassent pas mention, fut sa nomination en 1539 dans la commission chargée d'examiner les titres des évêques de Grenoble et de Valence et d'autres barons et seigneurs qui levaient des péages sur le sel voituré par le Rhône (*Actes de François I*, VIII,Paris, 1905, p. 686, no. 32856), puis en 1540 dans une autre commission chargée d'informer sur les malversations reprochées aux gardes péagers et fermiers du péage du Rhône (*Actes de François I*, VIII, p. 689, no. 32872): Du Rivail eut l'occasion de consulter alors un grand nombre de chartes anciennes, qu'il signale dans plusieurs additions portées sur le manuscrit de son histoire des Allobroges (pp. 333, 394–5, 405–6). En 1544 il se rendit à Paris, ayant été nommé parmi les

ouvrage, le *De Allobrogibus*, qui devait demeurer inédit jusqu'à sa publication par
A. de Terrebasse en 1844. On doit savoir gré à l'éditeur d'avoir exhumé ce texte,
et d'avoir reconstitué dans sa quasi-totalité le manuscrit (l'actuel Parisinus Latinus
6014), dont un utilisateur indélicat avait prélevé un certain nombre de cahiers,
parvenus heureusement eux aussi à la Bibliothèque royale. Un examen de ce
manuscrit permet de distinguer le texte primitif et des additions portées en marge
ou sur quelques folios insérés en un second temps,[145] de dater assez précisément
le texte et de corriger sur un point la préface de Terrebasse: 'l'auteur s'était
proposé d'écrire son *Histoire* en onze livres, mais chemin faisant il changea de
dessein, et son ouvrage n'en contient que neuf, d'une longueur fort inégale. Il
s'arrête à l'année 1535, peu de lignes après le récit de la mort de son fils aîné,
âgé de six ans, dont la perte lui inspire les plus amers regrets.'[146] En réalité, le
projet initial de Du Rivail était celui d'un ouvrage en sept livres, qui fut porté à
neuf en deux étapes, par la division du cinquième livre en livres V et VI
(respectivement 'Allobroges cum Burgundia ad Francos deuenere' et 'Regnum
Burgundiæ et Allobrogum cum Prouincia ad reges peculiares rediit'), puis par la
division du septième livre devenu huitième en livres VIII et IX (respectivement
'Delphini' et 'De translatione Delphinatus in Francos, et Delphinensium gestis sub
ipsis Francis'): la division primitive ne distinguait, après la période romaine, que
le royaume burgonde et la suzeraineté franque, avec l'intermède, illégitime aux
yeux de Du Rivail, de la domination germanique; la division définitive combine
plus habilement 'patriotisme' delphinois et 'patriotisme' français, en réservant des
livres séparés pour le deuxième royaume de Bourgogne et les Dauphins
indépendants. De cette modification en deux étapes témoignent les *incipit* des
livres VI à IX, les titres courants écrits au verso de chaque folio,[147] et enfin la
conclusion, qui dans sa première rédaction ne parlait que du septième livre, et
dans la seconde a corrigé 'septimi' en 'noni libri'. De même les premières lignes
de l'introduction étaient-elles primitivement: 'in animo est geographiam

---

juges du chancelier Poyet (Pilot, 'Aymar du Rivail' [n. 118 supra], p. 276; Vindry, *Parlementaires* [n. 118
supra], p. 110). En 1547 il fit partie d'une commission chargée de faire crier et publier la ferme du tirage du
sel sur les rivières de Rhône, Saône et Isère (*Actes de Henri II*, I, 09.26[1]). De 1547 à 1553, il fit partie d'une
commission chargée de procéder à l'aliénation d'une partie du domaine royal dans le Dauphiné (*Actes de Henri
II*, I, 12.10[2] et II, 01.31[5]). En 1548 ou 1549, il fut l'un des deux conseillers au parlement de Grenoble chargés
de se rendre dans le marquisat de Saluces, annexé par la France, pour y rédiger un réglement de police générale
d'après les coutumes locales (P. Granet, *Stylus regius Galliarum iuridicus olim Salucianis præscriptus*, Bourg-
en-Bresse, 1630, p. 244; Terrebasse, *De Allobrogibus* [n. 118 supra], pp. XVII–XVIII). Le *De Allobrogibus* fait
encore allusion à d'autres missions au cours desquelles Du Rivail plaida devant le duc de Savoie (pp. 55 et 350).
    [145] Le texte édité par Terrebasse est en général la version ultime du manuscrit, incluant toute les additions
sans les signaler d'aucune façon, mais contenant aussi un certain nombre d'indications, le plus souvent
biographiques, qui avaient pourtant été rayées dans un second temps.
    [146] *De Allobrogibus*, p. XVI; voir aussi p. 594 n. 3.
    [147] Ce sont ces titres courants qui marquent nettement les deux étapes, puisque ceux des folios 287–369
ont été corrigés à deux reprises: 'liber septimus', puis 'octauus', puis 'nonus'.

originesque et gesta [ces quatre derniers mots ayant ensuite été rayés et remplacés par "historiam"] Allobrogum VII libris amplecti'; mais la dernière des corrections successivement apportées ('octo', puis 'undecim libris') ne correspond pas au plan en neuf livres qui fut finalement adopté. C'est là le seul problème, mais on voit que Du Rivail n'a pas réduit à neuf livres un ouvrage qui aurait dû en comprendre onze: une nouvelle distribution de la même matière l'a fait passer de sept à huit et enfin à neuf livres; quant aux onze livres du premier folio, ils n'appartiennent pas à la rédaction primitive, et on y peut déceler l'indice d'un projet de prolongation de l'œuvre, ou tout simplement conclure à un lapsus de l'auteur. L'examen du folio 369 montre d'autre part que le texte s'arrêtait primitivement avec la mort du fils aîné de l'auteur, le 28 août 1531, immédiate-ment suivie de la conclusion générale. Une première mention de la crue du Rhône en septembre - octobre 1532 ne fut ajoutée que dans un deuxième temps, suivie d'une nouvelle rédaction de la conclusion générale. Enfin, en un troisième temps fut ajoutée une nouvelle rédaction, augmentée de renseignements sur l'épidémie de 1533–4, de lignes consacrées à la crue de 1532, et de l'indication de l'élévation de Didier de Tholon au rang de grand maître de l'ordre de Saint Jean de Jérusalem en décembre 1535. Que la rédaction primitive ait été achevée entre l'été 1531 et l'été 1532 est confirmé par le fait que tous les textes écrits après cette dernière date se trouvent dans des additions marginales ou sur des folios n'appartenant pas au manuscrit dans son état premier.[148] Inversement, les allusions que contient le texte primitif à l'ambassade de 1529 auprès du duc de Savoie et à la mort de Philibert de Chalon en 1530 montrent que la rédaction de l'ouvrage, et même du premier livre, n'a pas commencé avant 1530.[149] Le *De Allobrogibus* a donc été écrit entre 1530 et 1532. La mort du fils aîné de Du Rivail a peut-être contribué à en précipiter la rédaction, mais il ne s'agissait pas d'une œuvre de circonstance. Le projet fut certainement conçu avant 1531, car l'œuvre suppose plus de temps pour la lecture des sources et la réunion de la documentation, et sa non-publication n'implique pas non plus que Du Rivail ait immédiatement cessé de s'y intéresser: il continua d'y apporter des additions jusqu'après 1539, et peut-être même 1547.[150]

---

[148] 1535 dans une note marginale: p. 48 de l'édition Terrebasse = f. 24ᵛ du manuscrit; 1534 dans quelques lignes ajoutées en bas de page, dont l'écriture et le caractère erratique montrent bien qu'elles n'appartiennent pas à la rédaction primitive: p. 111 = f. 60ʳ; 1533 et 1535 dans un texte assez long ajouté en un second temps: p. 122 = f. 66ᵛ (folio collé sur le folio 66, de façon à recouvrir le verso primitif) et 66ʳ (en fait, folio inséré sous cette numérotation entre les folios 66 et 67, de sorte qu'il y a deux folios 66); allusion aux événements de 1536 dans le Chablais: p. 167 = f. 92ʳ (il s'agit là encore d'un folio 'bis', inséré entre les folios 92 et 93, de sorte qu'il y a deux folios 92); références à la mission de Du Rivail en 1539 dans des additions marginales: pp. 333, 394–395 et 405–406 = f. 190ʳ, 230ʳ et 237ᵛ.

[149] Voir respectivement, pour l'ambassade de 1529, p. 21 = f. 12ʳ et p. 152 = f. 82ᵛ; pour la mort de Philibert de Chalon, p. 95 = f. 51ʳ.

[150] C'est ce que me paraît impliquer (p. 406 = f. 237ᵛ) la formule 'diuus Franciscus rex christianissimus' pour désigner François I.

La date de la mort de Du Rivail reste incertaine. Son dernier testament, retrouvé par Giraud, date de 1557. On admet généralement qu'il était mort en 1560, quand son fils Aymar II devint à son tour conseiller au parlement de Grenoble, mais l'argument est sans valeur si Aymar II fut nommé sur résignation de son frère Philippe. Le seul *terminus ante quem* certain, comme l'a vu Vindry, est 1566, date de la mort du juriste et humaniste Antoine de Govea, lui-même auteur de vers sur la mort d'Aymar du Rivail.

Claude De Seyssel

A. C. DIONISOTTI

In 1978 Arnaldo Momigliano published an essay which, rather whimsically no doubt, adopts the style of a collective research project. The subject was to be 'The Historians of the Classical World and their Audiences'; numbered paragraphs outline the headings under which evidence might usefully be collected that 'would help us to understand where and on what occasions and by what kinds of people books of history were written and read'. The focus there was primarily on Graeco-Roman antiquity, but of course no one has taught more clearly than Momigliano that understanding the ancient historians involves not only 'reading and rereading the actual texts of the historians themselves—a duty that the projected collection does not intend to make lighter', but also inquiring into all their various successive audiences, from those they immediately addressed down to the present. The research project specified no deadline; indeed it even spelt out the terrible truth, which would be self-destructing in any 'real' research proposal, that 'the only work about which one can make some promise is the work already done'. So the project remains even now more real than most, and I have tried in what follows to contribute to it.[1]

* * *

Nowadays Claude de Seyssel is perhaps best known as a political theorist. On the accession of Francis I, in 1515, he wrote a slim work on *La Monarchie de France*; not quite so slim, nor of course so famous, as Machiavelli's *Prince* or More's *Utopia*, but an equally valid and distinctive interpretation of that world, as observed or imaginable, for better or worse. Initially the work found little acclaim. Its emphasis on the constraints, the *freins*, that should limit royal power, seemed drearily old-fashioned in the glittering new world of young monarchs: Francis himself, Henry VIII and Charles V. But it survived to re-emerge in contexts that might have surprised Seyssel. In 1548, adapted and translated into Latin, it was offered to Edward VI of England as a blueprint for a Protestant king. Later still, in the crisis of the French monarchy either side of St Bartholomew, Seyssel's vision of social harmony under a responsive and responsible monarch seemed newly relevant; and since the *Monarchie* antedated all the

[1] Momigliano's essay was first published partially in *The American Scholar*, 47, 1978, pp. 193–204, the full version with notes in *Annali della Scuola normale superiore di Pisa*, 3rd ser., 8, 1978, pp. 59–75, reprinted in his *Sesto contributo alla storia degli studi classici e del mondo antico*, I, Rome, 1980, pp. 361–76. I am much indebted and grateful to Jean-Louis Ferrary and Pierre Petitmengin for help with this paper.

current rifts, it could be cited almost as an ancestral constitution, of unimpeach-able orthodoxy and patriotism.[2]

However, this was only a fraction of Seyssel's literary output. Much the largest part of it, in bulk, was translation of ancient historians into French. In fact, modern editions of the *Monarchie* include the prefaces to two of his translations, those of Justin and Appian.[3] This rather concretely poses the question of what relationship there might be between the political analysis of the *Monarchie* and the work of translation from ancient historiography that preceded it. But before that question can be properly tackled, it may be useful to reconsider Seyssel's work of translation as such, in any case and by any criterion among the most important before Amyot.[4]

Seyssel himself offers us a start, in the introduction to his translation of Thucydides, completed in 1514 and dedicated to the king whom he had served for sixteen years, Louis XII of France. In view of Louis's laudable interest, he says in the preface:

> I have in the past laboured to make known to you a number of secular histories, which you had not previously seen or heard, inasmuch as they had not been translated into French; some were in Greek, like that of Xenophon on the expedition of Cyrus, and that of Diodorus on the successors of Alexander; others had originally been written in Greek and later translated into Latin, like that of Appian of Alexandria; others again were first written in Latin but had never been translated into French, like that of Justin... and later on, considering my ecclesiasti-cal state, I was moved to translate the ecclesiastical history of Rufinus of Aquileia [i.e. Eusebius]... And then, having nothing else to hand that seemed worthy of translation to present to you, I finally chose the history that Thucydides the Athenian wrote about the war in the Peloponnese, in eight books...

But, of course, Thucydides is not an easy author:

> ...indeed I thought I would repent and withdraw from this attempt, the more so since the translation from Greek into Latin by Lorenzo Valla seemed to me very obscure and difficult. And so in fact I would have done, had it not been for my lord Janus Lascaris... His promises and arguments added courage to my desire to be able to present you with something remarkable in itself and unknown to the French; so I undertook to complete the work, with the help of Lascaris's corrections and notes, without which indeed I would never have succeeded... and

---

[2] The relevant texts are gathered in Poujol's edition (see next note), pp. 225–37; Lambinus also cites it in his commentary on Nepos (*Aemilii Probi seu Cornelii Nepotis liber de vita imperatorum*, Paris, 1569, pp. 458–9 = *Vita Hamilcaris*, n. 25 in reprints).

[3] Claude de Seyssel, *La Monarchie de France*, ed. J. Poujol, Paris, 1961; *The Monarchy of France*, tr. H. J. Hexter and ed. D. R. Kelley, New Haven, 1981.

[4] Recent studies of translation seem to ignore Seyssel, e.g. Glyn P. Norton, *The Ideology and Language of Translation in Renaissance France*, Geneva, 1984, and V. Worth, *Practising Translation in Renaissance France*, Oxford, 1988.

I humbly beg that it may be your pleasure to welcome this translation and accept it as the masterpiece of my labours in this art of translation, namely in secular histories.[5]

Summing up, we have the seven books of Xenophon's *Anabasis*, nearly all of Appian's *Wars* and three books of Diodorus's *Bibliotheca*, supplemented by a couple of Plutarch's *Lives* that he does not trouble to mention, the whole of Justin's *Epitome*, Rufinus's *Ecclesiastical History* and finally Thucydides. That is a lot of ancient history; and it is also very Greek, for a country where Greek had barely begun to be taught. Yet it was not as a scholar, or professional translator, or even man of letters that Seyssel had served his king. Though an able propagandist, he was first and foremost *conseiller* and *maître des requêtes* of the king's household, an administrator and diplomat. In 1510 he was rewarded with the see of Marseilles, not the sort of benefice handed out to littérateurs. Thus it was that Seyssel was in Rome when he translated Thucydides, because he was engaged in delicate negotiations mending the war and schism that had unfortunately brewed up between the Papacy and the Most Christian King.[6]

How did Seyssel himself see his work of translation? What determined his choice of texts? The translations have been described as 'humanistic', because they involve classical, mainly Greek, texts.[7] But what sort of humanism is this? They are translations based on Latin versions (Seyssel knew no Greek), into a language, French, which at this date had absolutely no humanist credentials. Moreover, any humanism in this dawning sixteenth century, implies some relationship with Italian humanism. To what extent are these translations overtly or implicitly related to Italian humanist antecedents? And where do they fit, in

---

[5] Claude de Seyssel, *L'Histoire de Thucydide Athenien, de la guerre, qui fut entre les Peloponnesiens et Atheniens*, Paris, 1527, sig. ã vii: '…me suis cy devant parforcé de faire venir à vostre congnoissance plusieurs histoires mondaines, lesquelles n'aviez auparavant veu ne entendu, pour tant qu'elles n'avoient point esté translatees en langaige françoys, ains estoient les aulcunes en Grec, comme celle de Xenophon du voyage de Cyrus, et celle de Diodore des successeurs d'Alexandre, les aultres avoient esté escriptes premierement en Grec, et après translatees en latin, comme celle d'Appian Alexandrin; et aultres escriptes premierement en latin, mais jamais n'avoient esté translatees en françoys, comme celle de Justin…considerant mon estat ecclesiastique…fuz meu de translater l'histoire ecclesiastique de Ruffin Acquilesien… Et neantmoins depuis, non ayant aultre matiere en main que me semblast digne de translation pour vous presenter…ay finablement choisy l'histoire de Thucydides Athenien qu'il a escripte en huyct livres, de la guerre de Peloponnese…je me cuiday repentir et retirer de mon entreprinse; et d'autant plus que la translation qui a esté faicte de grec en latin par Laurent Valle, me sembloit moult obscure et difficile. Et veritablement l'eusse fait, n'eust esté Messire Jehan Lascary… Lesquelles promesses et persuasions me donnerent tel couraige, joinct le desir que j'avoye de vous povoir faire present d'une chose singuliere en soy, et non congneue aux françoys, que j'entreprins de la perfaire moyennant les annotations et corrections dudict Lascary, sans lesquelles à la verité jamais non fusse sceu venir à bout… Si vous supplie treshumblement, sire, que vostre plaisir soit prendre en gré ceste translation, et l'accepter pour le chief d'euvre de mes labeurs en cest art de translater, mesmement histoires mondaines.'

[6] The best work on Seyssel's career is A. Caviglia, *Claudio di Seyssel*, Miscellanea di storia italiana, 3rd ser., XXIII, Turin, 1928.

[7] P. Chavy, 'Les Traductions humanistes de Claude de Seyssel' in *L'Humanisme français au début de la Renaissance*, Paris, 1973, pp. 361–76.

the various cross-currents of French literature and scholarship in the reign of
Louis XII?

Seyssel spent a good part of his life in Italy, as student and teacher of law in
Pavia, as administrator of French rule in Lombardy, and elsewhere as ambassador.
No doubt he spoke and understood Italian fluently enough, and indeed a speech
that he gave in Italian to the Florentines (no less) survives, justifying his
appearance as the first of Émile Picot's *Les Français italianisants*.[8] But in fact
neither part of Picot's title really fits. Seyssel was not actually a Frenchman: he
was born into the ruling aristocracy of Savoy, his first allegiance was to the Duke
who held court in Turin, and indeed he died as Archbishop of Turin. On the other
hand, his family came from the French half of the Duchy, up near Geneva, it was
French-speaking and a strong supporter of the French, not the Piedmontese,
faction at court. Seyssel's upbringing is unlikely to have encouraged italianizing
of any sort. And once he had moved to the French court, it might be unwise to
flaunt Italian connections or an Italian culture (supposing he had one) on top of
a provincial origin. At any rate I know of no evidence that he did so. Already
under Louis XII there was no shortage of resident or visiting Italian humanists
at court: Paolo Emilio, Fausto Andrelini, Fra Giocondo, Mario Equicola,
Sannazaro, to mention only the most obvious. Nor did Seyssel, in celebrating that
court, lack opportunity to mention them. Yet he does not. And he in turn, so far
as I have seen, is not cited as of their company and does not figure among the
friends or patrons that they address.

Nor is he conspicuous in French humanist circles. True, he does appear in
Longueil's roll-call of French men of letters where, after a mixed bag of poets
(Guillaume du Bellay, Germain Brice, Valerand de la Varanne, Pierre de Burry,
'Jacobaeus'(?), Gilles of Delft, Julien Py, Olivier Conrard, 'Briandus'(?),
Guillaume Castel), we move onto more solid ground with writers of prose:

> dicet Budaeus diligenter, Briconetus leniter, narrabit aperte Scissellus, eloquetur
> graviter Tisardus, apposite Badius, Gaguinus luculenter, Pinus scite, duo Fernandi
> splendide, Erasmus copiose, acute, nitide, Faber Stapulensis philosophice, cuius
> incude expolita iam pure loqui didicit philosophia

followed by Clichtove, Charles de Bovelles, Guillaume Cop and Symphorien
Champier.[9]

---

[8] E. Picot, *Les Français italianisants au xvie siècle*, I, Paris, 1906, pp. 1–25, including a bit of the speech
on pp. 16–17; of course, the speech may well have been drafted or corrected for him.

[9] C. de Longueil, *Oratio de laudibus divi Ludovici atque Francorum, habita Pyctavii in coenobio Fratrum
minorum Anno domini 1510*, Paris, c. 1512, sig. cii^v. The whole passage is cited and annotated by Th. Simar,
Christophe de Longueil, Louvain, 1911, pp. 22–6: I have supplemented and corrected Simar's identifications
of the poets as far as I was able; presumably the two unknowns had, like the others, published some Latin verse.
I see no reason to doubt that the speech was delivered in 1510 as the title clearly states, see Ph. Aug. Becker,
Christophe de Longueil, Bonn etc., 1924, pp. 9–11; for the date of publication see *Inventaire chronologique des
éditions parisiennes du XVIe siècle*, II, Paris, 1977, no. 398.

Clearly, once Longueil had decided to be hung for a sheep and claim that the French could match the Italians in Latin eloquence (as well as beat them in everything else), he could not afford to be fussy: on most counts the list is generously inclusive. As regards Seyssel here, perhaps we should note two points. Firstly, that Longueil's phrase *narrabit aperte*[10] is a specific and not very ambitious claim. It echoes Cicero's prescription 'rem narrare, et ita ut veri similis narratio sit, ut aperta, ut brevis'.[11] It nicely suits Seyssel's London *Oratio* of 1506, which is indeed an apology for Louis XII skilfully dressed as a simple *narratio* of events; important in Seyssel's diplomatic career, but slight and low-key as a claim to humanism.[12] Secondly, it is noteworthy that the only person in Longueil's list with whom Seyssel is known to have had any direct dealings is the printer Badius Ascensius, to whom he entrusted the speech he had given in London, wretchedly misprinted there by Wynkyn de Worde, to be reprinted in 'its original correct, if not elegant, Latin'.[13]

Badius reappears many years later, in a context which at first sight seems to associate Seyssel with two others in Longueil's list, Lefèvre d'Étaples and Josse Clichtove, but in fact I think it is rather evidence to the contrary. While recovering from an illness in Rome in 1514, Seyssel had ventured to compose a meditative commentary on the first chapter of Luke's Gospel. By way of preface to the first edition (August 1514), there is a letter to Seyssel from Guillielmus Parvus (Parvy or Petit), expressing enthusiasm for the work and announcing that he has had it printed 'industria Iodoci Badii, boni apud nos nominis chalcographi et tuae dignitati noti.' For a second printing early in the following year, Parvy adds that among those to whom he has given a preview of the work are 'Raulinus et Clichtoveus nostri magno eulogio theologi et Iacobus Faber primarius philosophus'.[14] It was understandable that Seyssel, by now a bishop but with no theological training, should wish to consult an expert before publishing such a work. But it seems to me significant that the expert he chose, Parvy, was indeed *sacrae sapientiae professor*, but of all such the one most closely associated not with the university, but with the court: since 1509 he had been the king's

---

[10] So the original edition, not *apte* as in Simar and others since.

[11] *De oratore* 2.80; note also Pliny's comment on Isaeus 'prohoemiatur apte, narrat aperte, pugnat acriter' (*Epistulae* 2.3.3).

[12] Though the *Louenges* of 1508 claim in the title to have been 'Nouvellement composees en latin par maistre Claude de Seyssel...et translatees par lui de latin en français', no trace of a Latin text has been found, and Longueil is plainly referring to writings in Latin.

[13] Claude de Seyssel, *Ad serenissimum et potentissimum Angliae regem Henricum septimum oratio*, [Paris, 1506], sig. Aii^v: 'impressor ille Anglicus, parum (ut coniicio) latinarum litterarum gnarus, multos etiam...adiecit errores...cui morbo ut mederer per Parisios transiens doctissimo viro Iodoco Badio Ascensio reparandos tradidi. Isque tanta diligentia castigavit ut in primaevam formam restituens si non elegantem, latinam saltem, uti erat, nova impressione reddiderit'.

[14] The original editions are rare; the letter is conveniently edited in *The Prefatory Letters of Jacques Lefèvre d'Étaples*, ed. E. F. Rice, New York etc., 1972, pp. 338–9.

confessor.[15] And since we (as readers of the published letter-preface) are told that Seyssel knew the printer Badius, we would surely be told if there had been any kind of personal link between him and the more eminent trio from the university. Even with Badius, the link was not such that Badius ever thought to make him a dedicatee, for instance. Perhaps there was quite a simple reason for Seyssel's isolation from such scholarly circles, humanistic or otherwise: since the court was peripatetic, and Seyssel as diplomat even more so, he was very rarely in Paris. His library was not St Victor or the Sorbonne, but Blois.[16]

Parvy was a man of many parts and knew everybody. For the court he could write prayers in the form of 'blasons' and hymns set to fashionable tunes.[17] Budé wrote glowingly about him to Erasmus; he managed to entice the Hebrew scholar Agostino Giustiniani, if not Erasmus himself, to Paris; he had Valla's *De voluptate* published, in spite of Badius's shocked mutterings; and between 1511 and 1516 he supplied Badius with the manuscripts for a whole series of *editiones principes*, mainly of historical texts.[18] However, this is precisely where his humanism declares its independence as much from Erasmus as from the Italians. In that same summer of 1514, when Badius received and printed Seyssel's religious tract, he also hailed Parvy's tireless efforts to rescue all the best authors from wormeaten neglect and publish them for the common good of scholars: 'ad publicam studiosorum utilitatem optimos quosque auctores cum blattis et tineis decertantes in lucem emittendos nostro prelo committere'. This was the language that Poggio and other early Italian humanists had adopted to publicize the salvaging of such authors as Cicero, Quintilian, Lucretius and so on. But here it is deployed to herald the publication of 'four splendid historians all but obliterated by long neglect (quatuor luculentos historiographos paene situ victos)'; and who are they? They are: Gregory of Tours, Aimoin of Fleury, Paul the Deacon and Liutprand.[19] Today this might seem a useful step towards *Monumenta*

---

[15] In 1517 Budé remarked on Parvy's longstanding popularity as a preacher at court in a letter to Erasmus (*Opus epistolarum*, ed. P. S. Allen, II, Oxford, 1910, p. 444): 'Haud alio concionatore aula ac regius comitatus in magnis celebritatibus utitur, nec Ludovici Regis tempore usa est.'

[16] For completeness I suppose one should add that Seyssel twice figures among the addressees of Alanus Varenius (on whom see *Prefatory Letters* [n. 14 above], pp. 215–19, 385–6); but these vacuous dedications seem to be part of a blanket mailing of any potential patrons in southern France and scarcely imply any real contact.

[17] See his *Ave angélique salut* 'sur la chanson "Il fait beau veoir ces hommes d'armes"', and *Blasons des armes du pouvre pecheur*, both included in the collection *La Formation de l'homme*, Paris, 1538, pp. 138, 152.

[18] See J. K. Farge, *Biographical Register of Paris Doctors of Theology 1500–1536*, Toronto, 1980, pp. 367–73, and Ph. Renouard, *Bibliographie des impressions et des oeuvres de Josse Bade Ascensius*, Paris, 1908, Index, s.v. *Parvus*; the association with Badius seems to stop abruptly in 1516, it is not clear why. He had also collaborated with Jean Petit and Henri Estienne, see Victor Vitensis, *Historia persecutionum Africae*, Paris, [1511] (announcing other editions also), and Sigebert of Gembloux, *Chronicon*, Paris, 1513, described in F. Schreiber, *The Estiennes*, New York, 1982, p. 31.

[19] Dedication of *Liutprandi Ticinensis ecclesiae Levitae Rerum gestarum per Europam ipsius praesertim temporibus libri sex*, Paris, 1514, repr. in Renouard, *Bibliographie* (n. 18 above), III, p. 9.

Germaniae Historica or the like, but at the time it constituted first and foremost a cool dismissal of the whole concept of 'barbarism', a flat denial of classical Latin style as any criterion of value; and this without excuse or apology, not even that of patriotism.[20]

Thus the one French 'humanist' directly connected with Seyssel, besides being connected over a work that can scarcely be called humanistic, is anyway one who resolutely turned his back on the hall-mark of Italian humanism, mastery and pride in classical Latin style. In general, Seyssel might indeed find it difficult to go quite so far. So in his appraisal of Louis XII's achievements written in 1507–8, he evidently felt that the issue had to be faced, and that the best that could be claimed was an improvement and hope for the future:

> ...le royaulme de France, lequel auparavant estoit noté de n'avoir aucuns clercs qui sceussent bien parler latin, mais estoit leur langaige latin rude et barbare, et à ceulx qui en vouloient apprendre convenoit aller en Ytallie trouver des maistres, à present est pourveu d'hommes excellens tant en grec que en latin, de sorte que peu à peu se va perdant cest ancienne barbarisme, et si ce regne dure encores longuement...je ne doubte point que le parler latin ne soit aussi commun ou plus en France comme en Ytalie.[21]

Admittedly, barely a year later, in the preface to his translation of Justin, he suddenly seems to take a very different view: a giddy vision that French might inherit the mantle of Latin as a language of conquest and empire (long since propounded by Valla as an Italian form of imperial sway), and so impose itself even on Italy, just as William the Conqueror had imposed Norman on England:

> par le moyen des grandes et glorieuses conquêtes qu'avez faites en Italie, n'y a quartier maintenant en icelle, où le langage François ne soit entendu par la pluspart des gens: tellement que la où les Italiens reputoyent jadis les François barbares tant en meurs, qu'en langage, à present s'entrentendent sans truchement les uns les autres, et si s'adaptent les Italiens, tant ceux qui sont soubs vostre obeissance, que plusieurs autres, aux habillemens et maniere de vivre de France...[22]

This is rather akin to the bravado displayed by Longueil in the preface to his *Oratio*:

> Cur enim pluris fecerim Romanum suo vernaculo sermone disertum quam Francum gallica elegantia conspicuum? Sed turpe, ut ille ait, nescire Latine: turpe profecto Italis, nostratibus minime, non magis hercle quam si Persice nesciant aut Cantabrice, vel Romani ipsi Gallice.[23]

---

[20] The editions include texts of absolutely no nationalistic relevance, like Victor of Vita and Paulinus of Nola, and the initiative seems to me rather different in tenor from parallel moves in Germany, even if in some ways a reaction to them.

[21] Claude de Seyssel, *Les Louenges du roy Loys xii^e*, Paris, 1508, sig. c vi^v

[22] Seyssel, *La Monarchie*, ed. Poujol (n. 3 above), p. 66.

[23] Longueil, *Oratio* (n. 9 above), sig. a ii^r: 'Why should I admire a Roman speaking well in his own

But I doubt that we should read these statements as aspirations for a vernacular humanism, prognostics of Du Bellay's *Deffence et illustration* of forty years later. They are rather expressions of euphoric nationalism in the aftermath of the French victory at Agnadello in May 1509, and scarcely less ephemeral. It is indeed crucial to Longueil's bravado that he is writing stylish Latin and bandying Cicero like an Italian, only to call their bluff. And certainly the cult of classical Latinity in prose and verse, as a preeminent goal of humanism, only gained ground in France in the following decades.

Such a cult had not been a feature of Seyssel's own education, as he publicly declared in the preface to his London speech addressed to the apostolic protonotary and nuncio Pietro Grifo, who had also been there:

> For myself, I do not think that this speech deserves printing or spreading around Italy, least of all in Rome, the capital of the world crowded with the most learned and important people. I am well aware that it is altogether unpolished and semibarbarous, since, I am sorry to say, I never acquired even the most ordinary stylistic skill whether by rules or practice. For, virtually from the cradle, when I had scarcely grasped the elements of grammar, I devoted myself so completely to the study of law, that I never even had a teacher for literature, and spent my whole youth with commentaries on civil law that are anything but elegant.[24]

The disclaimer seems unnecessarily factual for a mere modesty-formula, and it is reiterated, more forcefully and with even less apology, in a quite different context many years later:

> There's little point in excusing my rough and boorish style, since rhetorical training is the last thing I could lay claim to, not having spent so much as one day with a teacher of it. Nor indeed did I study any other arts, apart from civil and canon law, to which I devoted myself exclusively from childhood on, immediately after basic grammar.[25]

---

language any more than a Frenchman eloquent in French? Ah, but it is disgraceful, as the great man said [Cicero, *Brutus,* 140], to be ignorant of Latin; disgraceful it may be for the Italians, but hardly for our people, any more than if they are ignorant of Persian or Iberian; or indeed for the Romans themselves if they are ignorant of French.'

[24] Seyssel, *Oratio* (n. 13 above), sig. Aii: [he does not think the speech deserves printing] 'ut per Italiam et ipsam praesertim orbis caput Romam, eruditissimorum gravissimorumque virorum turba refertissimam, circumferatur. Quippe qui nihil in ea non rude aut semibarbarum inveniri satis mihi conscius sum, quandoquidem neque arte neque exercitatione vel mediocrem dicendi peritiam (quod dolenter refero) umquam sim assecutus. Ab ipsis enim ferme cunabulis, grammatices rudimentis vixdum satis imbutus, ad legalem philosophiam me totum usque adeo contuli ut litterarum cultiorum ne umquam quidem praeceptor mihi fuerit; omnemque iuventam in hisce iuris civilis commentatorum codicibus ab omni prorsus elegantia abhorrentibus eatenus consumpsi'.

[25] Seyssel, *De divina providentia tractatus*, Paris, 1520, f. 151ʸ: 'Stili vero asperitatem et sermonis rusticitatem non est quod excusem, quippe qui artem nullam minus quam Rhethoricam profiteor, in qua ne diem quidem unum sub praeceptore consumpsi, sed neque in alia omnino ulla, praeter legalem et canonicam, quibus ab ipsa pueritia post suscepta statim prima grammatices rudimenta totus incubui.'

In fact Seyssel's Latin style is perfectly competent and no worse for a certain simplicity and directness. But the stance is significant. Seyssel recognizes the existence of humanistic standards of style, but categorically excludes himself from them. The most he concedes is perhaps at the beginning of his treatise on the collection of medieval law known as *Liber feudorum*, begun before he joined the service of Louis XII and never finished:

> Tanta est enim compilatorum huius operis in sermone atque stylo rusticitas obscoenitasque, ut neque ordo neque elegantia neque plena decidendi ratio, sed e contra confusio, barbaries et irrationabilis nonnumquam iniquitas ex his, quarum authoritati innitimur, constitutionibus deprehendatur.[26]

Even so, he goes on, this law has imperial sanction both in the courts and in the law-schools; it is too late to try to revise its language ('illorum itaque studium, qui constitutiones ipsas meliori elegantiorique stylo reficere conati sunt, aliquando utilissimum et paene necessarium, nunc vero temerarium atque perniciosum fore existimo'); better to accept it and do what one can to give it precision and clarity; so the treatise proceeds, with discussions of terms like *feudum, vassallus, homagium* etc. It is noticeable that the great Milanese jurist Jason de Mayno, hailed by Seyssel as 'mihi doctrina pater et praeceptor colendissimus', had not felt any need to make shocked noises about the language of the *Liber feudorum* when he lectured on it in 1483.[27] But another fact pointing the other way may be more significant. Seyssel allowed his lectures on the Digest, taken down by students in Turin back in the 1480's and 90's, to be published in Milan *tels quels*, long after his career had taken a quite different turn, in 1508.[28] They are written in the lawyers' traditional solid porridge of cross-reference and technical jargon. Later that same year and in Paris, Budé published his *Annotationes* on the Digest, where classical poets and orators crowd out the traditional commentators, cross-references and all. Of course Budé did not teach law, but neither, by now, did Seyssel.

For Budé, Italian humanism had culminated in the triumvirate of Politian, Barbaro and Pico, whose heritage now lay there for the taking. For Seyssel, this

---

[26] 'The compilers of this work were so appallingly unpolished in their language and style that there is no order or elegance or full argument to guide decision (?); on the contrary, what emerges from these constitutions on whose authority we rely can be confusion, barbarity and often unjustifiable injustice.' For editions see n. 28 below.

[27] See his *Lectura super primo...libro Codicis*, Pavia, 1491, sig. SS.

[28] Claude de Seyssel, *Commentaria in sex partes digestorum et Codicis, cum tractatu compendioso feudorum*, Milan, 1508, printed by Alexander Minutianus. This edition, more complete than the reprint Venice 1535, is very rare; besides the copy in the Brera library in Milan indicated by Caviglia (n. 6 above), pp. 38–41, Basel Universitätsbibliothek still has the copy which belonged to Zasius and presumably contributed to Thomas Guarinus's 1566 reprint of the *Speculum feudorum* (see *Amerbachkorrespondenz*, ed. A. Hartmann, III, Basel, 1947, p. 357; I am most grateful to Nicolas Barker and to Margaretha Debrunner for very kind and prompt verifications).

heritage would appear not to exist. He does occasionally mention individual Italian humanists; in the first place, obviously, those who had made Appian and Thucydides available in Latin, Pier Candido Decembrio and Lorenzo Valla. But, as we saw in the case of Valla, it is only to take them to task for being too often misleading, obscure or downright incomprehensible. Elsewhere we find references to Biondo's *Histories*, Platina's *Lives of the Popes*, Merula's history of Lombardy, Acciaioli's *Life of Charlemagne* (written for Louis XI): but all this in the manner of brisk bibliography, without wasting any adjectives, no decorative *vir doctissimus* or the like. Louis XII's patronage of men of letters is described only in general, naming no names. Against this background, the two exceptions, the only scholars who are both named and warmly praised as learned in Latin and Greek, stand out very sharply. They are both Greeks: Demetrius Chalcondyles in Milan, and Seyssel's close and constant collaborator in translation, Janus Lascaris.[29] On one level, it is easy enough to see why. Italian humanists were at best condescending in their attitude to French culture; the Greeks were homeless refugees who could not afford such condescension, and indeed had often themselves suffered it from those same Italian humanists. In fact, long before any influx of Greek immigrants, Petrarch had identified the envious Greeks who had carped at Rome in Livy's day, with the envious 'Gauls' of his own day. For Seyssel, however, this alliance with Greeks was no mere rhetorical flourish of mutual consolation; it had very positive and specific result in his translations—which it is high time that we turned to.

Many of the peculiarities of these are already manifest in the first of them, Xenophon's *Anabasis*. We perhaps think of this work as the first Greek text that a schoolboy would meet (in the days when schoolboys met Greek texts). But that is an altogether post-romantic phenomenon. In the fifteenth century no one was interested in it. A military adventure story, involving Greeks and Persians in an Eastern setting, it had no relevance to the history of Rome, no influence on Latin literature, no appreciable philosophical content (the one possible excuse for such Greekness). But Greekness was just what Seyssel pursued. Justin's *Epitome* of Pompeius Trogus is the one history in Latin that concentrates on Eastern and Greek history: not till Book 43, the penultimate book, does it get around to founding Rome. Likewise, the books of Diodorus that Seyssel chose to translate deal with the successors of Alexander in Greece and the East, and with Agathocles of Syracuse, excluding any Roman history. Thucydides, obviously, is

---

[29] Seyssel, *Les Louenges* (n. 21 above), f. c vi[v]: '...et si en a fait venir d'Ytalie et de Grece, mesmement messire Jehan Lascari, noble homme de la cité de Constantinople et tressavant en lectres grecques et latines...et entretient au surplus en sa cité de Millan grant nombre d'aultres hommes excellens esdictes sciences et entre aultres maistres Demetrio de Grece, le plus scavant en lectres grecques que l'on sache au jourdhuy nulle part, et neantmoins bien bon latin'. See also the dedication to Henry VII printed below (Appendix A, f. 18[v]), probably written at about the same time.

about as Greek as one can be. The *Ecclesiastical History* of Eusebius–Rufinus is universal, and in any case different. So the only real exception is Appian, but even that is a qualified one. For the way that Appian organized his history has combined with the accidents of its survival to create a work in which Roman power is seen fragmented round the Mediterranean in the books on External Wars, and destroying itself in the books on Civil Wars. At any rate Seyssel's preface to this translation emphasizes the negative lessons to be learned: he has chosen Appian, he says, 'because of all Greek and Roman writers he is the one who has given the fullest and most detailed account of the good and bad deeds of the Romans, but above all of their dissensions, seditions and intestine or civil wars.'[30]

To what extent was it Lascaris's choices and interests that guided Seyssel? Perhaps considerably. Already back in 1493, Lascaris had inaugurated his courses *in gymnasio Florentino* with a protreptic for the study of Greek, which had differentiated itself from other examples of that rather well-worn genre precisely by giving the Greeks priority not just in the areas where they had always been allowed it—the various arts and sciences, especially philosophy—but also in the arts that Roman tradition had denied them and claimed as typically its own: military valour and imperial power.[31] Certainly Lascaris was a scholar of impressive range and level;[32] but Seyssel also had a mind of his own, and a *doctor utriusque iuris* would not be easily overawed by a literary scholar. More important, I suspect, was the fact that Lascaris was not just a scholar but, like Seyssel, a 'noble homme', albeit dispossessed of his country.[33] Congenial attitudes and converging points of view perhaps best explain their somewhat unexpected, but evidently successful, partnership.

In fact, Seyssel is generous in acknowledgement not only of Lascaris's linguistic help, but also of his initiatives in unearthing new Greek texts for him. So the *Anabasis* is introduced as a joyful find when they were browsing together in the king's library at Blois. As we saw, Lascaris's encouragement is portrayed as crucial in Seyssel's decision to tackle Thucydides. Nor was that their last joint effort. For though it has always been thought that the Thucydides was Seyssel's

---

[30] 'Appien Alexandrin est celui qui plus amplement et plus particulièrement a donné connaissance de tous leurs faits bons et mauvais, mais surtout de leurs dissentions, séditions et guerres intestines et civiles' in Poujol's edition of *La Monarchie* (n. 3 above), p. 85.

[31] See Anna Meschini, 'La prolusione fiorentina di Giano Laskaris' in *Miscellanea di studi in onore di Vittore Branca*, III, Florence, 1983, pp. 69–113.

[32] For new material and a useful update on previous studies see Anna [Meschini] Pontani, 'Per la biografia, le lettere, i codici, le versioni di Giano Lascaris' in *Dotti bizantini e libri greci nell'Italia del secolo XV*, ed. M. Cortesi, E. V. Maltese, Naples, 1992, pp. 363–433.

[33] Also it may not be irrelevant that in 1501 René 'le grand bâtard de Savoie', patron of Seyssel's father, married Anne Lascaris de Tende, 'dont les ancêtres avaient régné sur Byzance et sur Nicée, lors de la quatrième Croisade': M. Bruchet, *Marguerite d'Autriche*, Lille, 1927, p. 38.

last translation, and indeed so he himself intended, the British Library has the dedicatory (and only?) copy of another translation that seems never to have been noticed (MS Harley 4939). In a long preface to the new king Francis I, Seyssel explains that he had no sooner finished the Thucydides when Lascaris appeared all excited with two previously unheard-of books of Appian, on the Spanish and Hannibalic Wars. Seyssel was actually at this point thinking he might attend to his ecclesiastical career (he had been bishop of Marseilles for five years without so much as visiting it), and was plainly not keen to embark on yet more translation; but once Lascaris had made a Latin version for him, he felt he could not refuse. The book must have strayed from the French royal library rather early, or perhaps was never even presented to its dedicatee. At any rate, whereas Seyssel's other translations were gradually published from the royal exemplars between 1527 and 1559, this work remained unknown and unprinted; as indeed were those two books of Appian, generally speaking, until they were re-discovered and re-translated some forty years later.[34]

In this last case it is clear that the impulse came from Lascaris, even though Seyssel took pride in these direct imports from Greece, unknown to the Latins (and he also remarks that Livy's account of the Hannibalic War does not make Appian's redundant, provided you care about substance in history, rather than rhetoric, see below Appendix B, f. 8^r). But it is a different matter in the case of the Diodorus; there we are told that Lascaris found the text, but in response to a request by Seyssel, who was looking for some fuller account of Alexander's successors. And I am sure that this was true, for a reason that I think helps us to understand the whole nature of his translating activity, its language and audience, the context and tradition for which it was envisaged.

Why should Seyssel be interested in the successors of Alexander? Ever since stories began, successful heroes have tended to create a demand for what happened next—to the hero, or his sons, or his companions, or, occasionally, back a generation, as *Gargantua* followed *Pantagruel*. This was how all the great legends had unfolded into ever-wider cycles of literary romance, from the Knights of the Round Table, the knights of Charlemagne, and the various heroes of the

---

[34] Not quite unknown, for besides some copies of the Greek text, there are also a number of (Lascaris's?) Latin translation: MSS Paris, Bibliothèque nationale, lat. 5787, apparently a much corrected rough draft, pages lost at the end; lat. 9685, complete, incorporates not quite all the corrections and adds some; Vatican City, Bibliotheca Apostolica, Vat. lat. 2968, ff. 9^r–82^r, copied from the first Paris MS after its loss of pages, and at some point bound with a translation from Polybius ascribed to Lascaris (see Pontani, n. 32 above, p. 432); Naples, Biblioteca nazionale, V.G.8, from Parrhasius's library (not seen, but with same incipit); Florence, Biblioteca nazionale centrale, Magliab. XXIII.4 (also not seen) apparently has at least a partial translation, ascribed to Basilius Chalcondyles and dedicated to Leo X (P. O. Kristeller, *Iter Italicum,* I, Leiden, 1963, p. 120). It could be that Lascaris collaborated in, or completed, a version by Chalcondyles's son, who died in Rome aged twenty-four in 1514 (precisely when Seyssel was there), mourned by Parrhasius his brother-in-law (then also in Rome) as well as by Lascaris his teacher: see G. Laskaris, *Epigrammi greci*, ed. A. Meschini, Padua, 1976, no. 45.

Crusades. Alexander the Great had been a hero of romance for three and a half centuries. For what happened after his dramatic death, Latin accounts were meagre, mainly Orosius and his source Justin. In the vernacular, various entirely fictional sequels were invented, like the adventures of Perceforest. In this context, a detailed account of what really happened, direct from the Greek, would be quite a scoop.

One might object that poor Diodorus has suffered quite enough abuse over the centuries, without now ending up on the same shelf as Lancelot of the Lake. And indeed, I am not suggesting that for Seyssel there was no difference. On the contrary, in recommending Xenophon's *Anabasis* he says:

> Et d'autant sont plus les histoires à louer quant elles sont composees par gens veritables et saiges, qui ont la verité ensuyvie à leur povoir. Car au regard d'aucunes fables que soubz couleur d'histoire ont esté jadis par gens oysifz composees, mesmement en langaige francoys, comme sont les livres de la Table Ronde, de Tristan, de Lancelot, de Maglonne, d'Olivier de Castille et autres semblables, qui ne contiennent sinon menteries et choses impossibles, elles ne sont point aucunement à louer'.[35]

Similarly, a Spanish translator of Appian in 1522 warns the noble dedicatee Rodrigo de Mendoza that he will not here find 'the windy fictions of Esplandian or the froth of Amadis, nor the dark smoke and thick fog of Tirante, nor the vain and fantastical thunderings of Tristan or Lancelot...all of which, as Petrarch so well said, fill paper with dreams'.[36] The allusion is to Petrarch's *Trionfo d'amore* (80–2):

> Ecco quei che le carte empion di sogni,
> Tristano e Lancellotto e gli altri erranti,
> Ove conven che'l vulgo errante agogni

albeit tactfully without Petrarch's too wounding pun associating the nobility's favourite reading with the 'vulgo errante'. We meet the allusion again in 1527, when Jacques Colin inaugurated the publication of Seyssel's translations with the Thucydides. There he admonishes his 'tresillustre et treshaulte excellence des princes et a la treshonoree magnificence des seigneurs et nobles Francoys', presumed to be his readers:

> ... De là est, mes tresredoubtéz et mes trehonoréz seigneurs, que en lieu des Tristans, Girons et Lancelotz et aultres qui 'emplissent les papiers de songes', et ou plusieurs ont souvent mal colloqué les bonnes heures, vous avez par le benefice

[35] Claude de Seyssel, *Histoire du voyage que fist Cyrus a l'encontre du roy de Perse*, Paris, 1529, f. I'.

[36] *Los Triumphos de Apiano*, Valencia, 1522, sig. a iiii: 'No estan aqui las ficciones ventosas de Esplandian, ni las espumas de Amadis, ni los humos escuros y espessas nieblas de Tirante, ni los vanos tronidos y estruentos fantastigos de Tristan y Lançarote, ni los incantamientos mintrosos que en estos libros que he dicho y otros como ellos falsamente se leen. Los quales totos (como Petrarca muy bien dize), hinchen las cartas de suennos'.

du Roy non moins fructueux que delectable passetemps, à cognoistre quelz gens furent Pericles, Nycias, Antigonus, Lysimachus, Eumenes, Hannibal, Scipion et plusieurs aultres saiges et vaillans capitaines, dont les gestes memorables sont descriptz es volumes dessus mentionnez.[37]

In short, the ancient historians are not equated with the romances but, when translated into the vernacular, they are presented as a substitute for them, directed at the same audience. An audience not of scholars, but of princes and nobles and those that would be like them; who would scarcely, at this date, read any ancient oratory or philosophy or even poetry; who in fact would mostly not read at all, but listen, for entertainment. Jacques Colin, who undertook the publication of Seyssel's translations, was at the time employed as the king's 'lecteur', responsible for choosing appropriate books and reading them aloud to the king and his court.[38] For a long time now, ever since the late thirteenth century, this audience's preference had been for prose narratives. Great quantities of the old chansons de geste had been 'dérimés', translated into prose.[39] Hence in the vernacular the borderline between romance and history was bound to be fluid and doubtful.

This audience, and this tradition, explain several features of Seyssel's translations, large and small. On the small side, the fact that in all cases he divided the text into short chapters, each with a heading summarizing the content; and these headings are then gathered together into a table at the beginning. I don't recall any Latin translation of a Greek historian doing this, but it is a standard feature of medieval historiography and of prose romances; one reason is probably that it is a great help when reading aloud.

Secondly, (something which puzzled me a good deal at first), the fact that Seyssel did not himself publish a single one of his translations. It was not any objection to the printing-press as such, for he was quick to publish other things, both Latin and vernacular. But the ancient histories were all dedicated to the king not just as works of translation, but very literally as book presents, finely produced for use at court. Later, some more were made as presents for the Duke of Savoy. And a copy of the Xenophon in the British Library was sumptuously confected, with lots of pictures (again a feature of romances), as a thank-you present for Henry VII of England. So the translations are an integral part of Seyssel's life as a courtier, their rarity and exclusiveness are part of their value.

Also it follows that for this audience any scholarly fussing would be out of place and indeed *infra dig*. Seyssel not only knew no Greek, he takes the fact absolutely for granted without a word of lament or apology: of course a nobleman

---

[37] Seyssel, *L'Histoire* (n. 5 above), sig. ã[v].

[38] See the fine work of V.-L. Bourrilly, *Jacques Colin*, Paris, 1905.

[39] See G. Doutrepont, *Les Mises en proses des épopees et des romans chevaleresques du 14ᵉ au 16ᵉ siècle*, Bruxelles, 1939.

from North of the Alps did not know Greek. He was much more worried about his French.[40] French was not a scholar's language but it was, par excellence and not only in France, the language of gentleman's history and romance.

Perhaps the most important question is the effect of such an audience on Seyssel's choice of texts to translate. For it was not just that the Alexander romance might prompt an interest in its sequels. Consider more generally the many histories and romances centred on the Crusades, in the Latin kingdoms of Greece and the East. For many noble families these represented their most immediate heroic past, and made all manner of history of that area acceptable. Unlike the humanist scholars reared on Petrarchan ideals, such an audience could readily identify with Xenophon leading his 10,000 men through the treacherous mountains of Asia Minor trodden by so many Crusaders. Both the spirit and the geography could make sense to them. Probably, in spite of humanist influences, such audiences also existed in the princely courts south of the Alps; after all it was a count Matteo Maria Boiardo, steeped in the traditions of romance, who translated Herodotus and Nepos's *Lives of Foreign Generals* into Italian for Duke Ercole d'Este. In fact this Duke commissioned a whole series of vernacular translations of Greek historians, including some of which there were no Latin versions.

It may well be that Seyssel knew of such precedents. They are precedents also in that they were exclusive products, existing only in one or two luxury copies. We might note in particular Decembrio's Italian translation of Appian's *Civil Wars* made for Duke Ercole in 1472, which, unlike his Latin version, draws on Plutarch's *Life of Antony* to give the story a proper ending, just as Seyssel was to do. It was not beyond Lascaris to suggest just this solution quite independently; but, given the close Este links with France, it is equally possible that he or Seyssel knew of Decembrio's work, even if the only copy was the illuminated parchment one made for the Duke.[41] However, such an enterprise inevitably had a different meaning when associated with the royal court of France. The influx of Italian humanist writing and classical scholarship into France continued apace, and was in many ways decisive. But in fact the Greek historians continued to have a rather special status compared with other classical texts, one particularly

---

[40] See in his preface to Xenophon's *Anabasis* (n. 35 above), f. III^r: 'et considerez que je ne suis pas natif de France et n'y ay hanté le tout comprins que trois ans au plus...parquoy n'est pas à merveiller si je n'ay le langaige francoys bien familier', followed by some interesting reflections on how difficult it is 'de coucher en beau stille une matiere qu'il fault translater d'une langue en autre', hence translated classical histories are never 'en si plaisant langaige comme...les histoires de Froissart, les croniques des Roys et autres telles'.

[41] MS Modena, Biblioteca Estense, α k.3.18 [= ital. 164], see P. O. Kristeller, *Iter italicum*, I, Leiden, 1963, p. 374, and II, Leiden, 1967, pp. 542–3. Seyssel spent a week in Ferrara in May–June 1509 (see Caviglia, n. 6 above, p. 159), and the Appian translation may well not yet have been completed; Chavy (n. 7 above, and in his *Traducteurs d'autrefois*, Paris–Geneva, 1988, s.v. *Seyssel*, but cf. s.v. *Appian*), gives various earlier datings, but I do not see on what evidence.

linked to the monarchy, and I think this was in good part due to Seyssel. The publication of his translations, beginning in 1527, was almost official, an act of royal generosity. Between 1544 and 1551 Robert Estienne, royal typographer, employed his splendid Greek types known as 'les grecs du roi', to print a whole series of grand first editions of Greek historians in folio, texts that Aldus had ignored, including the Diodorus, Appian and Eusebius that Seyssel had translated.

Perhaps Seyssel can also help us to understand France's most famous translator, Amyot. Of course times had changed: Amyot was no nobleman, and he was an excellent Greek scholar. But he too knew how to win favour at court. Plutarch was a banner under which all humanisms, Greek and Roman, historical and philosophical, could unite. But Amyot did not begin with Plutarch. Before that, he had translated Diodorus, the books preceding Seyssel's, including the account of Alexander; and earlier still, in 1547, another fine tale of eastern adventure, the *Histoire aethiopique* of Heliodorus. Amyot's 'Proesme du trans-lateur' presents us with a scholarly discussion of the nature and style of the work and apologies that his emendations of the Greek text may not always have been correct, not without a nonchalant reference to Politian's *Miscellanea*. Given this, he can of course afford to take the stern polemic of previous translators against the romances and stand it on its head. The text he is so learnedly translating is after all a 'fabuleuse histoire', a fiction, a romance. You might advise adults 'de ne s'amuser à lire sans jugement toutes sortes de livres fabuleux, de peur que leurs entendements ne s'accoutument petit à petit à aymer mensonge'; but we need relaxation, and while history can be pleasingly varied, its unvarnished truth can be a mite austere for the purpose. Anyway he cannot be blamed, he concludes in verse,

> Car si tu dis que telz songes escrire
> n'estoit besoing, ny de Grec les traduire

no one is forcing you to read them—an elegant, if by now rather easy, calling of Petrarch's bluff.[42]

Nonetheless, four years later, in 1551, a teacher of Greek in Paris offered Book I of Heliodorus to his pupils as a model of how to write history: exciting narrative, vivid descriptions, stirring speeches, it is all there. The truth of Heliodorus's account, he admits, is less clear; but then Greeks always were rather lax on this score, consider Herodotus.[43] And if Heliodorus can be history, why not

---

[42] *L'Histoire Aethiopique de Heliodorus... Nouvellement traduite de Grec en Françoys*, Paris, 1547, sig. aii[r]: 'Mais toutesfois encores a il semblé a quelques hommes de bon jugement, que la verité d'icelle [sc. histoire] estoit un petit trop austère pour suffisament delecter.'

[43] *Heliodori Aethiopicarum historiarum liber primus, Renato Guillonio interprete*, Chr. Wechel, Paris, 1552; the plain Greek text designed to accompany it has the date 1551. Both are rather rare: I know of copies at Besançon (with student notes), at the Bibliothèque Mazarine in Paris and (Greek only? not seen) at the Biblioteca Angelica in Rome. Guillon's preface borrows liberally from that of Vincentius Obsopoeus prefixed

Appian as romance? The catalogue of the Bibliothèque nationale lists under Appian an *Epistre de Cleriande la romayne a Reginus son concitoien*, by one Macé de Villebresme, 'l'ung des gentilhommes de la chambre du roy'. He was in fact a contemporary and fellow-courtier of Seyssel.[44] The work is a poem in the manner of Ovid's *Heroides*; but the situation is indeed drawn from Appian, a fine escape story from the Civil Wars (IV, 40). Unfortunately, in Appian's narrative Reginus's heroic wife is not named. Today's readers of Appian need no telling that, whatever her name was, it was not 'Cleriande'. But then we are only the latest of Appian's audiences.

---

to the *editio princeps* of the Greek text (Basel, 1534): he may have found it difficult to believe that Amyot, a vernacular translator, could know better than Obsopoeus.

[44] See K. Chesney, ed., *Oeuvres poétiques de Guillaume Crétin*, Paris, 1932, pp. xxi–xxii, 405–6.

APPENDIX

I print here two unpublished prefaces by Seyssel, though the second, especially, cries out for historical commentary that I am not competent to give.

In editing these texts I have benefited from the very kind, and essential, help of M. Pierre Petitmengin, who both alerted me to problems in my reading and punctuation of the texts and supplied me with *L'Édition des textes anciens XVIe–XVIIIe siècle* by J.-F. Belhoste *et al.*, 2nd edn, Paris, 1993, whose guidelines I have generally followed. Accordingly I have altered punctuation, distinguished i and j and introduced inverted commas and a limited range of accents as seemed helpful for the reader, whose interest is more likely to be in Seyssel's thought than in his (or his copyist's) scribal habits; but I have left the spelling (except obvious scribal slips), as recorded in the notes even when it seemed rather idiosyncratic: for instance 'prinpce' for 'prince', which Seyssel must have liked since it is found in presentation copies made for him by different scribes. Seyssel composed chapter headings for the historical texts, but not for his own prefaces: the English section headings here are invented by me to facilitate reading, nothing corresponds to them in the manuscripts. In the Appian preface there are some illuminated paragraph markers, and I have indicated where these occur by capital letters.

I have not attempted a palaeographical description of the manuscripts, but just noted features that reveal something of the audience and use that Seyssel envisaged for his translations. The Harley manuscript has only the illustrations noted, the Royal one is lavishly illustrated with half-page pictures of higher quality, but in both cases the authorship or provenance has yet to be properly investigated. I am most grateful to Miss J. M. Backhouse of the British Library for her advice. For the Royal manuscript and its relatives (MSS Paris, Bibliothèque nationale, fr. 701 and 702) see now F. Avril and N. Reynaud, *Les Manuscrits à peintures en France 1440–1520*, Paris, 1993, p. 345 (in fact, however, the copy for Henry VII must have preceded that for Charles of Savoy, as emerges from both prefaces).

A

Preface for a copy of Seyssel's translation of Xenophon's *Anabasis*: MS London, British Library, Royal 19.C. VI, c. 1506.[45]

This text is in fact only partly unpublished. It was written to present not the Xenophon translation as such, but this particular copy of it made for Henry VII

---

[45] Fully described (but misdated) in *Catalogue of Western Manuscripts in the Old Royal and King's Collections*, II, London, 1921, pp. 334–5.

of England, purportedly as a thank-you for hospitality on Seyssel's visit there in 1506. It nicely illustrates the function of these translations as courtly gifts, not intended for publication: for Seyssel's portrayal of Henry VII here is interesting and quite possibly sincere, but plainly for export only (note, in the last paragraph, '...a mon advis vous estes le prinpce sur la terre qui autant ou plus avez monstré par experience d'avoir des qualités requises pour regner...', etc.). Seyssel later recycled the first, more general, part of the preface in a presentation copy made for Charles of Savoy (MS Paris, Bibliothèque nationale, fr. 701); this (or a draft of it) happened to be used for the *editio princeps* of 1529, so it is found there and in later reprints. Nonetheless, it seems sensible to print the whole text as it was originally written for Henry VII.

Preliminaries

1^r–9^r Table of contents, giving chapter-summaries.

9^v A full-page picture of Louis XII receiving the book from Seyssel, is followed (10^r–15^r) by Seyssel's preface dedicating the work to Louis XII.

15^v, 16^r and an extra, ruled but unnumbered, page in between are blank.

16^v Full-page picture of the arms of England with Seyssel's arms in the border below, and in between the verses:

> Au plus saige prinpce qui soit sur terre
> Henry sixieme[46] regnant en Angleterre
> Claude de Seissel humblement fait present
> de ceste histoire tresrere au temps present.

17^r Half-page picture of Seyssel presenting his book to Henry VII, followed by the text of the Prologue:

> Prologue de messire Claude de Seyssel translateur de ce present livre au trespuissant et tressaige Roy d'Angleterre Henry vi^e de ce nom.

(Human understanding can only be fulfilled in study; but it is impossible to study all branches of learning)

Combien que l'entendement humain par sa nature et excellence soit capable de toutes sciences et intelligences humaines, treshault, tresexcellent et trespuissant prinpce, toutesfoys selon l'opinion d'Aristote et des Peripatetiques est besoing que par art et exercitacion il les apreigne; et mesme l'opinion de Platon et de ses suivans, qui ont dit que l'esprit humain que nous apellons l'ame[47] dés sa /17^v/

---

[46] I think the mistake is Seyssel's; it is repeated below. The MS seems to have 'sixiem', which perhaps should remain to represent a disyllable: the lines are hendecasyllables provided that final 'e's are pronounced, except before vowel or h.

[47] arme MS

creation en sa simple nature est parfaictement rempli de toutes lesdites sciences et intelligences, ne differe point en effect, quant à cecy, de la precedente, car ilz[48] ne nient point que pour l'indisposicion et empeschement des organes corporelz ne soit besoing pour luy en rendre la souvenance, qu'il s'exercite et travaille par le moyen desdites organes es chouses dont il desire avoir la cognoissance. Toutesfoys pour la multitude et profondité desdites sciences et pour la debilité des corps humains, est impossible que ung seul suppos<t> (tant soit bien composé et organizé de corps et douhé d'entendement pour peine qu'il saiche ne puisse prendre), soit parfaict, je ne diray pas en toutes sciences, mais à peine en une seule. Et non pourtant en y a de ceulx qui par continuacion d'estude et excellence d'engin ont bien grande cognoissance en plusieurs d'icelles sciences. Lesquelz d'autant sont plus à louer et priser, qu'ilz approchent plus à la perfection de leur esprit. À laquelle toutesvoyes nul ne peult pervenir en ceste vie mortelle, qui est la raison pour laquelle naturellement devons apeter la immortalité, affin de pervenir à la perfection de nostredit esprit, laquelle ne povons avoir sans la fruition de l'essence divine, comme dit le psalmiste (XVI 15), 'saciabor cum apparuerit gloria tua'.

(We should choose the study most suited to our abilities, but many choose what will give worldly advancement)
Considerant adonc nostre imbecilité, ne debvons pas entreprendre de plus scavoir que ne povons aprehender et encores debvons avoir regard de ne vouloir vacquer à l'aprehension de tant de chouses diverses qui engendrent confusion en nostre entendement. Comme font plusieurs qui de chascune chouse veulent scavoir ung peu et de tout ne scavent[49] rien. Mais puis que avons le chois et que cognoissons ne povoir tout embrasser, la discretion que l'on dit mere des vertuz nous doibt enseigner de nous appliquer à celle des sciences de laquelle sommes[50] plus capables, et par le moyen de laquelle povons pervenir à plus grande perfection /18ʳ/ d'entendement. Toutesfois l'on[51] voit communement que la plus part des hommes mortelz hebetés par la pesanteur du corps terrien et abusez aux chouses inferieures, applicquent tout leur entendement aux ars et sciences, desquelles ilz pensent plus amander en biens temporelz. Et quant ilz sont en jeune aage lorsqu'ilz ont l'esprit plus prompt et plus esveillé, ceulx qui devroyent les adresser aux vertuz morales et theologales, les font excerciter es ars mecaniques ou sciences questuaires, desquelles encores bien souvent n'apreignent pas tant qu'ilz en puissent user selon droiture, mais leur souffit en scavoir assez pour acquerir dignités et richesses.

[48] il MS
[49] scevent MS
[50] summes MS
[51] en MS

(Responsibility of kings for encouragement of true learning; the universities)
Et pour ce que le plus facile moyen de ce faire est d'avoir la grace et familarité
des grans prinpces et de ceulx qui ont le moyen d'en donner largement, et de
faire soudainement ung homme de pouvre riche et de abject honnoré, ceulx qui
à grans biens veulent pervenir en ce monde, se perforcent d'aprendre les chouses
que telz prinpces desirent scavoir ou esquelles ilz se delectent. Et quant les
prinpces sont si bons et si acomplis qu'ilz ayment toutes vertuz et desirent avoir
science des chouses convenables à leur estat, bien heureux sont leurs royaulmes,
pais et subjetz; car par ce moyen ilz habondent de toutes gens vertueulx et
scavans, comme l'on a veu à Romme, que du temps de Cesar et de Auguste et
d'aulcuns aultres bons empereurs tant de grans poetes et gens excellans en toutes
sciences ont esté, que jamais despuis n'en a l'on trouvé de telz; et jacoit[52] ce que
les prinpces des quartiers de pardeça, et presque tous les aultres despuis la ruine
et decadence de l'empire Romain, ne se soient gueres delectés aux lettres,
neantmoings plusieurs en y a eu, lesquelz voulentiers en eussent sceu, et aymoient
ceulx qui en scavoient, et les nourrissoyent et avançoyent, comme ont faict les
roys de France anciennement, qui ont assemblé moult grand nombre de gens /18ᵛ/
de science à Paris et ailleurs en leur royaulme, tant pour endoctriner les aultres
que pour jugier des differens d'entre les subjectz. Aussi ont fait plusieurs roys
d'Angleterre vos predecesseurs, sire, qui ont entretenu les universités qui encores
sont en vostre royaulme, honnoré et exaulcé les grans et scavens hommes, tant
en l'eglise que autrement. Qui a esté la cause que desditz pais et royaulmes sont
sortis tresexcellans personnaiges en toutes sciences.

(Louis XII and learning; Lascaris and the Xenophon translation)
Et là ou iceulx princes n'ont eu le scavoir pour entendre la lengue latine, ont quis
de faire translater plusieurs beaulx livres de lengaige latin en leur lengaige
maternel, et entre aultres de nostre temps le roy de France Loys xiiᵉ de ce nom,
vostre bon frere et allié et mon bon seigneur et maistre, a prins beaucoup de
peine pour avoir grand nombre de livres en toutes facultés et de tous quartiers.
Si en a faict ung tresnoble amas en une librairie qu'il a dressee en son chasteau
de Bloys. Et pareillement a quis et retiré de tous coustés gens excellens en toutes
sciences, lesquelz il entretient tant en divers lieulx de sondit royaulme que en sa
cité et duché de Millan, et mesmement en son université de Pavie qui est
aujourduy à ceste cause l'une des plus renommees que l'on saiche; et pour ce que
des livres qui sont en latin, mesmement contenans histoires qui est la chouse plus
convenable à luy et à tous prinpces, aujourduy il en avoit desjà grande foison, il
a bien taché d'en recouvrer des grecz et qui encores n'ont point esté translatés.
A ceste cause a dés long temps retiré en son service ung gentilhomme de

---

[52] iasoit MS

tresnoble et ancienne maison de Constantinople, lequel fuiant la cruaulté du Turch ennemy de nostre foy s'en estoit venu es quartiers d'Italie, et pour la grandeur et singularité de sa science tant en lengue grecque que latine, avoit esté par aulcun temps recuilly par certains grans personnaiges dudit pais; et se nomme messire Jehan Lascary, /19ʳ/ lequel pour satisfaire au desir dudit seigneur, et aussi à ma requeste, en cerchant et remuant plusieurs divers livres en lengaige gregeois, qui estoient en ladite librairie, trouva l'histoire que Xenophon le grant philosophe d'Athenes escript du voyage de Cyrus en Perse, que je desiroye dés long temps trouver, pourtant que j'avoye leu plusieurs livres d'histoires auctentiques qui en faisoyent mention; et aprés qu'il m'eut narré le contenu en ladite histoire, deliberames per ensemble la translater, luy de grec en latin et moy de latin en francoys, pour aprés en faire present audit seigneur, esperant qu'il luy seroit tres agreable, comme à la verité fut despuis; et tellement que pour la singularité du livre luy a semblé qu'il ne debvoit point estre divulgué, ains comme chouse tres rere estre communiqué à prinpces et grands personnaiges tant seulement; aussi a il bien voulu avoir une chouse que nul autre vivant ne vit jamais en ce lengaige françoys.[53]

(Seyssel's stay at Henry's court; reasons for offering him the Xenophon)
Mais dernierement estant de par ledit seigneur devers vostre royale maiesté et ayant veu vostre librairie, que je trouvay tresbelle et tresbien acoustree, entendant aussi que prenez grand recreation et passe temps à lire et ouyr histoires et aultres chouses apartenant à ung noble et saige prinpce, deliberay pour recognoissance en partie des grans honneurs et privees bonnes chieres que de vostre grace m'avez faict, vous faire present de ladite histoire, non aiant aultre chouse par laquelle vous puisse monstrer ne declairer la cognoissance que j'avoye de l'humain recueil et courtois traictement que m'avez faict. Esperant aussi que ledit present vous seroit agreable non point pour le lengaige, qui est rude, mais pour la matiere en soy, qui est à mon advis digne d'estre leue et entendue autant que histoire que j'aye veu. Car elle est toute plaine d'enseignemens et ung entendement eslevé comme est le vostre notera par le discours de ladite histoire presque autant de /19ᵛ/ bonnes sentences qu'il y a de parolles; aussi fut elle faicte par main d'ung des plus singuliers ouvriers que jamais fut.

(Henry's qualities as a ruler; why the Xenophon is bound to please him)
Et d'autant plus me suis persuadé qu'elle vous agreera, que à mon advis vous estes le prinpce sur la terre qui autant ou plus avez monstré par experience d'avoir des qualités requises pour regner. Et aussi de scavoir comme il fault conduire non pas tant seulement une armee, mais ung grand royaulme, soit en

---

[53] Thus far, with a few necessary changes, re-used for the dedication to Charles of Savoy.

paix ou en guerre. Par quoy ayant la plus part des enseignemens et cautelles que l'en peut noter par le discours dudit livre pratiqué et experimenté, il vous sera trop plus facile de les comprehendre que à nul aultre. Et à tout le moings pour la nouvelleté de la translation et l'antiquité de l'istoire ne peut estre que n'y pregnez quelque plaisir. Et finablement pour rarité du livre, dont nul n'a la coppie que ledit roy trescrestien et vous. Si vous supplie tres humblement, sire, que vueilles prendre en gré le present tel qu'il est, ayant regard au vouloir de celuy qui le faict, lequel sans point de faulte desire de tout son cueur vous pouvoir faire quelque service plus aggreable. Car vous l'y avez obligé grandement.

B

Preface to Seyssel's translation of Appian's *Iberica* and *Hannibalica*, early 1515: MS London, British Library, Harleian 4939.

This preface is wholly new and accompanies the equally unpublished translation of Appian's *Iberica* and *Hannibalica*. It was written soon after the accession of Francis I, so it is contemporary with the *Monarchie* and would deserve consideration in the light of that.

Brief Description

95 ff.; f. 1, with a full-page picture of Christ enthroned, does not belong to this book.

2^r A table of contents, giving quite full chapter summaries and relevant folio numbers, under the titles:

Cy commence la table de Appian Alexandrin des guerres des Romains en Espagne, translatee de grec en latin par messire Jehan Lascary et de latin en françois par messire Claude de Seyssel, evesque de Marseille.

and 4^v

Cy finit la table du premier livre de Appian Alexandrin des guerres d'Espagne. Et commence celle du second des gestes de Annibal en Italie.

This ends with a similar colophon on 5^v; 6^r is blank. On 6^v there is a full-page picture of angels holding the arms of Francis I with his motto 'nutrisco et exting<u>o'. The prologue begins on 7^r, under a half-page picture of Seyssel presenting his book to Francis I with attendant courtiers, and inside a richly ornamented frame, with the arms of Seyssel at the bottom.

The translation begins on 13^r, framed in another gold and painted border with the arms of Seyssel at the bottom, a half-page picture of siege and general carnage, and the rubricated title:

S'ensuit l'istoire de Appian Alexandrin des guerres des romains en espaigne, translatee de grec en latin par messire Jehan Lascary, et de latin en françois par messire Claude de Seyssel, evesque de Marseille.

Illuminated initials and paragraph-markers, rubricated summaries for each chapter and marginal notabilia guide the reader through the text. There are also original rubricated folio numbers. The *Iberica* end on 63ᵛ and the *Hannibalica* begin on the same page with an extra large initial. The text ends with a simple colophon on 95ʳ.

> Proheme de messire Claude de Seyssel, evesque de Marseille, en la translation de deux livres de l'histoire romaine de Appian Alexandrin nouvellement trouvéz, addressé au trescrestien roy de France François, premier de ce nom.

(Seyssel had intended to stop translating)

J'avoie proposé, trescrestien et tresheureux roy, ne me exerciter plus à la translation des livres latins en françois, tant par ce qu'il me sembloit non estre ormais convenable à mon eage et moings /7ᵛ/ à mon estat et profession, et mesmes aiant diverti ma fantasie à aultres estudes et exercices plus speculatifs et de plus grande importance, lesquelz sont du tout discrepans à telz ouvraiges, qui requierent l'homme oisif.[54] Et aussi me sembloit avoir faict mon chief d'oeuvre en la translation de l'histoire de Thucydides, et ne pouvoir plus faire chose en ce mestier que l'on peut gueres estimer aprés celle-la, ainsi que j'ay protesté au proheme de la translation d'iceluy.

(Lascaris brings him two new books of Appian)

Mais est advenu, moy estant à Romme ceste annee de par feu de bonne memoire le roy Loys xiiᵉ de ce nom, vostre predecesseur, devers nostre sainct pere pape Leon xᵉ de ce nom, que messire Jehan Lascary, lequel s'est moult travaillé en plusieurs aultres translations que j'ay faictes audit feu roy, m'avertit avoir trouvé en la librairie dudit sainct pere deux livres de l'histoire romaine de Appian Alixandrin, qui n'estoient gueres grans et ne se trouvoient en latin; assavoir le premier des guerres que eurent les Romains et les Cartaginois en Espagne, et le second de celles qu'ilz eurent en Italie du temps que Annibal y fut. Dont considerant le plaisir que ledit feu roy avoit prins aux aultres livres dudit Appian que j'ay translatéz, me pensay que pour rendre toute l'histoire dudit aucteur parfaicte, ne debvoie laisser ces deux livres. Si priay ledit Lascary qu'il les me voulsit translater en latin, ce qu'il fit tresvoluntiers pour le desir qu'il a tousjours eu de faire chose agreable audit feu roy.[55]

---

[54] Probably his *Explanatio moralis* on Luke's gospel, completed over the period 1514–18 and finally published as *Tractatus de triplici statu viatoris*, Turin, 1518.

[55] See n. 34 above.

(Worth translating even though Livy covers the same ground)
Mais depuis que je veiz ladite translation, fuz encores en doubte de la reduire en françois, pour ce que lesdites histoires me semblerent trop sommeres et abregees, saichant que on les trouvoit assez plus amplement couchees et en /8ʳ/ plus hault stille et plus difus mesmement en Tite-Live, qui est assez commun et familier; et par ainsi que l'on ne feroit pas grande estime de cestes-cy ainsi abregees. Toutesfois, aprés que j'euz tout consideré, me sembla ne debvoir frustrer ledit Lascary de ses labeurs, ne ledit seigneur roy defrauder de son intention. Et d'autant moings que, à bien prendre lesdits deux livres tout ainsi abregéz comme ilz sont, contiennent neantmoings les deux parties principales pour lesquelles l'histoire a esté premierement trouvee, assavoir la cognoissance des choses passees et l'enseignement pour celles qui sont advenir. Car la tierce partie, que est l'elegance du stille et l'agencement du lengaige, concerne plus l'art oratoire que l'histoire. Pour raison de quoy ceulx qui desirent avoir cognoissance de plusieurs choses, et qui appliquent plus leur entendement à la substance de l'escripture que à la lettre ne au lengaige, ayment trop mieulx l'abregé des histoires, pourveu qu'il ne soit par trop megre et troussé, qu'ilz ne font le long narré; ainsi que l'on voit par experience de l'abregé que a faict Justin de l'histoire de Trogue Pompee. Lequel abregé a esté trouvé si bon par ceulx qui sont venus aprés que l'on n'a plus tenu compte de ladite histoire estendue, combien qu'elle fust en beau et elegant stille, de sorte que les exemplaires en ont du tout esté perduz et y a desja bien long temps que l'on n'en treuve plus. Aussi à la verité, esdits deux livres de Appian en peu d'escripture l'on trouvera couchéz tous les points et passages de l'histoire qui sont à noter pour la substance d'icelle, et pour donner plusieurs grans et beaux enseignemens à tous prinpces et chiefs de guerre, tant pour l'art militaire que pour la conduicte des estatz.

(Portrayal of two republics, Carthage and Rome, and Rome's rise to power)
Car, premierement, par ladite histoire nous sont representéz /8ᵛ/ deux empires populaires, assavoir celuy des Romains et celuy des Cartaginois. Lesquelz de bien petite chose sont parvenuz à telle grandeur que, s'ilz se fussent acordéz ensemble, bien aiseement eussent peu dominer tout le monde. Et en tout evenement celuy des Romains, qui eut la victoire sur l'aultre, demoura par ce moien si grant et si puissant qu'il subjuga et destruisit la pluspart des grans roix, prinpces et peuples renomméz de la terre habitable, et mit les aultres en grant crainte et dangier de leurs estatz, sans avoir la pluspart du temps grant regart à raison ne à droicture, ne encores à plaisir et service que leur eussent esté faictz par aucuns d'iceulx, mais usant bien souvent de toutes tromperies, cruaultéz, violences et desloiaultéz, comme ceulx qui ne tendoient principalement à aultre fin que à l'acroissement

de leur empire et à eulx enrichir en particulier.[56] Ce qu'ilz firent en bien peu de temps, aprés qu'ilz eurent vaincu lesdits Cartaginois, jusques à ce qu'ilz obtindrent la monarchie du monde, comme dit est; tant par leur sens, conduite, vertu et cautelle, comme aussi par la pusilanimité ou inadvertence desdits prinpces et peuples qui furent de celuy temps. Lesquelz du commencement les laisserent acroistre petit à petit, mesprisant et contempnant leur naissance et debile puissance en telle sorte que aprés, quant ilz apperceurent leur grandeur, n'y peurent remedier, ce qu'ilz eussent du commencement faict bien aiseement. Qui est ung bel enseignement et exemple à tous grans roys et prinpces pour estre advertiz de penser et avoir regard aux estats populaires qu'ilz voient croistre autour d'eulx, d'auctorité, de force, de pais, de richesses, d'ambition et de convoitise. Car à bien considerer la naissance et le progres dudit estat des Romains, l'on en a veu depuis assez, et voit-on tous /9ʳ/ les jours en diverses regions, de trop plus grans et mieulx fondéz que n'estoit celuy du commencement ne encores long temps aprés, dont par raison sont beaucop plus à craindre.[57]

(Even the best republic acts only out of self-interest)

ET D'AUTANT encore plus que, entre tous les aultres estatz populaires dont il est memoire, celuy des Romains a esté le mieulx reglé et policié, et le plus raisonnable et tolerable, pourtant qu'il participoit de la monarchie par la puissance et auctorité grande que avoient leurs principaulx chiefz et gouverneurs, assavoir leurs consulz; et de l'aristocratie, qui est l'estat des gens sages et esleuz, pour la souveraine auctorité que avoit le senat, lequel estoit continnuellement garny de grans notables et vertueux personnaiges acompliz de toutes vertuz et sciences. Et si usoit de si bonnes loix et disciplines que encores aujourduy la pluspart du monde les ensuit et allegue pour les meilleurs et plus civiles que l'on saiche. Dont, si ce nonobstant l'on trouve—par le recit de leurs histoires mesmes, et par le tesmoignage des plus grans personaiges d'entre eulx, comme de Cicero, tant en ses oraisons que en ses epistres et aultres traictéz—que leurs chiefs de guerre et aultres officiers, et encores le senat ensemble tout le peuple, ont souvent usé de tous moiens incivilz, iniques, inhumains et desraisonnables pour leur convoitise et ambition, trop plus sont à craindre les estatz populaires qui n'ont loix, ordonnances ne statuz, si non à leur proffit, et ne sont gouvernéz par gens vertueux et raisonnables, ne ont aucun estude ne exercice de vertu sinon l'art

---

[56] The Spanish campaigns of Licinius Lucullus and Galba in 151/0 BC (Appian, *Iberica*, 51–5, 59–60) are notable examples of 'toutes tromperies, cruaultéz' etc. largely for the sake of personal gain. But Seyssel generalizes what Appian censures as individual behaviour unworthy of Romans. See also *Iberica*, 100.

[57] The subtext to this and the following disquisition on 'estats populaires' is perhaps most likely the rise of the Swiss cantons. Seyssel was employed on several tricky and largely unsuccessful negotiations with them; their independence and expansion since 1499 and major role in wiping out the French conquests in Italy in 1512–13 must have seemed to him to bode ill. They got their come-uppance at Marignano (September 1515), but this preface must have been written earlier, or we would certainly have an allusion to it.

militaire, dont ilz usent indiscremment et à tous propos sans avoir regard fors à leur proffit particulier.

(A danger to all monarchies)
ET SI n'est possible prendre seureté es promesses et traictéz de telz estatz qui sont subgetz /9ᵛ/ à la pure et absolue volunté d'ung peuple rude, incivil et voluntaire, qui de sa nature est ennemy des prinpces, des nobles, des riches et de tous ceulx qui ont sens et auctorité; et au surplus n'est le plus souvent capable de verité et de raison, ains est enclin à toute violence, vilennie et convoitise, ainsi que l'on peut appercevoir par la presente histoire de l'estat des Cartaginois, et par aultres de celuy des Atheniens. Parquoy est chose tresdangereuse à tous prinpces de permettre telz estatz populaires eslever et acroistre autour d'eulx, s'ilz ne voient eulx povoir bien asseurer de leur amitié, car il y peut avoir dangier de leurs estatz et monarchies, ainsi que, oultre l'exemple des Romains dont nous parlons, l'on a veu de plusieurs aultres peuples et nations, que pour semblables occasions ont en divers temps occupé la plus grande partie de l'Europe et de l'Asie, comme les Gaulz[58], les Grecz, les Gotz et aultres nations barbares; et de fresche memoire les Turcz et les Sarrasins, encores que aucuns d'eulx aient aprés faict roys et tenu forme de monarchie.

(Philip of Macedon prevented growth of Greek republics and so made possible Alexander's unrivalled success)
Considerant lesquelles choses, les prinpces sages et aviséz qui voient telz estatz trop elever autour d'eulx et ne se povoir asseurer d'eulx par bonne et entiere amitié, doibvent tacher d'eulx asseurer par aultres moiens, ainsi que fit jadis le roy Philippe de Macedoine. Lequel, voiant l'estat populaire de plusieurs cités de Grece venir à telle grandeur et puissance, depuis la victoire qu'ilz eurent contre les Persiens, que si on ne les rabaissoit, luy et les aultres prinpces leurs voisins viendroient du tout en leur subjection, et seroient par eulx oppresséz et malmenéz, comme desja estoient, tint telz moiens envers eulx qu'il les remit presque à sa subiection ou à tout le moings les affoiblit, /10ʳ/ de sorte que Alixandre son filz le fit aprés bien aiseement. Et jacoit ce que, en ce faisant, il usast de plusieurs cautelles et tromperies qui ne sont jamais à louer mesmement à ung roy, TOUTESFOIZ, aiant à besoigner avec gens qui usoient envers luy et tous aultres de telz artz et malices, faict aucunement à excuser; car il n'estoit question si non qui en scauroit mieulx jouer. Et s'il eut failly à ce faire, il ne seroit aucune memoire du plus vaillant, du plus heureux et du plus puissant prince que jamais fut sur la terre, assavoir du grant Alixandre, ne de plusieurs aultres grans et

[58] Gaulx MS

vertueux roys qui luy succederent, dont la renommee demourra tant que le monde durera.

(A monarch should not be advised to engage in deceit, but he should guard against it)
Et si ne doibt l'on pourtant à mon advis conseiller ne persuader à homme vivant, mesmement à ung grant prinpce, de user de aucune tromperie et desloiauté envers personne qui vive, mais tresbien de soy garder d'estre deceu ne engigné, et au remenant preveoir de loing les choses qui peulent pour l'avenir redonder à la ruyne, honte et dommaige de son estat et y pourvoir par amitié et alliance ou par aultres moiens, de sorte qu'il mette son estat en seureté. Et c'est assez quant à ce point.

(Military discipline)
L'ON TROUVE pareillement esdits deux livres de Appian combien vault la discipline militaire au faict des armes et de la guerre, et aussi le sens et la conduite d'ung bon chief, par plusieurs faictz vertueux et cauteleux d'aucuns empereurs et chiefs de guerre, tant des Romains que des aultres qui sont nomméz en icelle histoire, et principalement de trois, assavoir de Viriatus,[59] de Annibal[60] et sur tous de Scipion Affrican;[61] lequel par ses sens, vertu et conduite, avec le mesmes exercite qui avoit souvent esté veincu soubz la /10ᵛ/ conduite des aultres empereurs et ducz romains qui les avoient gouvernéz et conduitz sans ordre ne discipline suffisante, veinquit aprés les mesmes ennemis qui les avoient au paravant veincus, principalement pour les avoir reduitz à la vraie discipline; qui est donner clerement à cognoistre que la bonne conducte et discipline des chiefs est plus cause de la victoire que la force et le nombre des souldars. Et a l'on veu souvent et de fresche memoire que—quant les chiefz ne sont obeiz ou ne veulent user de leur auctorité à faire garder l'ordre et la police et discipline, et que les gens de bien ne sont estiméz et remuneréz selon leurs vertuz et merites, et les laches et meschans puniz et chastiéz selon leur deserte—l'audace et licence croit aux mauvais, et les bons perdent le couraige, dont s'en ensuivent tous desordres et inconveniens, là ou gardant la police et discipline adviendroit tout le contraire. Car les mauvais perdroient l'audace, et aux bons croistroit le cueur, dont toutes bonnes choses s'en ensuivent; tant au faict de la guerre pour le combat (car trop plus sont vaillans et bons combatans et tiennent meilleur ordre et par ce moien sont plus crains et estiméz de leurs ennemis, comme aussi au faict de la police, pour vivre entre les amis et subjectz sans reprehension et sans querelle. Qui est

---

[59] *Iberica*, 61–75.
[60] *Hannibalica*, 20–6.
[61] I.e. Aemilianus at Numantia in 134/3 BC: *Iberica*, 84–6.

la principale cause de les faire aimer, là ou vivant mal ilz sont haiz, dont il advient qu'ilz ne peuvent prendre fiance aux amis et subjectz, mesmement nouvellement conquis, ains saichant estre haiz d'eulx, les creignent quant il survient quelque affaire autant que les propres ennemis. Et à ceste cause sont constraintz quelquefoiz abandonner à bien petite occasion les pais et provinces qu'ilz ont conquis à grans coustz, dangiers et labeurs, qui redonde aprés à grant honte et /11ʳ/ meschief, non pas à eulx seulement, mais à leurs princes et seigneurs.

(Discipline and morale)
UNG AULTRE enseignement de grande vertu et constance peuvent aprendre tous princes et gouverneurs de gros estatz à ce que fit le senat romain quant il refusa de rachapter les prisonniers que Annibal avoit prins au petit camp des Romains aprés la bataille de Cannes.[62] Car combien que par la perte que le peuple et empire romain avoit faicte en ladite bataille et aux deux aultres precedentes, ilz fussent si affoibliz mesmement de bons combatans qu'ilz n'estoient plus pour resister aux champs à leurs ennemis, ne à peine pour deffendre leur cité, et que les parens et amis qui estoient citoiens de Romme de tous estatz fissent toute instance d'obtenir dudit senat permission et licence de rachapter lesdits prisonniers de leurs propres deniers, ne volut toutesfois le permettre, ains ayma mieulx perdre ung tel nombre de bons citoiens, tous gens de guerre, en tel besoing et dangier, que de relaxer la discipline et severité acoustumee; tant pour non monstrer aux ennemis avoir perdu le cueur, comme pour non donner mauvais exemple et trop grande confiance de misericorde aux aultres citoiens et gens de guerre, qui restoient de leur party. Qui est une chose à mon advis à quoy tous princes magnanimes doibvent bien prendre exemple, de ne perdre pour affaire que leur vienne le cueur, ne faire ou consentir chose qui soit derrogante à leur honneur et reputation. Car si comme l'on doibt tenir à legiereté et oultrecuydance de mespriser son ennemy, encores qu'il soit le plus foible, l'on doibt aussi reputer à pusilanimité et faulte de cueur de l'estimer tant, encores qu'il soit le plus fort, que l'on decline à chose deshonneste et reprehensible. Pourtant que en ce faisant, oultre la plaie que l'on faict à l'honneur, que est /11ᵛ/ le vraye tresor des princes, l'on double le cueur et la hardiesse aux ennemis, et le diminue l'on d'autant aux amis, dont trop mieulx vauldroit estre forcé et perdre quelque partie de sa terre, soy estant mis en son debvoir de la deffendre, que de la garder en faisant chose qui fut tenue à lascheté, pourtant que la terre ne faict à comparer à l'honneur, et si se peut recouvrer, et l'honneur non.

---

[62] *Hannibalica*, 28.

(Attack of an enemy country the best form of defence against it)
L'ON PEUT au surplus cognoistre evidemment par ladite histoire, que trop
mieulx vault aler assaillir son ennemy en sa terre, encores qu'il soit le plus
puissant, si on le peut faire, que de l'attendre en la sienne propre. Et que le
souverain remede de delivrer son pais de guerre, est la mouvoir ou faire mouvoir
en celuy de qui l'on se doubte, comme fit Annibal quant il entreprint la guerre
en Italie, et encores plus à propos Scipion, quant il l'entreprint en Afrique.[63] Et
oultre l'experience, l'on peut en ladite histoire veoir les raisons que ledit Scipion
allegua au senat et peuple romain, et Annibal aux Cartaginois, en celle guerre;[64]
et depuis la destruction de Cartage, au roy Anthiocus, et avant eulx Agathocles
tyran des Syracusains à ses amis et souldars quant il se partit de sa cité de
Sarragosse,[65] que les Cartaginois tenoient assiegee, pour aler faire la guerre en
Affrique, comme l'on peut veoir en l'histoire que j'ay translatee de Dyodorus
Siculus (XX 3). Et sans aler chercher exemples anciens, l'on en a de nostre temps
veu assez par lesquelz est bien apprové ce que dit est.

(Dedication to Francis I)
PLUSIEURS AULTRES bons et notables enseignemens pourra noter et recuillir
quiconques vouldra soigneusement lire et bien peser ladite histoire, que je ne
veulx cy reciter, pour non exceder par trop la mesure convenable à ung proheme.
Jacoit que je reputasse trop plus utile recuillir la moille et le sug de toutes
histoires par telz /12ʳ/ enseignemens et notables, ainsi que fit jadis Valere
Maxime, que de les lire et exposer textualement, mais à ce supplira la diligence
et prudence du liseur, qui pourra espoir prendre en ce faisant quelque goust à la
presente histoire; laquelle pour ces raisons, sire, fuz meu de translater, esperant
en faire present audit feu roy à mon retour de Romme. Toutesfois dieu, qui faict
toutes choses pour le mieulx, n'a voulu que arrivasse à temps pour luy faire
rapport de ma charge, ne present de ma translation; ains arrivay le jour propre
dont la nuit il avoit rendu l'esperit au createur. Et non pourtant considerant, sire,
que en cela et toutes aultres vertuz vous avez esté et estes imitateur et vray
successeur dudit feu roy, tout ainsi que estes de la coronne, et que de son vivant
mesmes preniez autant ou plus de plaisir à lire telles histoires, et tous aultres
livres ou l'on peut apprendre quelque chose vertueuse et honneste, que luy, et
mesmes lesdits livres que je luy ay translatéz, m'a semblé que autant vous seroit
ledit present agreable qu'il eut esté à luy. Et si satisferoie à l'intention dudit
Lascary en le vous presentant, tout ainsi que si je l'eusse presenté audit feu roy
par les mesmes raisons. Car vous estes pour luy en scavoir autant de gré et faire

---

[63] *Iberica*, 9; *Hannibalica*, 55.

[64] For Scipio *Libyca*, 7 seems more relevant than anything in these two books; for Hannibal *Iberica*, 10,
Hannibalica, 3.

[65] This and similar forms for 'Syracuse' were current.

autant ou plus de guerdon que ledit feu roy eut faict. QUANT au regard de moy, encores que j'eusse beaucop de grans debvoirs et obligations à iceluy bon prince, principalement pour l'amour et confiance qu'il a monstré en plusieurs choses avoir à moy, dont tout le temps de ma vie me repute tenu et obligé à prier dieu pour son ame, et exaulser son nom de mon povoir, toutesfoiz j'en avoie d'aultres envers vous desjà au paravant que parvinsiez à la coronne, qui ne sont pas moindres, comme bien scavez. Et par /12ᵛ/ ainsi estant trestous lesdits debvoirs et obligations confonduz en vostre personne par vostre advenement à la coronne, me repute ne povoir satisfaire à iceulx en tout ne en partie par cecy ne par aultre service que vous sceusse faire.

ET NEANTMOINGS vous supplie treshumblement, sire, qu'il vous plaise prendre en gré ledit present, aiant regard principalement au bon vouloir qui est de vous faire service et chose agreable en toutes les sortes que je pourroie, jusques au dernier de ma vie. Et non aiant aultre moien de ce faire, à tout le moings prieray incessamment dieu le createur qu'il vous doint longuement gouverner et regir ce royaume à sa louenge, au bien et contentement des subiectz, et à vostre perpetuelle gloire et renommee, comme chascun espere, pour les grans dons de nature et de grace que l'on voit excellemment assembléz en vostre personne. Et pour la grande demonstration et apparence de toute vertu et bonté que l'on a cogneu en vous à cestuy vostre nouvel avenement à la coronne, estant encores en si jeune eage, qui à peine en est capable. Dont par succession de temps venant à plus grande maturité et perfection, tant par le commun cours de nature estant en eage plus rassis, comme par l'experience des choses si grandes qu'il vous convient manier cy aprés, l'on peut raisonnablement esperer plus de felicité et de prosperité en ce roiaume de vostre regne que l'on n'y a veu de nul aultre temps, moiennant l'aide du createur duquel tout bien procede, et auquel l'on doibt rendre la louenge de toutes choses.

From Philology to History: Ancient Historiography between Humanism and Enlightenment

C. R. LIGOTA

In his article 'Ancient History and the Antiquarian'[1]—largely the source of inspiration for this colloquium—Arnaldo Momigliano sets in opposition two types of historical scholarship: a literary or historiographic type, seeking to recover the past in a chronologically structured narrative of events, and an antiquarian one, the collection and systematization of material remains for the purpose of reconstructing institutions. Momigliano sees this dichotomy as originating in Antiquity and acquiring a new lease of life in Renaissance Humanism. He sees the two strands coming together in the eighteenth century, notably in Gibbon's *Decline and Fall*.

I should like to offer a footnote to this model by suggesting that one of its components transgresses the line of demarcation between the historiographic and the antiquarian, and that it is a change in the status of this component that brings about, or helps to bring about, the coming together of the two. The component I have in mind is ancient historiography, the texts of ancient historians accessible to the humanists. It will be my contention that the humanists treated these texts on a par with material remains, i.e. as primary evidence and not as interpretation, and that it is the eventual coming into view of this latter aspect of ancient historiography that helped to historicize Graeco-Roman Antiquity, i.e. to establish a self-consciously non-ancient standpoint from which to recount it, the historiographical text so engendered drawing upon and interpreting the evidence offered by the various antiquarian disciplines.

* * *

The notion of surveying the past from a standpoint external to it, i.e. in the present, and marked as such, had existed in mediaeval historiography. Two quite distinct features define it: 1) the stated awareness of writing at a particular point in the temporal span between the Creation and the Last Judgment; 2) the practice of having historical works officially certified or approved conferring on them the status of a public instrument—which implied that their validity derived not from the evidence of the past as such but from a recognition of it in the present. Let me illustrate each of these, in reverse order.

The practice of, as it were, receiving historical works into the canon. In the eighties of the twelfth century, Godfrey of Viterbo, notary and chaplain at the

---

[1] A. Momigliano, 'Ancient History and the Antiquarian', *Journal of the Warburg and Courtauld Institutes*, 13, 1950, pp. 285–315; repr. in *Contributo alla storia degli studi classici*, Roma, 1955, pp. 67–106.

court of the Emperors Frederick Barbarossa and Henry VI, wrote the *Pantheon*, a compendium of world history, compiled, as he informs us, from the Old and the New Testament and from 'almost all histories' ('de omnibus fere historiis': these are subsequently listed). He decided to submit it to the Pope for pre-publication approval. He expounds his reasons in the dedication addressed to Urban III.[2] Emperors and kings are accountable solely to God and to the pope. They are above the law, their only guide to right action is historical example. It is appropriate, therefore, that a work of history should derive its validity and authority from the power that binds and looses on earth and in heaven, the power, moreover, without whose mediation no passage of the Scriptures can be known to be authentic. This idea of authenticity as validation concluding a historical process rather than as an attribute sought for at origin will resurface later in my text.

Bernard Guenée has studied the mediaeval usage of the term 'authentic' in relation to historical writings.[3] Both in Latin and in French it occurs as an equivalent of 'received', 'authorized' or 'canonical', and as the exact synonym of 'approved'. Guenée's main example is the dispute which came to a head in 1410 between the monks of St Denis and the canons of Notre Dame concerning the relics of the saint. Both sides produced as evidence the *Grandes chroniques de France*, a historiographical patchwork held in the highest esteem by virtue of its official status. The dispute turned on the authority of a particular section of the *Chroniques* dating from the reign of Philip Augustus: was its author in fact Rignotus or Rigordus, and if so was his title of 'regum Francie cronographus' genuine, or had it been substituted for 'ecclesie Sancti Dyonisii cronographus'? The latter was more important than the former, but neither was essential to the monks' case, as one of their counsel observed. The section qualified as 'historia approbata et auctorizata' on the strength of 'publicacio coram principibus' and of the place of custody which was the public archive.

Now for awareness of writing at a particular point of time. Sifrid of Balnhusin, a Thuringian cleric writing at the beginning of the fourteenth century, declares in the preface of his *Historia universalis*[4] that the work stretches from the beginnings of Creation to the year 1304. He has relied on earlier writings, not only the *Biblioteca Hieronymi*, that is the Bible, but the *Historia scholastica*, the

---

[2] See J. B. Migne, *Patrologia latina*, CXCVIII, col. 877; *Monumenta Germaniae historica, Scriptores*, XXII, 133; *Lexikon des Mittelalters*, IV, 1607–8.

[3] See B. Guenée, 'Authentique et approuvé. Recherches sur les principes de la critique historique au Moyen Age' in *Actes du colloque sur la lexicographie du latin médiéval* [1978], Paris, 1981, pp. 215–28, reprinted in B. Guenée, *Politique et histoire au Moyen Age. Recueil d'articles...*, Paris, 1981, pp. 265–78.

[4] *Monumenta Germaniae historica, Scriptores*, XXV, pp. 685–6; see H. Hofmann, 'Artikulationsformen des historischen Wissens in der lateinischen Historiographie des hohen und späten Mittelalters', *Grundriss der romanischen Literaturen des Mittelalters*, XI, 1: *La Littérature historiographique des origines à 1500*, I, 2, Heidelberg, 1987, pp. 387–8.

Chronica of Eusebius and Jerome etc., and only for the most recent events added his own account. He has called it *Historia universalis* 'because it is a compendium of universal histories to which I and those who will come after me can add new events in the succession of times until the end of the world'. So, both a clearly defined point up to which—which is also the point from which—the history has been written and a projection of similar points into a finite future. Sifrid stresses, as one expects a mediaeval historian to do, that all he has done is to excerpt recognised authorities. He has put in nothing new, nothing uncertain or doubtful. So *nihil novi*—except the point in time.

A century and a half earlier, Otto of Freising, writing his tale of two cities, is quite emphatic about the stage in time he is writing from. It is almost the end of time: 'Nos autem, tamquam in fine temporum constituti...'[5] Otto's work is in eight books. The last deals with Antichrist, the resurrection of the dead and the end of the two cities. Book VII, the last historical book bringing the story up to 1146, the year of writing, closes with a section on the religious orders. Otto has decided to end—also in the sense of marking a turning point, 'metam et articulum ponamus'[6]—his tale of misery and turbulence by opposing to it an account of monastic existence, the regulated peacefulness of which gives a foretaste of the rest on the seventh day—and thus provides a transition to the eschatology of Book VIII.

*   *   *

It hardly needs saying that the humanists had little use for such a view of history. But in rejecting it they lost a critical tool, or at least the basis for one: the notion of recovering the past from a distinct standpoint in time. What replaced it was a massive value judgment: the excellence of Antiquity, the darkness of what came after it. Classical Antiquity fascinated the humanists in the strict sense of the word. Its material remains—coins, gems, inscriptions, buildings—seemed to recreate it for them in a phantasm of immediacy. Charles Mitchell has evoked the phenomenon in his 'Archaeology and Romance',[7] convincingly suggesting that the *Hypnerotomachia Polifili* was here emblematic.

The recovery of ancient literary texts was a more sophisticated affair: it occurred in the medium of language. The outstanding testimony for this is the work of Lorenzo Valla. Language, that is, for all practical purposes, Latin, is for Valla the supreme or the fundamental reality, of heavenly descent, a sacrament. It is the medium of perception and the *locus* of truth. He expounds this view *ex*

---

[5] Otto Frisingensis, *Chronica sive historia de duabus civitatibus,* recogn. A. Hofmeister, *Scriptores rerum germanicarum*, Hannover, 1912, i prol., p. 7, 15–16.

[6] Ibid., VII, 34, p. 369,13

[7] C. Mitchell, 'Archaeology and Romance in Renaissance Italy', *Italian Renaissance Studies. A Tribute to ... C. M. Ady*, ed. E. F. Jacob, London, 1960, pp. 455ff.

professo in the *Elegantiae* and the *Dialectic* but it underpins every branch of his intellectual activity. Aristotle's thesis that 'more' and 'less' apply to quality but not to substance is ruined by showing that linguistic usage is against it. The interpretation of law is vitiated by bad Latin. History cannot perform its function of imparting wisdom by example—the highest function in Valla's scale—unless the historian has a perfect mastery of the language and of the stylistic requirements for the genre.

In history Latin reigns supreme, not in a flat chauvinistic sense but almost as an ontological proposition.[8] Rome as empire has disappeared but Rome as Latin lives on. Valla systematically casts literary activity in political and military terms drawn from episodes of Roman history, claiming that it is only as so applied that they come into their own: 'Quousque tandem, Quirites—I am calling upon men of letters and supporters of the Roman tongue, for they are the true and the only Quirites, the others were more like *inquilini*, resident aliens—quousque inquam Quirites urbem vestram, non dico domicilium imperii, sed parentem literarum a Gallis esse captam patiemini, id est Latinitatem a barbaris oppressam?'[9] Valla goes on to parallel various literary activities with the dispersed location of Roman forces outside Rome during the Gallic invasion and calls for a Camillus to lead them back, to refound Rome, that is to restore Latin to its excellence—a fundamental undertaking which is that of the *Elegantiae*. 'Camillus qui signa in patriam referat', as the *Aeneid* (vi, 825) has it—the interposition of a Vergilian filter is a palmary stroke here.[10] In connection with his emendations of Livy, Valla describes restoring classical texts as a 'restitutio in patriam'.[11]

Language informs reality: restoring Latin, clarifying points of grammar und usage, is like converting a labyrinth into an amphitheatre. Valla uses this comparison to describe what he has achieved in his treatise on the pronominal forms *sui* and *suus*.[12] He extends the comparison, in all humility, to what Pope Nicholas V has achieved architecturally in the Vatican—and asks Giovanni Tortelli to whom the treatise is dedicated, to seek papal approval for publication; for is not the pope the *moderator* and *princeps* not only of the Roman Pontificate and of the Roman Empire, but of Roman speech—*Romani eloquii*—as well ? An unprecedented cumulation of high offices, of which the last is the highest. Neither the Papacy nor the Empire can do without Latin. Latin can dispense with both.

---

[8] See H. B. Gerl, *Rhetorik als Philosophie: Lorenzo Valla*, Humanistische Bibliothek, I, 13, Munich, 1974, pp. 242ff.

[9] Lorenzo Valla, *Elegantiae*, bk 1, praefatio, in Valla, *Opera omnia*, Basel, 1540, repr. vol. I, Turin, 1962, pp. 4–5.

[10] Loc. cit.

[11] See Lorenzo Valla, *Antidotum in Facium*, IV, 3, 8, ed. Mariangela Regoliosi, Padua, 1981, p. 323.

[12] Valla, *Opera* (n. 9 above), I, pp. 248–9.

The contrast with Godfrey of Viterbo's request for papal authorization of his historical work tells its own story.

Valla's notion of Latin as the 'seminary of all doctrine'[13] is also at the root of his conception of history, both when he writes it himself—the *Gesta Ferdinandi regis*—and when he emends Livy. He can be observed in both capacities in the *Antidotum in Facium*. He rebuts Facio's pompous and ill-informed cavils by showing, with the help of copious and pertinent quotation from ancient authors, that his usage in the *Gesta* is semantically, grammatically and rhetorically correct, and that this correctness makes for historical truth. In the *Proemium* to the *Gesta*, rejecting the traditional hierarchy, he establishes the superiority of history both to philosophy and to poetry—to the former because it teaches by example, to the latter because it teaches by true example: 'tanto robustiorem esse historiam quanto veriorem'.[14] And it is the activation of the resources of the language that at once uncovers historical truth and makes it communicable.

Concerning the *Emendationes in Titum Livium*, just two remarks. 1) Valla prefers conjecture to collation. He practises the former to brilliant effect and boasts of his successes. As for the latter, though, as Mariangela Regoliosi has shown,[15] he *may* not have been innocent of cross-manuscript reference, he never mentions it for himself, while imputing it to his adversaries as a sign of their inferior ability in the few instances of agreement with their emendations. 2) In matters of factual information Valla, anticipating the Protestants, also prefers internal criticism—correcting Scripture from Scripture—as the *disputatio* he devotes to the problem of the Tarquins shows.[16] Against Livy's statement (i, 46, 4) which records his own uncertainty and accepts the opinion of others to the effect that Lucius and Aruns were the sons rather than the grandsons of Tarquinius Priscus, Valla demonstrates from other passages in Livy the improbability of this, and therefore the near certainty of the alternative being the case. And he repeatedly insists that he has obtained his result from internal evidence alone, 'sua ipsius [i.e. Livy's] confessione', without benefit of the corroborating opinion of Dionysius of Halicarnassus which came his way subsequently.

I think both these traits go with Valla's 'linguistic turn'—*sit venia verbo*. A historical text is for him a product of language in so massive and so articulate a

---

[13] Valla, *Opera* (n. 9 above), I, p. 249.

[14] *Gesta Ferdinandi regis Aragonum*, Proemium, ix, ed. O. Besomi, Padua, 1973, pp. 5, 19–20.

[15] M. Regoliosi, 'Lorenzo Valla, Antonio Panormita, Giacomo Curlo e le emendazioni a Livio', *Italia medioevale e umanistica*, 24, 1981, pp. 299ff.

[16] 'Duo Tarquinii Lucius ac Aruns, prisci Tarquinii filiive an nepotes fuerint, adversus Livium disputatio'; 'In Benedictum Morandum confutatio prior'; 'In Benedictum Morandum confutatio altera' in Valla, *Opera* (n. 9 above), I, pp. 438ff; 445ff; 455ff.

way that other perspectives—relationship to textual tradition, relationship to outside reality—are either internalized or blocked out.[17]

Internalization abolishes temporal distance between text and referent. The presence of the former entails the presence of the latter, and the latter integrates the former: a historiographical text surviving from Antiquity, what with its linguistic and rhetorical excellence on the one hand, and the vicissitudes of its passage through the intervening darkness on the other, is so eminently part of that Antiquity that its specific function which is that of interpretation, with all that this implies of apartness and partial obscurity, is lost to view.

A hyperbolic statement—no less significant for that—of the identification of text and historical reality occurs, appropriately enough, in the first printed Livy, 1470. The editor, Giovanni Andrea Bussi, casts his praise of the historian in the form of a sustained parallel, suggesting a kind of congenerousness, between Livy and Rome. 'Will anyone be found to praise Livy adequately? The most eloquent of all historians, he had such urbanity, excellence and renown that, standing equal to the Empire of Rome, he equalled its glory by telling of it'.[18] This equality or congruence is then developed and clinched—'orationis cardo'—by asserting that the reconstruction of either could only be self-reconstruction. Only Rome, were it to flourish again, could raise Rome from its ruins; only Livy, were he to come back from the dead, could restore the lost books of Livy[19]—Scripture from Scripture.

This paramountcy of language must not be taken too literally. Even Valla's emendations are not purely linguistic or exclusively intralivian, as for example in the episode of the vote on the malpractices of the tax-farmer Marcus Postumius, where Valla replaces a meaningless corruption and counters a gratuitous and historically mistaken conjecture of the Neapolitans by drawing on Cicero's reference to voting procedure in the *De natura deorum*.[20]

In the sixteenth-century archaeological discoveries, notably that of the Capitoline Fasti, lead to a decidedly 'external', non-linguistic approach to the text—enough to mention Sigonio's *Scholia* to Livy in his edition of 1555 and following. But the approach remains philological: information extracted from new finds is brought to bear on the text by way of supplement and commentary. There is no idea of constructing an alternative historical view—or to see the historian's text as representing a view. One set of remains is made to shed light on another.

---

[17] See C. Ligota, 'Von der Autorität zur Quelle: Die humanistische Auffassung des Textes', *Wolfenbütteler Beiträge*, 8, 1988, pp. 18–19.

[18] See G. A. Bussi, *Prefazioni alle edizioni di Sweynheym e Pannartz…*, a cura di M.Miglio, Milan, 1978, p. 30.

[19] Ibid., p. 32.

[20] Valla, *Antidotum in Facium* (n. 11 above), IV, 8, 3, pp. 364–5.

In his *Institution du prince*, 1547, Guillaume Budé praises the invention of printing as the 'instauration et perpetuation de l'Antiquité': the 'haultes et magnifiques sepultures de literature' which ancient historians had erected to ancient rulers are now certain not to perish.[21] This is the text as monument. As one edition of Livy succeeds another, reissuing earlier commentaries and adding new ones, the historian's text becomes more and more like a piece of ancient architecture undergoing extensive restoration. The magnificent 1568 Frankfurt Livy includes the *Observationes* of Wilhelm Godelaevaeus. He praises earlier commentators for helping the reader not to lose his way, for keeping him on the right path in pursuit of the knowledge that the text has to offer—'in recto expeditoque tramite suscepti itineris'. Finding one's way around a text—to us a clinically dead metaphor but to the humanists perhaps a live one. Let us recall Valla's treatise on *sui & suus*: the reference for his architectural comparison—converting a labyrinth into an amphitheatre—is the labyrinth in *Aeneid*, v, with its 'inextricabilis' or 'inremeabilis' 'error' and its 'parietibus textum caecis iter'.[22]

* * *

Now for the change in the status of ancient historiography. I cannot offer a film, only a few stills, with no assurance of continuity. And I begin by leaving historiography altogether for a brief visit to biblical scholarship and classical philology. My hosts are, respectively, Richard Simon and Friedrich August Wolf. The influence of the former on the latter, via Johann Salomo Semler, can perhaps be supposed.[23] Anthony Grafton has shown that Wolf's comparisons with the Massoretes should be taken seriously.[24] I have nothing new to say about either Wolf or Simon, it is only that their work documents in a particularly coherent way the problem under discussion.

The common element in the achievement of Simon and Wolf can perhaps be described as a theory of textual descent which does away with the notion of original: it recognizes historical generations only and declares primeval ancestors beyond its ken. Simon, more than a hundred years before Wolf, appears to have been the first to hit on the idea that texts have a history—*Histoire critique du*

---

[21] Guillaume Budé, *Institution du prince*, Paris, 1547, repr. Farnborough, 1966, cap. XV, p. 63.

[22] See Valla, *Opera* (n. 9 above), I, pp. 235; 248.

[23] See J. D. Woodbridge, 'German Responses to the Biblical Critic Richard Simon: from Leibniz to J. S. Semler', *Historische Kritik und biblischer Kanon in der deutschen Aufklärung*, 18. Wolfenbütteler Symposion... 1985, ed. von H. Graf Reventlow *et al.*, Wolfenbütteler Forschungen, XLI, Wiesbaden, 1988, pp. 65–87; G. Hornig, *Die Anfänge der kritisch-historischen Theologie. Johann Salomo Semlers Schriftverständnis und seine Stellung zu Luther*, Forschungen zur systematischen Theologie und Religionsphilosophie, VIII, Göttingen, 1961, pp. 182ff.

[24] See A. Grafton, 'Prolegomena to Friedrich August Wolf', *Journal of the Warburg and Courtauld Institutes*, 44, 1981, pp. 101–29 (119–26); F. A. Wolf, *Prolegomena to Homer 1795*, transl. with introd. by A. Grafton *et al.*, Princeton, N.J., 1985, 18ff.

Vieux Testament, 1678; *Histoire critique du texte du Nouveau Testament*, 1689; *Histoire critique des versions du Nouveau Testament*, 1690, are the titles of his main works. The assumption underlying Simon's comprehensive survey of the textual tradition of the two Testaments is the belated and derivative character of the earliest texts in relation to what they narrate, and the complexity and discontinuity of their subsequent transmission. For the Old Testament he has the theory of public scribes—all anonymous except for Ezra—which disposes of the problem of authorship, and eliminates the very notion of an original. The books of the Old Testament as we have them began life as extracts or summaries of much fuller records kept in the state archives of the Republic of the Hebrews. The scribes who compiled them, also called prophets, were divinely inspired. This made them truthful and accurate but not infallible and did not determine their judgment as to what and when to extract. Scripture as Scripture is a purely human affair, neither entirely reliable as a record nor exempt from alteration, both deliberate and unwitting. It needs to be read critically, as Augustine, and Jerome's lady-friends knew.

The Old Testament as a corpus was assembled by Ezra after the return from Babylon. One can only speculate how much had survived from before the Captivity and how much he had to reconstruct. It was his editorship as scribe and prophet that conferred authority on the collection. Canonicity, not originality, made it authentic.

But even this very derivative stage is not easily accessible. Quite apart from subsequent changes in Hebrew and the intrusion of Aramaic, the Massoretes of Tiberias, working in Simon's view over a span of time—late Antiquity and early Middle Ages—interposed yet another filter, especially by the introduction of pointing. For Simon the Massoretic text conveys the Word of God. He is concerned to show that this is not incompatible with its composite, occasionally defective and non-definitive character.

As for the New Testament, Jesus wrote nothing himself and instructed his disciples to spread the word by preaching, not to write it down. The Gospels are a record not of the story they tell but of the Evangelists' preaching embodying versions of that story. This is the case for Matthew and Mark. Luke and John were composed to counter heretical versions. The formation of the New Testament is inseparable from the oral tradition of the early church and the only way to establish an authentic text is from attestations—Simon calls them *Actes*—of what was the received text in the main churches at any given time. No personal intuition, no communing with the text, however deeply informed by faith, can be a substitute for this indirect approach. The text cannot be explained from the text, it is not a self-contained entity governed by internal correspondences. It is never immediately present because no state of it can be original. It is always being added to and subtracted from. It is a product of history.

What Simon did for the Bible, Wolf did for Homer. His specific contribution is not the vanishing oral Homer—the idea had been in the air for over a century—but the deutero-Homer of the Homeric text. The oral stage is beyond recall—this disposes of author and original. Several centuries elapse before the poems are first set down in writing—in late sixth-century Athens. A complex history of the text begins, marked by irretrievable losses and alterations. Wolf quotes a line from Lucan about even ruins perishing[25]—appropriately enough it refers to Troy when Caesar visited the site. With all the massive scholarly apparatus, enriched by the recently discovered Venice scholia, that Wolf is preparing to deploy, he sets his sights no higher than the reconstitution of what would have been acceptable to 'Longinus'—for Wolf Cassius Longinus, third century A.D.—'or some other ancient critic who knew how to handle the materials of the Alexandrians'—not an ideal, perfect text but 'norma eruditae antiquitatis', where 'eruditae' means both learned and attested.[26]

The Homeric vulgate is relatively uncorrupt—not a sign of genuineness but of uncritical aestheticizing. The specious beauty needs to be unmasked—not just the occasional *Schönheitsfehler* cured by *ad hoc* emendation and random recension but the entire text submitted to systematic recension, so that only what is historically documented, i.e. attested in reputable exemplars—*ad fidem testatae antiquitatis*—can be retained. Wolf sums up his idea as follows (I quote Anthony Grafton's translation): 'The Homer that we hold in our hands now is not the one who flourished in the mouths of the Greeks of his own day, but one variously altered, interpolated, corrected and emended from the times of Solon down to those of the Alexandrians. Learned...men have long felt their way to this conclusion by using various scattered bits of evidence; but now the voices of all periods joined together bear witness, and history speaks'.[27]

* * *

What are the consequences of this historicizing of the text for the status of ancient historiography? I shall end by looking quickly at the work of Johann Christoph Gatterer who prepared the ground, and that of Barthold Georg Niebuhr who drew the conclusion.

Gatterer, active in Göttingen from the 60's to the 90's of the eighteenth century, was a late offspring of seventeenth-century polymathy. He combined three lines of interest: antiquarian studies, universal history, and the structure of historical narrative, 'der historische Plan', as he called it. The combination gelled: it led Gatterer to the postulate of 'nexus rerum universalis', or 'die Vorstellung

---

[25] *Pharsalia*, IX, 969: F. A. Wolf, *Prolegomena ad Homerum*, XLIX, ed. R. Peppmüller, Halle, 1884, repr. Hildesheim, 1963, p. 204.

[26] Wolf, *Prolegomena* (n. 25 above), VII, pp. 15–16.

[27] Wolf, *Prolegomena* (n. 24 above), XLIX, p. 209.

des allgemeinen Zusamenhangs der Dinge in der Welt'.[28] Universal history was the romance of this postulate, in the antiquarian domain it engendered the 'Historische Enzyklopädie'—not only a course of university lectures but also a programme of research, gathering the various antiquarian disciplines into a system as the auxiliary sciences of history—and at the level of historical narrative it suggested to Gatterer the notion of a standpoint from which history is written. He arrived at it via an analysis of the specific character of historical causality, distinct from natural causality in that a cause does not determine its effect but brings it about by calling forth responses which are not logically necessary, only historically probable. This is where the historian comes in. He establishes the responses as facts and traces the connections between them. Ideally everything is connected with everything else and the ideal historian stands at the point of 'nexus rerum universalis'. In practice, of course, he has to select and he does so from a standpoint the whereabouts of which are both less obvious and less reputable. But they can be determined and the historian can strive to free himself, at least partly, from his limitations. Gatterer reflects on this in an essay entitled 'Vom Standort und Gesichtspunckt des Geschichtsschreibers oder der teutsche Livius'.[29] The German Livy intends neither a translation of Livy into German nor a history of Germany in a Livian mode but a history of Rome from the standpoint of an eighteenth-century German—Gatterer, in fact, for the sake of the argument—that is not a native but a foreigner, not attached to Rome but indifferent towards it, not a pagan but a Christian, a Protestant, not a politician but a university professor, etc., etc.

So a project for a historiography that presses the antiquarian disciplines into service and envisages Antiquity from a historically defined, self-consciously non-antique standpoint.[30]

Finally, Niebuhr. Niebuhr was very much aware of writing Roman history from a non-Roman standpoint. He meditated the example of Gibbon, and decided to do for early Rome what Gibbon had done for the later Empire. In the lectures of 1810–11 he still pays homage to the humanist view: the ancient historians are unsurpassed in style and moral excellence, and it would be foolish and pointless to embark on a history of Rome had Livy and Tacitus survived entire. But then he goes on to announce his programme: he intends to investigate the built-over and hidden foundations of the ancient Roman people and its state on which such

---

[28] J. C. Gatterer, 'Vom historischen Plan und der darauf sich gründenden Zusammenfügung der Erzählung', *Allgemeine historische Bibliothek*, I, Halle, 1767, p. 82.

[29] Ibid., V, 1768, pp. 3ff.

[30] It is not without interest that about fifteen years before Gatterer's 'Teutsche Livius' Johann Martin Chladenius put forward the hermeneutical notion of 'points of view' (*Sehepunckte*)—see J. M. Chladenius, *Allgemeine Geschichtswissenschaft...*, ch. 5, Leipzig, 1752 (repr. Vienna etc., 1985), pp. 91ff.

ancient authors as are extant shed no light.[31] He amplifies this point in the following year: our exalted view of ancient historians rests on an illusion. We contemplate Antiquity like a mountain range at a distance. It consists of several chains standing in depth but for us the furthermost merges with the nearest. We forget that Roman historians writing in the chaos of the falling Republic or under the new order of the Empire are as remote from some of the events and institutions they describe as we are from the Minnesängers. What they have to offer is not direct witness but a reconstruction—incomplete, tendentious and often wrong.[32] Roman history, especially early Roman history, needs to be investigated anew. Niebuhr has undertaken to do so.

---

[31] B. G. Niebuhr, *Kleine historische und philologische Schriften*, I, Bonn, 1828, repr. Osnabrück, 1969, pp. 85–7.

[32] Ibid., II, 1843/1969, pp. 14–15.

William Camden's *Britannia*: History and Historiography

CHRISTIANE KUNST[*]

Arnaldo Momigliano's article 'Ancient History and the Antiquarian', which he called a 'provisional map' of the field of antiquarian studies, is, in its general approach to the subject, still rather like the only map of hidden wells in a desert. Writing in 1950, Momigliano deplored the lack of a 'history of antiquarian studies'. So far the condition has not been remedied, though a few detailed studies have thrown some light on various aspects of a complex field. At least no one has challenged Momigliano's belief that the investigation of local studies is one key to an understanding of antiquarian thought.

In sixteenth- and seventeenth-century England, it was political and religious exigencies that fostered the concern with British antiquities. Its salient characteristic was a dichotomy, manifesting itself in a variety of ways, between a general interest in history and work with a strong national or regional connotation.[1] The acknowledged leader in antiquarian research in his own day and for a couple of centuries to come was William Camden, the son of a London painter, born in 1551. He was one of the first to set standards for investigating the local antiquities of Britain.[2] Earlier, John Leland had devoted most of his life to a similar project; but it was Camden who introduced Romano-British studies to England and fostered a vivid interest in the classical tradition of history writing. Moreover, in contrast to Leland, Camden succeeded in actually *writing* the first antiquarian textbook on British history ranging from prehistory to Elizabethan England.[3] *Britannia*, first published in 1586, was a sixteenth- and seventeenth-

---

[*] I wish to thank Michael Crawford and Christopher Ligota for help and advice.

[1] See F. S. Fussner, *The Historical Revolution. English Historical Writing and Thought, 1580–1640*, London 1962, pp. 92ff.; F. J. Levy, *Tudor Historical Thought*, San Marino, Calif., 1967, pp. 124ff.; A. Ferguson, *Clio Unbound: Perception of the Social and Cultural Past in Renaissance England*, Durham, N.C., 1979, pp. 51ff., 78ff. (see G. R. Elton's review in *History and Theory*, 20, 1981, pp. 92–100); E. Cochrane, *Historians and Historiography in the Italian Renaissance*, Chicago 1981, ch. 15; J. M. Levine, *Humanism and history. Origins of Modern English Historiography*, Ithaca, 1987, pp. 73ff.; D. R. Woolf, 'Erudition and the Idea of History in Renaissance England', *Renaissance Quarterly*, 40, 1987, pp. 11–48; *idem, The Idea of History in Early Stuart England. Erudition, Ideology and 'the Light of Truth' from the Accession of James I to the Civil War*, Toronto, 1990.

[2] As late as 1838 the newly founded Camden Society explained its name 'as at once a symbol of the importance and value of the subjects to which the attention of the Society will be directed, and a pledge that its designs [the publication of early historical and literary remains] will be prosecuted with zeal, learning and judgment'—quoted by M. Powicke, 'William Camden', *English Studies*, 1948 (=*Essays and Studies Collected for the English Association*, n.s. 1), p. 75.

[3] Leland had set the scene, outlining the tasks to be performed by the antiquarian: see Levy, *Tudor Historical Thought* (n. 1 above), p. 22; but he never managed to put his vast collection of data into the projected book, *De antiquitate Britannica*.

century bestseller. Six editions, each substantially enlarged, came out in Camden's lifetime.[4]

For political as well as religious reasons the Tudors encouraged pride in an independent national past. So it is no accident that Camden emphasized the significance of local studies, castigating those 'who wished to be strangers in their own city, in transit through their own land, and in knowledge always children'.[5]

Camden declared the purpose of the enthusiastically received *Britannia* to be:

> that I bring to light our ancient Britain: that is, that I restore antiquity to Britain, and Britain to her antiquity, that I renovate the old, illuminate the obscure, and resolve the doubtful; and that, as far as can be, I bring back from exile, truth in our affairs, proscribed whether by the carelessness of the historians or the credulity of the public.[6]

In writing thus, Camden was echoing Cicero's appreciation of the antiquarian achievements of Varro, whom he deeply admired.[7]

But how does Camden turn out to be such an influential figure in English scholarship? The question needs to be investigated in the context of his two different approaches to history. On the one hand, there is his conscious application of modern historical methods, on the other a constant attempt to employ ancient history as an instrument for education and national stability.

Britannia, at least in so far as it followed the format originally devised by Abraham Ortelius, was primarily intended to elucidate the topography of Roman Britain; so it is particularly important to study the model Camden established to interpret the Roman past. Simultaneously, our attention will have to focus on the surprising phenomenon that *Britannia* lost none of its attraction for the British

---

[4] The two later major revisions and enlargements, one by Edmund Gibson in 1695, the other by Richard Gough in 1789, 'form significant milestones in the history of British antiquarian thought from the Renaissance to the Regency': S. Piggott, 'William Camden and the *Britannia*', *Proceedings of the British Academy*, 37, 1951, pp. 199–217; reprinted as an Introduction to the reprint of Gibson's edition, Newton Abbot, Devon, 1951; also in S. Piggott, *Ruins in a Landscape*, Edinburgh, 1976, pp. 33–53; quotation above from the opening paragraph.

[5] '...qui in urbe sua hospites, in patria sua peregrini, et cognitione semper pueri esse velint': *Britannia*, 1586, 'Benevolo lectori'.

[6] '...ut Britanniam nostram illustrarem: hoc est, ut Britanniae antiquitatem, et suae antiquitati Britanniam restituerem, ut vetustis novitatem, obscuris lucem, dubiis fidem adderem, et ut veritatem in rebus nostris, quam vel scriptorum securitas, vel vulgi credulitas proscripserunt, quoad fieri posset, postliminio revocarem': *Britannia*, 1586, dedicatory letter to Lord Burghley.

[7] See Augustine, *De civitate Dei*, vi, 2 (Cicero, *Academica*, i, 3, 9): 'Nos in nostra urbe peregrinantes errantesque tamquam hospites tui libri quasi domum reduxerunt, ut possemus aliquando qui et ubi essemus agnoscere. Tu aetatem patriae, tu descriptiones temporum, tu sacrorum iura, tu sacerdotum, tu domesticam, tu publicam disciplinam, tu sedem regionum locorum, tu omnium divinarum humanarumque rerum nomina, genera, officia, causas aperuisti'. Camden draws on this passage by antiphrasis: 'Si qui vero sint, qui in urbe sua hospites, in patria sua peregrini, in cognitione semper pueri esse velint, sibi per me placeant, sibi dormiant...': *Britannia*, 1586 and 1607, 'Lectori'. Camden refers to Varro as 'doctissimus Romanorum': *Britannia*, 1607, p. 5 and *passim* (probably after Seneca, *Consolatio ad Helviam*, viii, l; elsewhere he quotes vii, 7 and adapts vii, 5; Varro sets the standard for him which, he says, he does not always achieve: *Britannia*, 1607, 'Lectori'.)

reading public after Camden's interpretation of Romano-British antiquities had been devalued and had undergone a profound change in the debate over the British past during the political upheaval of the early Stuart period.

Camden had an eminent share in applying the more advanced scholarly methods of his day to British material.[8] Although, as Antonia Gransden has pointed out, the study of literary sources, documents, topography and antiquities had a continuous tradition in medieval historical writing,[9] the application of this method to ancient history was new, as was the revival of what Momigliano has called the Varronian idea of *antiquitates*—the 'idea of a civilization recovered by systematic collection of all the relics of the past'.[10] The *sacrosanctitas* of Livy, Tacitus and other ancient historians deterred the modern scholar of antiquity from historiographical attempts, but no such restriction operated in the field of *antiquitates*. The investigation of these could supplement the ancient authors either by filling in what they did not mention or replacing lost accounts. Camden may have been influenced by medieval scholarship, but his immediate concern was to point out that he modelled himself on ancient antiquarianism.

Since the province of Britain had received no more than episodic attention from historians in antiquity, it offered a rich field for investigation. One model for studying the ancient world was its geography.[11] Camden never wearied of pointing out that his original design had been to write a chorographical description of Britain,[12] with the central aim of identifying ancient placenames, using philology and topography as his tools.[13] He felt that this research required training or at least the acquisition of specific skills. Thus he learned Welsh and Anglo-Saxon, and toured England extensively, venturing even into the dangerous border country near Hadrian's Wall to collect first-hand topographical information. *Britannia* represents an antiquarian tour of Roman Britain along the lines of Flavio Biondo's tour of Italy.[14]

---

[8] See F. J. Levy, 'The Making of Camden's Britannia', *Bibliothèque d'humanisme et Renaissance*, 36, 1964, pp. 70–97, esp. 76ff.

[9] A. Gransden, *Historical Writing in England 550 to the Early Sixteenth Century*, II, London, 1982, pp. 426ff. See also A. Gransden, 'Antiquarian Studies in Fifteenth-Century England', *Antiquaries Journal*, 60, I, 1980, pp. 75–97.

[10] A. Momigliano, 'Ancient History and the Antiquarian', *Contributo alla storia degli studi classici*, Rome, 1955, p. 73.

[11] See G. Strauss, 'Topographical Historical Method in Sixteenth-Century German Scholarship' in *Studies in the Renaissance*, Publications of the Renaissance Society of America, V, 1958, pp. 87–101, esp. p. 88.

[12] For the distinction between chorography and geography see Ptolemy, *Geography* i, l, l; 4.

[13] 'Hoc enim mihi imprimis propositum susceptumque fuit consilium, ut loca illa quorum Caesar, Tacitus, Ptolemaeus, Antoninus Aug., Provinciarum Notitia, aliqui vetusti scriptores meminerunt, et TEMPUS caeca quadam caligine nominibus extinctis, mutatis, aut corruptis circumfudit, indagarem et e tenebris eruerem. In his indagandis, ut minus comperta asseveratione non affirmo, ita quae probabilia haud quaquam subticeo': *Britannia*, 1607, 'Lectori'.

[14] For an example of how Camden combined travel information with archaeological evidence, see *Britannia*, 1607, p. 439.

The reintroduction of geography as a factor in history had two aspects: Camden not only travelled around the country to look for antiquities, search for them or enquire about oral traditions, but he also formed an opinion as to what extent geographical conditions had influenced historical events. He was interested in social as well as in economic matters.

But, unlike Leland's, Camden's antiquarian travels were intended to collect specific information and not to accumulate encyclopaedic knowledge. 'I took Pliny's advice and often re-read the title of my book, asking myself again and again what it was I had undertaken to write'.[15]

In line with his belief in specialist knowledge, Camden advocated academic cooperation on a national as well as an international scale. The first edition of *Britannia* was primarily addressed to the international community of scholars as the professionals of the trade.[16] On the national level Camden sought the cooperation of competent local antiquarians,[17] declaring his readiness to learn from their more accurate observations.[18] He was very conscious of being a pioneer, looking at his work as an initial contribution to knowledge and not as a final interpretation: 'For me it is enough and more to have made a start, and I will consider it a gain if I have attracted others into this field, be it to write more or to amend what I have written'.[19]

The collaborative approach, however, became obsolete in Romano-British studies in the following centuries, partly because the field was taken over by the learned amateur, partly because a general outline of interpretation was canonized. William Stukeley's statement in the preface to his *Itinerarium curiosum*, written in 1724, may serve as an example of the anti-erudite attitude: 'I avoided prejudice, never carrying any author along with me, but taking things in the natural order and manner they presented themselves',[20] and as late as 1907,

---

[15] '...titulum (quod monet Plinius) saepius legi et identitidem me interrogavi quid scribere inceperim': *Britannia*, 1586, 'Benevolo lectori'. Woolf, 'Erudition' (n. 1 above), p. 22, sees the refusal of Tudor writers to attempt a general history from non-narrative sources as a consequence of Leland's failure—'the Marley's ghost of Tudor historical writing'.

[16] 'Quid praestiterim dicant qui recte iudicare norunt, ne illi facile diiudicent', and further: 'Me autem et mea scripta omnia piorum et doctorum iudicio in singulis, ea qua par est reverentia, demisissime submitto et subiicio...': *Britannia*, 1607, 'Lectori'. The idea is first frankly expressed in the 1600 edition, 'Ad lectorem' (postface, sep. pag.), p. 30.

[17] 'Angliam fere omnem peragravi, versatissimum et peritissimum quemque in sua regione consului': *Britannia*, 1607, 'Lectori'.

[18] 'Locorum peculiaria alii qui incolunt accuratius observent, si monuerint in quo erraverim, cum gratia corrigam; quod imprudens omiserim, adjiciam; quod minus explicaverim, edoctus plenius edocebo': *Britannia*, 1607, 'Lectori'.

[19] 'Alia aetas, alii homines alia in lucem indies proferent. Mihi satis superque incepisse, et in lucro ponam me alios in hanc arenam provocasse, sive denuo scribant, sive mea emendent': *Britannia*, 1607, 'Lectori'.

[20] W. Stukeley, *Itinerarium curiosum. Or an Account of the Antiquitys and Remarkable Curiositys in Nature or Art Observ'd in Travels thro' Great Brittan*, Centuria I, London, 1724/25, Preface.

Francis Haverfield, in an attempt to reorganize Romano-British studies, denounced the absence of cooperation and specialized training in the field.[21]

Camden explicitly distinguished *Britannia* from 'history' and called it a 'chorographical description', partly to differentiate his historical-antiquarian work from the more dramatic genre of history, partly to indicate that the evidence came to a very large extent from non-literary sources.[22] The title *Britannia sive florentissimorum regnorum Angliae, Scotiae, Hiberniae, et insularum adiacentium ex intima antiquitate chorographica descriptio* shows various influences. There is a clear link with Biondo's *Italia illustrata* and the German geographers around Conrad Celtes who developed the idea of chorography in their project of a *Germania illustrata*. Another model may have been Leandro Alberti's widely known *Descrittione di tutta Italia* (1550). Alberti adopted the form of a geographical survey in order to combine *descriptio* and *narratio*. The work was less scholarly but, in its Latin translation, very popular all over Europe (eight editions in twenty-five years).

In his *Annales rerum Anglicarum et Hibernicarum, regnante Elizabetha*, Camden admitted that only war and politics were proper subjects for history, and he went on to explain why he had incorporated 'antiquarian' issues. It was perhaps Camden's most important achievement to have merged historical and antiquarian subjects in both *Britannia* and the *Annales*, and thus to have introduced a new mode of historical writing in England.[23] He also established a model for original research. Completeness of documentation was at the heart of his scholarly work because he believed it possible to reconstruct a true picture of the past by piecing together all available evidence.

Beyond that, he felt the need to define what reliable evidence was.[24] In his dispute with Ralph Brooke he showed that historical questions could not be solved without recourse to source material.[25] To establish its reliability Camden

---

[21] See F. Haverfield, *The Roman Occupation of Britain*, ed. G. McDonald, Oxford, 1924, pp. 59–88, esp. p. 85. In modern Romano-British studies the pendulum has swung back towards depreciating all non-archaeological sources of historical knowledge by turning Haverfield's demand for archaeological research: 'the spade is mightier than the pen; the shovel and pick are the revealers of secrets' (ibid., p. 28), into the war-cry: 'text hinders archaeology'.

[22] See *Britannia*, 1586, p. 123. For a recent study concerning the problem of the distinction between history and antiquities see Woolf, 'Erudition' (n. 1 above).

[23] Woolf, *Idea of History*, p. 7, argues for a strict separation between history and antiquarian studies in all fields before the eighteenth century. Camden 'did not recognize the essential similariity of his two masterpieces' (ibid., p. 26). I think the distinction should not be pressed quite so far (see also Momigliano, 'Ancient History' [n. 10 above], pp. 75, 77f.): *Britannia* is not entirely descriptive, nor the *Annals* merely narrative. At least when dealing with institutional history, as in the case of the provincial administration of Roman Britain, Camden had a clear idea of historical change during the Roman occupation.

[24] 'I may have been led into error by the authority of writers, and of others whom I reckoned I might safely rely on' (Fieri potest ut ex scriptorum authoritate et aliorum quos fide dignissimos existimavi, erraverim): *Britannia*, 1607, 'Lectori'.

[25] One outcome of the Brooke controversy was that henceforth quotations from non-classical sources were

distinguished between original documents, contemporary historians, and non-contemporary historians:

> There are two instruments for confirming or refuting any matter, reason and authority. It is true that in the study of antiquity authority carries far more weight, and the knowledge of things past is placed on a solid footing not by the power of argument but by the authority of texts. For the most sacred and solemn authority, as all know, attaches to public records which we call archives, together with monastic registers, furthermore to the writings of historians, first those of their own age, secondly later ones who have distinguished themselves by judgment and diligence in the pursuit of truth.[26]

He applied this method when verifying the historiographical tradition of Geoffrey of Monmouth concerning early British history.[27] First, he challenged the historical existence of Brutus by what he called the argument *ex tempore* based on Varro's three stages of the past—ἄδηλον, μυθικόν, ἱστορικόν.[28] On a second level he showed the lack of 'authoritas scriptorum idoneorum', defining as 'idonei' writers 'quorum ut vetustas et eruditio maior, ita fides potior'. Geoffrey of Monmouth's claim to have drawn his *History* from a very old book in the British tongue which began with Brutus, king of the first Britons, was invalidated by the statements of earlier authors, such as Gildas and Nennius, complaining of the absence of native sources.[29] Finally, Camden looked to the authority of the modern learned community and explained that the most erudite contemporary authors were doubtful of Brutus's existence, as indeed had been earlier British scholars of repute. This set of arguments suggests that Camden considered history a serious and professional business which implied access to well stocked libraries,[30] the collection and interpretation of documents, and a constant exchange of information among the learned.

identified.

[26] 'Quod duo sunt instrumenta ad res omnes aut confirmandas aut impugnandas, RATIO et AUTHORITAS: verum in hoc Antiquitatis studio longe plurimum posse Authoritatem, et rerum praeteritarum scientiam non rationum momento, sed scriptorum authoritate solidissima corroborari. Sanctissima autem et gravissima, ut omnes sciunt est authoritas tabularum publicarum quae Archiva vocamus, quibus etiam adiungantur Monasteriorum Registra, deinde Historicorum pro sua cuiusque aetate, postremo recentium scriptorum qui in veritate indaganda iudicio et diligentia prae ceteris excelluerunt.': *Britannia*, 1600, 'Ad Lectorem' (postface, sep. pag.), pp. 2–3.

[27] Camden claimed that he was only applying the mode of argumentation used by the learned men of his age: see *Britannia*, 1607, pp. 4–5.

[28] See *Britannia*, 1607, p. 25, for the argument of a historical past.

[29] *Britannia*, 1607, p. 6. What early British sources Camden read, and what he made of them, requires further investigation. For his use of Nennius see D. N. Dumville, 'The Sixteenth-Century History of Two Cambridge Books from Sawley', *Transactions of the Cambridge Bibliographical Society*, 7, 1977–80, pp. 438–9, reprinted in *idem*, *Histories and Pseudo-histories of the Insular Middle Ages*, Aldershot, 1990.

[30] For a partial catalogue of Camden's library see R. De Molen, 'The Library of William Camden', *Proceedings of the American Philosophical Society*, 128, 4, 1984, pp. 327–409, esp. 336ff.

In line with humanist scholarship Camden's main emphasis was clearly philological and rested on written evidence in the broadest sense. Next to written documents,[31] he particularly valued coins[32] and inscriptions. He was the first to accumulate a corpus of Roman inscriptions in Britain which he arranged topographically.[33] In using epigraphic material to supplement the list of Roman governors he correctly identified Sallustius Lucullus as the successor of Gnaeus Julius Agricola against the prevailing consensus that it was Cn. Trebellius.[34] He further identified Nonius Philippus as governor under Gordian the Younger.[35] In general, his purely archaeological interests were limited, though he was well aware of archaeological features such as crop marks,[36] pottery deposits or burial sites, and employed basic stratigraphy when drawing conclusions about the age of the Roman walls of London from coin evidence.[37]

Camden's archaeological achievements have been underrated by students of the history of archaeology who tend to trace the beginnings of archaeological thought almost entirely to the influence of the natural sciences at the end of the seventeenth century.[38] It is hardly necessary to point out against this that the humanist philological tradition had a strong interest in chronology and classification based on a concept of anachronism rooted in the study of palaeography.

Camden's method is based on the verification of hypotheses. In *Britannia* the Trojan myth is confronted with the results of comparative antiquarian studies. In establishing that Britain was peopled from Gaul, Camden lists geographical arguments and evidence from ancient writers. He describes similarities in religious rites,[39] in the form of government, in customs, again drawing particularly on linguistic evidence. The nucleus of *Britannia*, the identification of ancient

---

[31] Thus Camden turned to the *Codex Theodosianus* for an explanation of features of provincial administration of Britain.

[32] 'Cum vero inter omnes doctos in confesso sit plurimum lucis ad historias antiquas illustrandas ex antiquis nummis exoriri, placuit numismata...lectori hic exhibere': *Britannia*, 1607, p. 61. Several tables of British, Roman and Saxon coins appear in the work. Camden recognized that the ancient Britons had their own coinage, and even had some success in interpreting the legends by establishing that the inscriptions VER and CAM indicated mints.

[33] For contemporary discussion of the respective merits of a systematic and a topographical classification of inscriptions see I. Calabi Limentani, 'Note su classificazione ed indici epigrafici dallo Smezio al Morcelli: antiquità, retorica, critica', *Epigraphica*, 49, 1987, pp. 177–202.

[34] *Britannia*, 1607, p. 43.

[35] *Britannia*, 1607, p. 50.

[36] *Britannia*, 1607, pp. 241, 449, for Richborough and Wroxeter.

[37] *Britannia*, 1607, p. 304.

[38] See G. Daniel, *A Short History of Archaeology*, London, 1981; B. G. Trigger, *A History of Archaeological Thought*, Cambridge, 1989, chap. 2: 'Classical Archaeology and Antiquarianism', mostly follows Daniel. For a stimulating contribution see M. Hunter, 'The Royal Society and the Origins of British Archaeology', *Antiquity*, 65, 1971, pp. 113–21; 187–92.

[39] *Britannia*, 1607, pp. 9ff.

place names, was also philological:[40] following a suggestion of Plato, Camden was convinced that place names could be traced back to an original British language.[41] Moreover, he recognized that merely reading the ancient sources was not enough, and he adopted an archaeological approach in pointing out that the stations of the Antonine Itinerary could only be correctly identified by tracing on the ground the military roads that connected them.[42]

Camden's willingness to undertake field studies in order to establish the reliability of sources has to be seen against the passionate debate on the reality of early British history. In 1577, when Camden set about organizing his material for publication, Tudor antiquarians were to a great extent still discussing the question whether Britain had been founded by the Trojan Brutus. Geoffrey of Monmouth's account was taken at face value.[43] *Britannia* shifted attention to the Roman period, where Geoffrey's history could be checked against ancient historians. In thus placing the British past on a historical footing, *Britannia* established the common ground that history was verifiable and historiography subject to criticism.[44]

The general scheme of *Britannia* was to present a picture of the Roman province of Britain with reference to its development through Saxon and mediaeval times. Camden saw the history of England embedded in, and determined by, the continuing physical structure of Roman Britain. The markers 'pre-' and 'post-Roman' gave a new focus to the periodization of British history.*Britannia* also attempted to show continuity, glorify the present through the past, and let the present appear as the result of a continuous linear development. Furthermore, Camden contributed significantly to the creation of an atmosphere of historical writing in England which looked to the nation—its development and growth—as the framework of historiography by centring attention on national antiquities. Whereas the 1586 edition with its emphasis on place names was a contribution to international scholarly debate, the following editions focused increasingly on the demands of an English reading public interested in questions

---

[40] G. C. Boon, 'Camden and the Britannia', *Archaeologia Cambrensis*, 136, 1987, pp. 1–19, esp. p. 14, calls this Camden's 'etymological gymnastics'.

[41] 'Plato in Cratylo iubet ut nominum origines ad Barbaricas linguas, utique antiquiores revocemus: ego ad Britannicam sive Wallicam (ut iam vocant) linguam, qua primaevi et antiquissimi huius regionis incolae usi sunt, in Etymis, et coniecturis semper recurro': *Britannia*, 1607, 'Lectori'.

[42] 'Qui ad has igitur vias in Antonini Itinerario memorata non quaerit, a vero et a via proculdubio aberrabit': *Britannia*, 1607, p. 25.

[43] For a discussion of the debate on British history, see T. Kendrick, *British Antiquity*, London, 1950, pp. 78ff.; for Leland's role, see Levy, *Historical Thought* (n. 1 above), p. 131.

[44] '...liceat mihi Romanorum in Britannia historiam non e fabellis quas vani esset scribere, et imperiti credere; sed ex incorruptis priscae antiquitatis monumentis summatim et carptim perstringere', *Britannia*, p. 25.

of local topography in connection with the history of the leading families, of landholding and of heraldry.[45]

* * *

Britannia reflects the values of the Elizabethan establishment at a moment of crisis. Not only had the Reformation shaken the foundations of the Tudor world. The Tudor monarchs had deeply compromised the social and political structure of the country. This had sharpened people's perception of the past as a process of constant change. Again, the Tudors were dependent on attempts to legitimize their rule in historical terms in order to show that the newly formed world rested on foundations justified by an ancient past. With Elizabeth the need became particularly acute. Antiquarian studies were well-suited to meet it because their main interest bore on institutions as well as civil history. Camden stated in *Britannia*:

> It may benefit the reader if we insert here a chorographical table of Britain (as it was when a Roman province) together with the ancient names... if you learn nothing else from it, it will at least teach you that there are continual changes in the world; new foundations of cities are laid, new names of nations arise, while earlier ones become extinct.[46]

For Camden change did not represent the wheel of fortune but happened in a man-made world for varying reasons.

Britannia provided an intellectual justification for Elizabethan rule because it emphasized the organic, historical continuity of England, the existence of an ancient und unchallenged monarchy, and traced the independent cultural tradition of the British Church back to the Roman Empire.[47] It is not surprising that both

---

[45] The first translation, by Philemon Holland, came out in 1610, the revised edition in 1637. Holland added to Camden's text though claiming to publish an authorized version; this is doubtful. A new translation was published by Edmund Gibson (Bishop of Lincoln from 1716) in 1695, in one folio volume; revised edition in 1722, in two folio volumes; a further edition in 1772 with a few corrections and additions by Gibson's son-in-law, George Scott. The last substantial revision to date, with a new translation, is by Richard Gough, three folio volumes, 1789; second edition 1806, in four folio volumes. The Victoria County History project abandoned any revision of *Britannia*. There are critical editions, by G. J. Copley, for Surrey/Sussex and Kent, based on Gough's 1789 text (both London, 1977), designed, presumably, for local historians. Gibson's edition (1695) is available in facsimile, with an introduction by Stuart Piggott, Newton Abbot, 1971 (see also n. 4 above). Gough's four-volume edition of 1806 has been reprinted as vol. 73 of the series *Anglistica et Americana*, Hildesheim, 1974.

[46] 'Lectoris etiam interesse putamus Chorographicam Britanniae tabellam (cum fuerat Romanorum provincia) priscis nominibus hoc in loco inserere, non quidem illam accuratam. Quis enim praestabit? Sed e qua si nihil aliud hoc tamen ediscas, quotidie aliquid in hoc orbe mutari, nova urbium fundamenta iaci, nova gentium nomina extinctis nominibus prioribus exoriri...': *Britannia*, 1607, p. 76.

[47] Camden's account of the British king Lucius who introduced Christianity to Britain in the middle of the Roman occupation (*Britannia*, 1607, p. 47) remained almost unchallenged for another hundred years.

Elizabeth's Chancellor, William Cecil (Lord Burghley), and her Primate, Matthew Parker, devoted themselves to the patronage of antiquarian studies.[48]

Camden replaced the myth of Brutus by a model of the legitimacy of power in England that was congruous with the Tudor ideology of empire. Henry VIII had broken away from Rome by virtue of the authority he held as successor of the Roman emperors. In this context England was styled as an ancient *imperium/empire*.[49] In contrast to the development on the Continent, Henry and Elizabeth looked at themselves as the direct descendants of the Roman emperors in Britain and not just their legal successors.[50]

Whereas Henry VIII's claim was mainly theoretical, Elizabeth made every effort to employ history as a ground for her legal rights.[51] One line of argument was rooted in the Welsh Tudors' claim to have restored the ancient British monarchy. Though Elizabeth's adaptation of antiquity lacked consistency, she identified *inter alia* with Constantine, the son of the allegedly British princess, Helena.[52]

The model of derivation of royal power from the Romans was still current in England at the beginning of the seventeenth century. Camden improved on it by transposing the origin of feudal rights in England to the times of the Roman emperor Alexander Severus, thus giving a Roman complexion to the most striking feature of the mediaeval legal system.[53]

Unlike Samuel Daniel who stated that native royal authority continued through the Roman occupation,[54] Camden put forward a much more historical argument by developing the concept of the Romanization of Britain.

---

[48] For Camden's relationship with Burghley see H. Trevor Roper, *Queen Elizabeth's First Historian*, Neale Lecture in English History, London, 1971.

[49] See R. Koebner, *Empire*, Cambridge, 1961, for England esp. ch. 2, pp. 18ff.; *idem.*, 'The Imperial Crown of this Realm: Henry VIII, Constantine the Great and Polydore Vergil', *Bulletin of the Institute of Historical Research*, 26, 1953, pp. 29–52.

[50] For a change in the argument concerning the divine right theory see J. P. Sommerville, 'Richard Hooker, Hadrian Saravia and the Advent of the Divine Right of Kings', *History of Political Thought*, 4, 1983, pp. 229–45.

[51] For an analysis of the general phenomenon in Europe, see F. A. Yates, *Astrea: the Imperial Cult in the Sixteenth Century*, London, 1975, pp. 29–112.

[52] J. Foxe, *Actes and Monuments*, which appeared in 1563 in the first English version, emphasized the Constantine image in relation to Elizabeth and included her in the line of martyrs since antiquity. After 1571 the book was found in every Anglican church. See W. Haller, *Foxe's Book of Martyrs and the Elect Nation*, London, 1963, p. 119.

[53] 'Cum tamen Alexander Severus Imp<erator> (ut est apud Lampridium) *sola quae de hostibus capta erant limitaneis ducibus, et militibus donasset, ita ut eorum essent, si haeredes illorum militarent nec unquam ad privatos pertinerent, existimans attentius eos militaturos, si etiam sua rura defenderent:* (verba haec velim notes, nam hinc vel species *feudi*, vel origo *feudorum* deducatur)...': *Britannia*, 1607, p. 651 (*Historia Augusta*, Alexander Severus, 58, 4).

[54] 'All Kings from Lucius to Vortigern were Roman Governors': S. Daniel, *The First Part of the Historie of England*, London, 1612, p. 19.

He considered the transformation of Britain into a Roman province, observing that this process was achieved not only by making her subject to Roman law and administration. He found that the army had an important share in Romanizing the country. Finally, he stated that Romans and Britons had grown into a single nation through close contact and intermarriage over five hundred years.[55] Camden saw early British history clearly in a Romano-European context. This attitude is linked to the view he shared with many scholars of his time that a common past could serve as a model for reconciling the religious schism in Europe.

It was in the course of the seventeenth century—mainly as a result of the constitutional dispute—that a new standardized view of early British history was established. The new historiography distanced itself from the tradition of the Renaissance and from the Society of Antiquaries, as we shall see in a moment.

Another factor was continuous war in Europe which disrupted personal relationships and intellectual exchange. It made England appear a blessed country, remote from the turmoil on the Continent, and thus fostered the emphasis on national history. The later seventeenth and early eighteenth centuries considered the Roman occupation merely as a prelude to national history, and denied any Roman component in the emergence of the nation.

* * *

This change in historical thinking took place in James's reign and was linked with the simultaneous reinterpretation of the 'law' of England. Sir Edward Coke accomplished the transformation of the heterogeneous common law into a homogeneous legal system.[56] The underlying historical position consisted in the claim that the law in England was of immemorial antiquity,[57] which provided a blueprint for the redefinition of early British history.

The dispute over the interpretation of the British past was closely linked to the fundamental political issue of the early Stuart period, whether it was the King or Parliament that exercised sovereignty in the state.[58] Under political pressure, the monarchy took refuge in a set of arguments comprising elements taken from the Monmouth tradition as well as from Roman history.

One of the reasons why the idea of a Roman component in the makeup of the nation was eventually discredited was that the Stuarts, in their attempt to

---

[55] 'Communis illa mater enim, ut inquit ille, Roma, cives vocavit *Quos domuit, nexuque pio longinqua revinxit*': *Britannia*, 1607, p. 61.

[56] See Ferguson, *Clio* (n. 1 above), p. 278.

[57] For a detailed interpretation of the 'common law model', see J. G. A. Pocock, *The Ancient Constitution and the Feudal Law*, Cambridge, 1987.

[58] See W. Nippel, *Mischverfassung und Verfassungsrealität in Antike und Früher Neuzeit*, Stuttgart, 1980, pp. 211ff.; G. A. Ritter, 'Divine Right und Praerogative der englischen Könige 1604–1640', *Historische Zeitschrift*, 196, 1963, pp. 584–625, repr. in *idem, Parlament und Demokratie in Grossbritannien*, Göttingen, 1972, pp. 11–58.

strengthen regal authority, used the Roman model to elaborate a concept of reason of state[59] which derived from a common European context and the history of the Romans in Britain.

Another aspect of the ideological relevance of Roman Britain was the notion of a distinct *orbis Britannicus* found in the ancient authors. James's triumphal entry into London in March 1604 marked the integration of this idea in the mythology of the Stuart state.[60] 'Orbis Britannicus, divisus ab orbe',[61] together with the Trojan descent of the Stuarts was a prime motif on the triumphal arches put up for the occasion. Trojan ancestry could easily be connected with the idea of empire, since the Trojans were the progenitors of empire in the West. Along these lines James not only identified himself with Augustus's ideology of peace but drew a more distinctly British parallel by seeing himself as another Constantine, the British born emperor. Constantine was a useful model for James because he had established and defended the true faith, presiding over the early councils of the Church to achieve uniformity of doctrine.[62]

The allusion to Vergil's motto for Roman Britain[63] suggested that even the Romans had felt that a special destiny was in store for Britain. According to Ben Jonson, once a pupil of William Camden, the iconography of James's entry into London was intended to 'shew that this empire is a world divided from the world'.[64]

But the phrase 'toto divisos orbe Britannos' received a completely different meaning in the first quarter of the seventeenth century. The historical argument used in the controversy between King and Parliament disengaged Britain from the European historical context and declared the apartness of her past, thus undercutting the Stuart position on divine kingship and ancient monarchy.[65]

---

[59] See D. S. Berkowitz, 'Reason of State and the Petition of Right', *Staatsräson. Studien zur Geschichte eines politischen Begriffs*, ed. R. Schnur, Berlin, 1975, pp. 165–212.

[60] See G. Parry, *The Golden Age Restor'd: the Culture of the Stuart Court 1603–1642*, Manchester, 1985, pp. 1–39.

[61] The central figure on the facade of the first arch represented the British Monarchy, seated beneath the two crowns of England and Scotland, and bearing in her lap a globe inscribed: 'Orbis Britannicus. Divisus ab Orbe.'

[62] Constantine served as a precedent for James to call the Hampton Court Conference in 1604. For Constantine as a role model see Joseph Hall, 'An holy panegyrick. A sermon preached at Paul's Crosse upon the anniversarie solemnitie of the happy inauguration of our Drad Sooveraigne Lord, King James, March 24, 1613' in *The Works of J. H...*, I, London, 1628, pp. 482ff.

[63] 'Et penitus toto divisos orbe Britannos': Vergil, *Eclogues*, 1, 66.

[64] 'The King's Entertainment' in *Ben Jonson*, ed. C. H. Herford and P. and E. Simpson, VII, Oxford, 1941, pp. 84–5.

[65] The Petition of Right was looked upon as a confirmation of Magna Carta functioning as a confirmation of the laws of Edward the Confessor. Together these served as the 'fundamental and immemorial lex terrae'. In the debate over the Petition Coke said: 'No other state is like this. *Divisos ab orbe Britannos*. We have a national appropriate law to this kingdom. If you tell me of other laws you are gone. I will speak only of the laws of England. This question is a question of law... It is not I, Edward Coke, that speaketh it. I shall say

As early as 1610, and again in 1615, John Selden[66] had drawn attention to early British history. *Analecton Anglobritannicon* prepared in 1607, published in 1615, was designed to illustrate an 'ancient constitution'. *Jani Anglorum facies altera* went to press in 1610.[67] Here the Roman conquest was, in contrast to Camden's understanding, viewed as the enslavement of the native Britons and a break in constitutional development.

Selden presented a pre-Roman constitution, relying to a large extent on the accounts of Roman historians; he followed Camden's argument that the institutions, customs and laws of the early Britons were best understood by studying the evidence from Gaul.[68] The emerging picture left no room for a king to have established civil society or to have given laws to England. Instead, the evidence appeared to reveal a considerable dispersion of political power.[69]

In 1583, Thomas Smith, looking at the same evidence in his *De republica Anglorum*, had come to quite different conclusions:

> By olde and auncient histories that I have red, I cannot understand that our nation hath used any other and generall authoritie in this realme neither *Aristocraticall* nor *Democraticall*, but onely the royall and kingly majestie which at the first was divided into many and sundrie kings, each absolutely reigning in his countrie, not under the subjection of other...[70]

But according to Selden it was common law and religion that gave cohesion to society in early Britain, not a single political authority. The political power left to kings was executive only and was exercised on a very small scale.[71] Selden devoted only a very few pages to Roman rule in Britain. He acknowledged that Rome brought Southern Britain under one jurisdiction,[72] and transformed Britain

---

nothing, but the records shall speak', *Commons Debates 1628*, II, ed. by R. C. Johnson & M. Jansson Cole, New Haven, 1977, pp. 100–101.

[66] For Selden see P. Christianson, 'Young John Selden and the Ancient Constitution, ca. 1610–18', *Proceedings of the American Philosophical Society*, 128, 4, 1884, pp. 271–315; J. P. Sommerville, 'John Selden, the Law of Nature and the Origins of Government', *Historical Journal*, 27, 1984, pp. 437–8; Pocock, *Constitution* (n. 53 above), p. 295; for the importance of Selden as a historian see Woolf, 'Erudition' (n. 1 above), pp. 33ff.

[67] J. Selden, *Analecton Anglobritannicon*, London, 1615; *idem*, *Jani Anglorum facies altera*, London, 1610.

[68] See J. Selden, *The Reverse or Back Face of the English Janus*, London, 1683, p. 16.

[69] Ancient Britain was ruled by a number of monarchs who came together in assemblies to discuss such matters as foreign relations or war and peace. Since the kingdoms were extremely small Selden called them aristocracies rather than monarchies. See Selden, *Jani...facies* (n. 67 above), p. 25 (1683, p. 17); *idem, Analecton* (n. 67 above), p. 20.

[70] Sir T. Smith, *De republica Anglorum*, bk. I, ch. 9, ed. M. Dewar, Cambridge, 1982, p. 56.

[71] Selden, *Jani...facies* (n. 67 above), pp. 123–33 (1683, pp. 93–9).

[72] In his edition of Fortescue (1616), Selden dealt at length with Fortescue's claim that the Romans did not change British law while they occupied Britain but maintained British jurisdiction having recognized its superior worth. Though Selden refutes Fortescue's claim, he argues that Roman rule had no lasting effect in Britain. See Sir J. Fortescue, *De laudibus legum Angliae.. hereto are ioind the two summes of Sir Ralph de Hengham... Notes both on Fortescue and Hengham are added* [by John Selden], London, 1616, pp. 11–12.

culturally. Thus he saw the revolt of Boudicca and generally British resistance to
Rome in the context of British resentment of Roman culture. For instance, when
the Romans tried to extirpate the Druids, their underlying aim was to destroy
British religion as well as British law, because the Druids guaranteed the stability
of both and thus functioned as the guardians of British culture.[73]

* * *

The *Jani Anglorum facies altera* is an offshoot of the tradition of the Society of
Antiquaries. It is here that we first meet debates on the history of English
political institutions on the basis of documentary evidence.

Camden's humanist philologico-historical method seems to have been a major
influence in Selden's work, even though Selden presents a new historical
interpretation and literally creates a historical image of the ancient constitution
which, unlike Coke and Fortescue, is not rooted in idealizing anachronisms. On
the other hand Romano-British studies suffered from a general trend in
scholarship. Selden was a philologist interested in law and not in fieldwork. On
the Continent antiquarians now, after geography and philology, discovered law
as an object of study. But these were insufficient tools for writing a history of
Roman Britain.

The debate over British history affected Romano-British studies in two ways.
Interest in the political implications of Roman rule gave way to denying the
Roman past altogether, while a new importance was attributed to antiquarian
studies which gained political and social recognition. Antiquarian pursuits became
a suitable pastime for the 'complete gentleman'.[74] Whereas Selden was a highly
trained professional, antiquarian studies in general fell into the hands of the
learned amateur. Camden's *Britannia* continued to be read but, as the appearance
of English versions suggests, it had acquired a new constituency.[75]

Interest in local history developed within the framework of the new, self-
confident, national state, though its principal motive was parochial pride in
opposition to the court doctrine of central government. The supporters of local
autonomy looked to history for the substantiation of their claims. They turned up
their Camden who had arranged his material by shires as they now were, in the
belief that they corresponded to the tribal boundaries of Roman Britain. *Britannia*
became the basic grid for organizing the results of work in British history,
archaeology, genealogy and topography until the beginning of the twentieth
century. The great venture of the *Victoria County History* was an offspring of this

---

[73] See Fortescue, *De laudibus*, Selden's notes, p. 12. For the interpretation of the Druids' function see
Selden, *English Janus* (n. 68 above), pp. 13–16, 93, and *idem, Analecton* (n. 67 above), chap. 4.

[74] See Henry Peacham, *The Compleat Gentleman*, 2nd impression, London, 1634.

[75] See n. 45 above.

tradition. Francis Haverfield was the first to try to break out of it. Onthe other hand the concept of Romanization was lost until Haverfield revived it for Britain and gave it a name.

William Camden, whose work linked two important periods in English history, stands at the beginning of a British academic tradition in the study of antiquity. He investigated all aspects of the past, drew on every possible source and called for the unity of history. But he also stands at the beginning of the specialization of learning, its fragmentation into sectional disciplines. For Camden the past was not only a collection of artefacts, he was interested in man as a social being.

The most striking feature in Camden's work was the combination of a scientific interest with its emphasis on well defined methods of research, and a strong sense of history as a factor of political stability. Camden claimed that the nation shared a common historical past at a time when the idea was threatened by the emergence of a variety of partial views of the past, such as the Anglo-Saxon tradition, the ancient church tradition etc. This is reflected in the fact that *Britannia* as a piece of history writing combines several different historiographical and antiquarian traditions, which to explore in detail would need another paper.

Camden was not, as Ralphe Brooke would have us believe, an isolated schoolmaster beating boys. Though he never left his native country, he was in touch with the wide world of European scholarship, a connection based on the idea of a common European past. The connection was severed in the following century because, as a result of political circumstances, the idea was discarded in favour of a British history unlike any other, with little use for a European context.

The story of Romano-British studies in England has, to a large extent, been one of dependence on the general political and cultural position Englishmen have, over the centuries, adopted in relation to the Continent. The crucial question today is how does England see herself—as part of Europe or as Orbis Britannicus.

Legal Historians and Roman *Agrimensores* in the First Half of the Nineteenth Century

L. CAPOGROSSI COLOGNESI

Taking its cue from the contributions of Alfred Heuss and Arnaldo Momigliano, recent research on Niebuhr has highlighted the key importance, in his work on Roman history, of the problem of Roman land systems and the different uses of private land and *ager publicus*.[1] It is in this perspective that Niebuhr's strong interest in the writings of the Roman land-surveyors is to be evaluated. I shall not, on this occasion, go into the more strictly philological aspects in any detail even though these are immediately relevant to the problems I shall be considering. Suffice it to mention that, in the first edition of the second volume of his *Römische Geschichte*, Niebuhr published an appendix devoted to the *gromatici veteres* with a detailed discussion of the problems posed by the textual tradition.[2] He shows his dissatisfaction with the existing editions, essentially that of Goes,[3] and expresses the hope that 'some scholar possessing the philological spirit of our age, along with the learning and the industry of the French school of the sixteenth century' will devote himself to 'these venerable ruins', and produce a satisfactory edition.[4]

Niebuhr's reference to the great French jurists of the sixteenth century which I have reported *verbatim* is not a vain flourish; it represents a considered opinion. Niebuhr wanted to use these authors in order to promote a detailed, thorough understanding of Roman society. French scholars had been so successful in the study of Roman legal and institutional history mainly because of their deep knowledge of ancient literature and of juridical documents, as well as of other kinds of sources, especially epigraphic and archaeological.

---

[1] A. Heuss, *Barthold Georg Niebuhrs wissenschaftliche Anfänge*, Abhandlungen der Akademie der Wissenschaften in Göttingen, Phil.-hist. Klasse, III, 114, Göttingen, 1981; A. Momigliano, 'Alle origini dell'interesse su Roma arcaica: Niebuhr e l'India', *Rivista storica italiana*, 92, 1980, pp. 561–71, reprinted in *Settimo contributo alla storia degli studi classici e del mondo antico*, Roma, 1984, pp. 155–67; and the review of Heuss, ibid., pp. 167–70. See now G. Bonacina, *Hegel, il mondo romano e la storiografia*, Firenze, 1991, ch. 1 and 2; and J. Q. Whitman, *The Legacy of Roman Law in the German Romantic Era*, Princeton, 1990, pp. 155ff.

[2] B. G. Niebuhr, *Römische Geschichte*, II, Berlin, 1812, pp. 532–62.. The appendix was omitted in the second edition (1830) but partially retained in the English translation (*The History of Rome*, transl. J. C. Hare and C. Thirlwall), II, Cambridge, 1832, Appendix 2, pp. 631–41; see also Appendix 1 in the same volume, pp. 617–30, differently oriented but equally rich in quotations from the *gromatici*.

[3] Niebuhr, *History* (n. 2 above), II, pp. 638–9: 'What Rigaltius did for the *agrimensores* is of great value; the laborious work of Goesius, of hardly any'. For a new critical edition it would consequently 'be necessary to separate [*abtrennen*] the matter added in the later editions'.

[4] Niebuhr, *History* (n. 2 above), II, p. 638; see also at p. 633 what he says about his intention to 'excite others to take the same interest [as he has done] in it' [i.e. the text of the *agrimensores*].

Niebuhr rightly thought that a real understanding of the techniques of land surveying and of the system of land settlement (and of the relationship between town and country) was possible only in terms of the legal and economic consequences of these procedures. Only with a sufficient knowledge of this wider framework was it possible to understand the original meaning of the writings of the *gromatici*.

It should be said that, despite his deep interest in the writings of the *agrimensores*, of which the reference to Renaissance scholarship is an indication, Niebuhr did not achieve what he had postulated. Instead of reconstructing the legal and gromatic organization of Roman territory, he limited himself, at least in the *Römische Geschichte*, to investigating the more strictly institutional aspects, for which he drew on the evidence supplied by the *gromatici*. This enabled him to make sense of the scant and at times obscure testimony of the ancient historians. I refer to the question of Roman agrarian legislation and its relationship to the *ager publicus*. The new material was not, as we know, to lead Niebuhr to conclusions different from those reached by Heyne in his well-known essay on 'Leges agrariae pestiferae et execrabiles'. What is new is its major role in Niebuhr's historiographical undertaking, the reconstruction of the Roman Republic.[5]

Another novelty is Niebuhr's comparative approach. He discerned parallels between the writings of the Roman land surveyors and what the English had recently found out about agrarian relationships in India.[6] Furthermore, Niebuhr thought that the articulation of the land described by the *gromatici* could to some extent be traced in the modern Italian landscape. This was a major insight which was to find subsequent confirmation.[7]

There is a romantic flavour in this approach with its emphasis on elements of continuity over thousands of years. It can be related to Niebuhr's other attitudes and interests, especially during his years in Rome. While in Rome he found relevance in the image, formed at first hand and described with feeling, of a free and proud country people—in the Castelli Romani or in Tivoli—exploited by absentee landlords. These same places in Latium offered evidence of a related phenomenon, the concentration of landed property, which had started in the late Middle Ages and was still operative in Niebuhr's day. He could use this to

---

[5] Niebuhr's early researches, opened up to scholarship through Heuss's monumental work, are directly connected with later developments in the first and second edition of the *Römische Geschichte*. The substantial treatise on the *ager publicus* and the *leges agrariae* in the second edition of volume II can be seen as the conclusion of a sustained effort going back to the beginnings of Niebuhr's interest in Roman history.

[6] See Heuss and Momigliano in n. 1 above.

[7] Niebuhr, *Römische Geschichte* (n. 2 above), II, p. 633. See also Niebuhr's letter to Savigny, of 17 Oct. 1816, and to Jacobi, of 11 Jan. 1817: Niebuhr, *Briefe, Neue Folge, 1816–1830*, ed. E. Vischer, I, 1, *Briefe aus Rom, 1816–1823*, Bern etc., 1981, pp. 89; 124.

illuminate the development of big Roman landholdings to the detriment of small ones in Republican times.[8]

However, it seems somewhat implausible that these modern conditions, observed during Niebuhr's stay in Rome but conceived of already before his Italian sojourn,[9] could shed light on the nature and pattern of the relationships between patricians and plebeians under the Republic. But, whether valid or not, the parallel can be seen as an element in Niebuhr's contribution to the opening of new historiographical horizons through the identification of documentary material which had until then remained outside the purview of students of Roman history and of Roman law, with the partial exception of French sixteenth-century scholars and, in their wake, the practitioners of *Elegante Jurisprudenz*.

Niebuhr's views had immediate repercussions, as can be illustrated by two French works which appeared within a year of each other on almost the same subject: the history of landed property in ancient Rome. Both Charles Giraud's *Recherches sur le droit de propriété chez les Romains*[10] and the broader work of Edouard Laboulaye, *Histoire du droit de propriété foncière en Occident*,[11] fully acknowledge Niebuhr's interpretation of the Roman *leges de modo agrorum*. The date of the first work is 1838, that of the second, which was to have a more lasting success with European specialists, 1839.

It was Biagio Brugi, an Italian expert on the *gromatici*, who noted the strict adherence of these two works to Niebuhr's approach, primarily on the ground of their 'enthusiastic' use of gromatic evidence.[12] Especially in Laboulaye this adherence seems almost slavish: as in Niebuhr, the writings of the *gromatici* are used only, or pre-eminently, to shed light on, and stress the historical importance of, Roman agrarian laws.

Given its emphasis on legal history within the European framework, Laboulaye's book was bound to enjoy lasting success. It is extensively quoted in later literature. One point of interest may be noted: Laboulaye's attempt to draw together, within the Roman system, several different types of property, of which the *dominium ex iure Quiritium* constitutes the most important but not the only variety.[13]

---

[8] C. C. J. Bunsen, C. A. Brandis & J. W. Loebell, *The Life and Letters of Barthold Georg Niebuhr, with An Essay on His Character and Influence,* II, London, 1852, pp. 139ff.

[9] Niebuhr, *Römische Geschichte* (n. 2 above), II, p. 633: 'I have never been in Italy, where without doubt, especially in the Campagna, a number of peculiar customs with regard to the partition of land and the marking of boundary stones must be subsisting down to this very day, though unnoticed by travellers and even by natives.'

[10] Charles Giraud, *Recherches sur le droit de propriété chez les Romains sous la république et sous l'empire*, Aix, 1838.

[11] Edouard Laboulaye, *Histoire du droit de propriété foncière en Occident*, Paris, 1839.

[12] B. Brugi, *Le dottrine giuridiche degli agrimensori romani comparate a quelle del Digesto*, Verona etc., 1897, p. 35.

[13] Laboulaye, *Histoire* (n. 11 above), pp. 73ff., 87ff., 93ff.

But this perspective was destined to fade away. The growing importance of the distinction between 'private' and 'public' law in nineteenth-century juridical science left the specialists of Roman private law as all but the sole authorities on the central themes of property. As a result, research in this field concentrated on the system of *ius civile* identifying Roman property with *dominium ex iure Quiritium*. It is significant that Laboulaye's knowledge of the *agrimensores* helped him to widen the category of land ownership in Roman law, so as to include legal forms other than the classical *dominium ex iure Quiritium*. Half a century later the same road was to be followed by a more successful author—the young Max Weber in his *Römische Agrargeschichte*.

Giraud's book is far more fragmentary and uncertain in its results. It is only a part of a much more extensive project, as the author himself points out.[14] In tone and content it is completely different from Laboulaye. But for Giraud too the link with Niebuhr is close and, at the same time, problematic. This is shown, for example, by the radical, if polite, criticism of the use of Indian agrarian structures to interpret land relationships in ancient Rome.

Not that Giraud rejects the Indian parallel altogether. He adduces the laws of Menu to refute the validity of the role assigned by Niebuhr to the Indian *Zemindar*[15]—even though a reference to the most ancient Indian legal traditions to support an interpretation of what the English found in India in the eighteenth century might seem far from convincing. It is not so much the criticism of Niebuhr as the reference to the laws of Menu that is of interest. It introduces in 1838 what will become a recurrent theme among European jurists and legal historians throughout the century. But the book has yet more to offer. From our point of view two aspects stand out: first the way the individualistic form of landed property is unhesitatingly assigned to the very beginnings of Rome and the other great civilizations of the ancient world—India in the East, Egypt and Greece in the Mediterranean.[16] Such a view provides a historical basis for what cannot but appear, in the final analysis, as a scale of values: what is refuted is not so much the Niebuhrian notion of the exclusion of the plebeians from primitive ownership as the hypothesis of a possible form of collective land ownership.

This immediately leads us to another, yet more interesting aspect of Giraud's work, his forward-looking tendency to single out aspects of institutional mechanisms which were by and large to remain outside the purview of the Historical School of law in Germany. Giraud achieves an integration of the study of juridical and institutional forms of ancient societies in relation to other cultural

---

[14] Giraud, *Recherches* (n. 10 above), p. 67 of the Appendix; see also p. III of the Introduction.

[15] Giraud, *Recherches* (n. 10 above), pp. 16ff.

[16] Some form of communal land exploitation is allowed by Giraud, *Recherches* (n. 10 above), pp. 4ff., in the lower stages of human societies. By the time the great civilizations begin 'la théorie de la communauté des biens ne présente...plus que l'attrait du roman' (ibid., p. 15).

aspects. In particular, such forms appear associated with—if not actually based on—the presence of a religious element which ends up by assuming a key significance. On this point Giraud's essay can be said to anticipate the approach of Fustel de Coulanges's *Cité antique*, the success of which was to be amply justified by its superior quality and depth. The question is still open as to the extent of the influence on Giraud of Creuzer's interpretation of the religious aspects of Graeco-Roman antiquity.

Giraud's use of the *gromatici* appears broad and systematic. But, as in Niebuhr, there is an absence, if anything more clearly marked, of any inclination to use the *gromatici* to reconstruct the territorial organization of ancient Rome, that is to exploit what constitutes in fact the main value of the document, as a later generation of scholars would do.[17] Giraud's interests comprise a variety of topics: we are told about the relationship between augural science, with its Etruscan origins, and religion;[18] about the different social roles of the land-surveyors, and the various functions they perform;[19] and we encounter meticulous, penetrating analyses of the religious value of boundaries and their archaic regulation.[20] However, on the last mentioned point, Giraud's approach is not very different from that of antiquarians and earlier students of ancient history.

By far the most interesting aspect of the book is the key importance attributed to religion as the very foundation of the patriarchal family, as well as of private land-holding and other social institutions. The analysis of the cult of Vesta as the basis of the primitive family, of the role of the Penates and the god Terminus in establishing the individual possession of land is perhaps where the book is at its best and where it advances furthest against earlier accounts.

But, for all the wealth of material and the wide scope of the investigation, such an approach could only have established itself—as it was to do with Fustel—if the author had carried through his overall design. As we have seen this did not happen. Giraud's work remained a torso, a fragment of the cultural history of an institution. The analysis of the more strictly technical and juridical aspects was reserved for a second volume which never saw the light of day.

Giraud's use of the *gromatici* falls far short of what they have to offer. Rather than create a model of cultural interpretation of institutional phenomena, it settles for little more than a series of commonplaces. We have to move to a new generation of scholars, and once again to Germany, to find a deeper and more productive exploitation of the *agrimensores*. It is interesting that the protagonist here, A. Rudorff, is also the leading light of one of the two divergent tendencies

---

[17] Giraud, *Recherches* (n. 10 above), pp. 52ff.

[18] Ibid., pp. 102ff.

[19] Ibid., pp. 123ff.

[20] Ibid., pp. 118ff.; also pp. 74ff. on the relevance of religious elements (i. e. the cult of Vesta and of the god Terminus) in archaic family relationships and primitive ownership.

that emerged from the school of Savigny—the historical one—while it is almost symbolic that the leader of the opposite tendency, G. F. Puchta, should have attacked, with fairly substantial arguments, not only the famous theory of Savigny and Niebuhr about the origin of the *interdicta possessoria*, but also Niebuhr's view of the original scope of the *lex Licinia de modo agrorum* as referring only to the ownership of the *ager publicus*.[21]

With Rudorff, the historiographical perspectives opened up by Niebuhr, and extended by Savigny, come into their own. The commentary he wrote for his edition of the *gromatici* can be considered as the first—and, so far, in many respects the only—systematic treatment of Roman land-surveying. Rudorff uses the data of land-surveying to analyse the organization of Roman territory in all its aspects, both in terms of what is on the ground—types of division, boundaries etc. —and of juridical classification. He takes into account the effects of the types of land exploitation, of the role of the state and local authorities, as well as relationships between private individuals, regulated by what we may call the 'private law' of Rome. Moreover, he covers a broad period of time spanning evolutionary processes from primitive forms of organization by villages to the end of the municipal order and the emergence of the *saltus*, the great latifundia of the late Roman Empire.[22]

The writings of the land-surveyors provided Rudorff with various types of information regarding territorial organization, but also on the more specifically economic aspects of landed property. This differentiation led him to identify two areas of research which we associate respectively with the names of Mommsen and Weber. Mommsen opened up new possibilities for the understanding of Roman institutions in his commentary on the *Libri coloniarum* which appeared together with Rudorff's commentary on the *gromatici*.[23] He was fashioning a new analytical instrument for the investigation of Roman *Staatsrecht* which would enable him to delineate not only the central political government of the Roman State but also the numerous local institutions, taking into account the great variety of land and human settlement on Roman territory and the legal statutes regulating them. Here was the foundation on which he was to raise his subsequent great achievements—the *Corpus inscriptionum latinarum* and the *Staatsrecht*.

---

[21] For views on the origin of the *interdicta possessoria*, see my 'I gromatici nella storiografia dell '800', *Die römische Feldmesskunst. Interdisziplinäre Beiträge zu ihrer Bedeutung für die Zivilisationsgeschichte Roms*, ed. O. Behrends and L. Capogrossi Colgnesi, Abhandlungen der Akademie der Wissenschaften in Göttingen, Phil.-hist. Klasse, 3. F., 193, Göttingen, 1992, pp. 9–25. For Puchta's criticism of current ideas on the *lex Licinia de modo agrorum* see his *Cursus der Institutionen*, 1, 9º, ed. P. Kruger, Leipzig, 1881, §57, where he follows Huschke's criticism of Niebuhr's interpretation of the *lex Licinia de modo agrorum*. See E. Huschke, *Ueber die Stelle des Varro von den Licinien (de re rust. 1, 2, 9)*, Heidelberg, 1835, pp. 3ff.

[22] A. Rudorff, 'Gromatische Institutionen' in *Die Schriften der römischen Feldmesser*, ed. F. Blume, K. Lachmann, A. Rudorff, II, Berlin, 1852, pp. 227–464.

[23] T. Mommsen, 'Die *Libri coloniarum*' in Blume *et al.*, *Schriften* (n. 22 above), II, pp. 143–220.

The other area of research was to mature much later, with the famous essay on Roman agrarian history by the young Weber (1891). Mommsen saw this study of the *gromatici* as opening for Weber the possibility of creating a new department of ancient history: the economic history of Rome. It seems to me important to stress the influence of Rudorff on Weber in the way he quite deliberately integrates economic history with institutional and legal analysis.

Both Rudorff's commentary and Mommsen's analysis of the *Libri coloniarum* appeared in 1852, in the second volume of the edition of the *agrimensores* by Blume and Lachmann. In the systematic treatment of their material they accomplished what Niebuhr had so clearly foreshadowed—a break with the tradition of *antiquitates*.

Niebuhr's reference to French sixteenth-century jurists may prompt reflection as to why it was students of Roman law, which both Rudorff and Mommsen were, that achieved these results. It can immediately be observed that the new approach to the *gromatici* led necessarily through Roman law. Enough to mention problems of historical topography which could only be solved with the help of legal documents and in terms of juridical notions. It is perhaps more interesting to examine the imposing picture of the 'gromatische Institutionen' conjured up by Rudorff. The very structure of Rudorff's commentary is typical of this kind of scholarship and testifies to its high level.

Not that the 'Institutionen' were exclusively an outcome of legal paedagogy. It is obvious, however, that they could not have been written without the systematic premises established in legal thought already in the eighteenth century and enriched by the historicizing tendency of Savigny and his school, or the techniques of analysis of the texts of the *Corpus iuris civilis* developed by European jurists since the end of the Middle Ages. Rudorff's method postulated the use of many different kinds of sources. But, unlike the antiquarians, he integrated these sources in a systematic, sophisticated analysis, the aim of which was to reconstruct the territorial and legal organization of ancient Rome by means of an organic and generalizing model. He achieved this by a procedure that could be described as half systematic and half historical, imposing co-existence on two kinds of approach whose incompatibility had not—and has not—been formally resolved.

Considering this quite peculiar product of the discipline of Roman law in the nineteenth century, one is tempted to remark that this stimulating new departure which gave rise to new developments in various directions and the creation of new departments of knowledge occurred at the very time when the discipline began to lose the solidity of its age-old social function. Perhaps students of Roman law need not despair of their work being of some use both to ancient historians and to modern legal theory.

Index